The Museum Effect

Dear Paul —
As Lisa said, this really is your fault! I cannot thank you enough for all you've done for us over the years. So many great times and so much reussetorte (sp!). I hope you enjoy this!
Love, Jeff

The Museum Effect

How Museums, Libraries, and Cultural Institutions Educate and Civilize Society

Jeffrey K. Smith

ROWMAN & LITTLEFIELD
Lanham • Boulder • New York • Toronto • Plymouth, UK

Published by Rowman & Littlefield
4501 Forbes Boulevard, Suite 200, Lanham, Maryland 20706
www.rowman.com

10 Thornbury Road, Plymouth PL6 7PP, United Kingdom

Copyright © 2014 by Rowman & Littlefield

British Library Cataloguing in Publication Information Available

Library of Congress Cataloging-in-Publication Data
Smith, Jeffrey K.
 The museum effect : how museums, libraries, and cultural institutions educate and civilize society / Jeffrey K. Smith.
     pages cm
 Includes bibliographical references and index.
 ISBN 978-0-7591-2294-9 (cloth : alkaline paper) — ISBN 978-0-7591-2295-6 (paperback : alkaline paper) — ISBN 978-0-7591-2296-3 (electronic) 1. Museums—Educational aspects. 2. Museums—Social aspects. 3. Libraries and education. 4. Libraries—Social aspects. 5. Education—Social aspects. 6. Arts and society. 7. Community life. 8. Museums and community. 9. Libraries and community. I. Title.
 AM7.S63 2014
 069'.15—dc23

                                                                2014004944

∞™ The paper used in this publication meets the minimum requirements of American National Standard for Information Sciences—Permanence of Paper for Printed Library Materials, ANSI/NISO Z39.48-1992.

Printed in the United States of America

Contents

Acknowledgments

I have many people to thank for their assistance and support in writing this book. Charles Harmon from Rowman & Littlefield has been incredibly patient and supportive; I greatly appreciate his calm perseverance throughout the project. Next, my former student and good friend Izabella Waszkielewicz, in searching for a PhD thesis topic, came to me and said, "You know how you have that good feeling when you come out of a museum, kind of like when you come out of church? I want to study that." I did know that feeling, and I had seen it in many others, and thought it would be a great idea to study it. It was Izabella's dissertation research that formed the real, direct empirical evidence that the Museum Effect exists, and I thank her for all the great work she did on that dissertation and the other studies we did together.

I'd like to thank David Carr, who got me started working in museums and libraries, and who was instrumental in providing the motivation to write this book. I thank Pablo Tinio, with whom I have spent hours and hours on "iChat" discussing aesthetics, museums, boxing, and recipes, mostly with me in Dunedin, New Zealand, and Pablo in Vienna, Austria. Thanks also to Paul Locher, Helmut Leder, and James Kaufman, who have provided insight, inspiration, and camaraderie. They are all great scholars and great friends.

Within the museum field, we have encountered so many wonderful people along the way that I cannot thank them all. But I would like to mention a few in particular. At the Met, there is Richard Mühlberger, who hired me and supported the establishment of the Office of Research and Evaluation; Kent Lydecker, with whom I've enjoyed many great conversations about art and about museum visitors; and Nick Ruocco, now departed, who was the very essence of a museum educator and who taught us all about how important museums can be in the lives of children. Also, while we were at the Met, many people made our work better, easier to get accomplished, and more fun. Thank you to Nancy Posternak, DeWayne Phillips, Elyse Topalian, Bill McCabe, Hazel Rodriguez, and David Rosen.

Outside of the Met, I'd like to thank Kathryn Potts, who has always been eager to learn more about the folks who come to visit the Whitney, and has been great fun to work with. Beau Vallance, Ellen Giusti, and Deborah Schwarz have been lifelong leaders in the field of museum education and great friends and colleagues.

This book was written during a sabbatical leave from the University of Otago, in New Zealand; I appreciate the freedom to work and encouragement to explore what I think is important here in my adopted home.

Closer to home, I'd like to thank Leah Smith for editing this work, Benjamin Smith for reconstructing graphs into readable forms, and to both of them for coming with me on so many museum visits!

Finally, to Lisa, my partner in research, travel, aesthetics, adventure, and factor analysis, thank you, my love.

Preface

"I know mornings like that."

On the cover of this book a lone magpie sits on a farm gate on a winter morning with the snow resting heavily on the wattle fence and barren trees. The picture was rejected by the Salon of Paris in 1869, a fate not uncommon for Impressionist works. It is renowned for the way Monet, not yet thirty years old when he painted this scene, depicted the long shadows on the snow. But I think that if you stand in front of this work in the incredible Musée d'Orsay in Paris, the first thought that is most likely to go through your mind is: "I know mornings like that."

You can go from that work to see *Le Déjeuner Sur L'Herbe*, or *Olympia* by Manet, *The Card Players* by Cezanne, *The Gleaners* by Millet, and *The Absinthe Drinker* by Degas. And many, many more.

But what if museums did not exist?

What if, by some historical slip or accident, the concept of the museum had never been invented? There is no British Museum, no Louvre, no Metropolitan Museum of Art, no American Museum of Natural History, no Prado, no Uffizi, no Exploratorium, no Smithsonian. And let us include libraries in this thought experiment as well, and small museums in towns and neighborhoods as well. None of these exist. How would life be different?

There would be no great collections of art, nor of dinosaurs, no single location where one could follow the evolution of flight, no locus for understanding scientific discovery, no place for historians or archaeologists to contemplate the objects of their study, no place to see modern art that pushes the boundaries. There would be no way for a community or organization to say, "This is who we are; these are the artifacts that define our town."

Furthermore, there would not be a place to go for a Sunday afternoon, or a Tuesday over lunch to go immerse oneself in the presence of genius, to be able to stand before works that inspire, enlighten, illuminate. There would be no place to go choose any of thousands upon thousands of great works of literature and take them home to read, for free. We would have fewer opportunities to remove ourselves from our workaday lives and reflect upon our current status and our aspirations. How great would our diminishment be?

If we can contemplate how much we would lose if we did not have our cultural institutions, we can appreciate how much we gain because we do have them. To put it simply: *museums matter*. My purpose in this book is to explore how museums matter to us. We can all have a sense of how museums matter at a societal level. Museums collect, preserve, interpret, and present the objects that are important to us. These objects are great works of art, historical artifacts, and cultural icons. We might also include institutions that nurture and present living objects such as arboretums, botanical gardens, zoos, and ecosanctuaries. Museums are a hallmark of civilized society. Museums tell us that our history is important to us, that the arts are important to us, that we will remember the great things of our heritage and the less noble as well. They bind us together and permit us to experience firsthand those things that are precious to us not as individuals, but as groups of people, as communities and societies.

I think that we have some idea of the importance of major museums and cultural institutions. One cannot think of Paris for long without thinking of the Louvre. The Guggenheim has fundamentally changed the image of Bilbao. Museums help to define the locations in which they reside, both in terms of broad public image and perception, but also in how the members of the city or town think about themselves.

Museums (and by that I mean cultural institutions in general, but "museum" is a bit less clunky than "cultural institutions") exist because *we want them to exist*. They exist when people have decided that they are not just a collection of individuals; they are a community and they want to share the important objects of their community among themselves and with visitors. That community might be a neighborhood or small town; it might be an organization or a religious group; or, it might be as large as a country. At some point, a group of people found their affiliation with one another to be so strong that they decided that it was important that objects of shared value be housed and displayed for all members to see. To be sure, some museums are the result of a wealthy donor, and others rose up around a historic event, but in each case, there is the notion that the museum represents some community of people, and it almost always represents what this community feels is best about them.

A museum proclaims, "There is a community here. And these are the things that define our community."

We see the importance and impact of museums at a public and communal level, but what about at an individual level? How do museums affect us one person at a time? What happens when a firefighter or a schoolteacher or a retired botanist stands in front of a Botticelli and contemplates his or her life? How is a person affected when she moves from that Botticelli to a Michelangelo, or a Giotto? And as that person takes a walk through the museum, seeing dozens, or even hundreds of works of art, what is the effect that accrues in that person? How is that person different from what she was when she walked into the museum two hours earlier?

I believe that museums have a civilizing effect on society that can affect not only as communities, but also one person at a time. That is, people who visit museums and use the opportunity of that visit to reflect upon their lives and society become "better" people as a result of that visit. This is a somewhat daring claim, but I believe it to be true, and hope to convince you of that in the ensuing pages. I don't believe it happens with every visitor, or with any visitor on every visit, but I think it is a phenomenon that occurs frequently within the halls of the museum. And thus, I call it the *Museum Effect*. I think the Museum Effect occurs within different kinds of cultural institutions, including libraries, but my focus will be on the art museum. It is where I've done the most research and spent the most time.

I first started going to art museums when I was a sophomore at Princeton in 1969–1970. I would go to the Princeton Art Museum during the school year and to the Art Institute of Chicago when I was home during the summer. It was a very strange and unsettled time in America. You could look it up. But I found in the Princeton Art Museum one object that was a particular source of serenity and peacefulness and that took me away from the burning issues of the day: a painting of a meadow in Giverny by Claude Monet. I would go to the art museum on the way back from class and spend a few minutes looking at the Monet. I would look at other works as well, but I'd always come back to the meadow by Monet. It carried me away to a different time and place. I imagined being Monet on the day he painted that meadow. I wondered what it would be like to live in Paris in the 1890s. In the Art Institute there was another painting by Monet, of the railway station at St. Lazare, and also a Caillebotte painting of a rainy street scene in Paris. I would invent other lives as I looked at those works.

Sometimes I wondered if I were looking at a work properly. Was I supposed to be seeing things that I didn't see? Was I supposed to stand close or at a distance? Was it OK if I thought about things that were only tangentially related to the painting as I stood in front of it? Was it pretentious of me to think that I should even be allowed to view this painting, as I had no background in art history?

In writing this preface, I looked up the Monet painting at Giverny online, and was amused to find that it didn't look like I remembered it. I had reconstructed it over the decades, and laughed when I saw it. In fact, at first I was pretty sure that this wasn't the same painting, but eventually I realized it was. And as I looked a bit longer at the image on my computer screen, the old familiarity began to come back. I was taken back to a time where the world was unsteady, but my future seemed unbounded.

The ideas that form the basis of this book come from nearly twenty years of being the head of the Office of Research and Evaluation at the incredible Metropolitan Museum of Art. During that time and since, I also have had the opportunity to work with a number of other extraordinary institutions, including the Philadelphia Museum of Art, the St. Louis Art Museum, the Brooklyn Museum, and the American Museum of Natural History, among others. "Museum people" are great people to work with; they are passionate about their field, dedicated to their jobs, and horribly underpaid. It has been an honor to be associated with them.

I've written this book primarily for the people who work in cultural institutions, people who might see their own visitors in the stories I tell and the studies I present. In addition to people currently working in such institutions, I hope that people studying to become museum professionals might read this as well. I have tried to either document my arguments with prior research, or make them sufficiently logical that they can be accepted where the documentation is not all that I would like it to be. I don't see this as a finished product so much as an invitation to join with me in thinking about museums and their effects on individuals, as I have joined with others who study our cultural institutions.

I have tried to write in an informal fashion, for two reasons. First, I believe it is easier to read, and second, because I enjoy writing in this style. I hope you will excuse me if you find too many anecdotes, and are able to stay with me when I present some material that may be a bit quantitative at times. I have aimed for a middle path in both regards, but I may have colored outside the lines once or twice along the way.

To my great joy, my journey in exploring museums and the people who come to visit them has not been a solitary one. I have been joined almost every step of the way by my wonderful wife, Lisa, who is a scholar of aesthetics and museum studies of the first rank. We might have written this book together had she not been so busy being the dean of the College of Education at the University of Otago (and hence my boss!). Throughout the book, I talk about work that "we" have done, our ideas that "we" have explored.

I do not mean the royal "we" or the rhetorical "we"; I mean "Lisa and me." Sometimes I mean those of us who work in the museum field, but mostly I mean "Lisa and me."

There are seven chapters in this book. I start with an introduction to the general topic, and then look at the research on who comes to museums and why. Then, in chapter 3, I examine three concepts that are important to understanding the Museum Effect: time, flow, and the unit of analysis. In chapter 4, I lay out the argument for the Museum Effect, considering a number of models that have preceded this effort. In chapter 5, I examine how the Museum Effect might be extended to other cultural institutions and libraries. It is a very interesting exercise to think about how a history museum differs from an art museum, and how a botanical garden differs from both of them. In chapter 6, I look at how the Museum Effect might be enhanced by looking at the wealth of possibilities that exist for augmenting museum visitation. And then in chapter 7, I present some ideas on how the Museum Effect and related research might be examined by others who are interested in this work, or have burning questions of their own that they would like to study. Although this chapter only scratches the surface of conducting research in museums, I hope it provides some insight into the methods of the social scientist.

1

Introduction—Who We Are, Who We Were, Who We Might Become

"That's the baby Jesus."

These words came from a beautiful young Hispanic girl visiting the Metropolitan Museum of Art from a shelter for families who could not afford housing; they were spoken softly and to herself. Or perhaps she was speaking to Raffaello Sanzio da Urbino ("Raphael") who painted the altarpiece that this girl was viewing (Figure 1.1). Or perhaps, she was simply speaking to the baby Jesus.

Her reverie was temporarily broken by her big brother who informed her, "That ain't no baby Jesus. Why you say such things?" He then walked away, but the spell was cast. She turned once again to the altarpiece and affirmed with a smile, "That *is* the baby Jesus." Across five centuries, Raphael could still put joy into the hearts of the faithful.

This is what art does. It is what museums do. And, I will argue in the pages to follow, this ability to inspire us in our lives may well extend to other cultural institutions and libraries as well. These institutions show us *who we are, who we were, and who we might become.* Simply put, they make us better people. They are critical in the lives of those who visit them and to the communities in which they reside. This is a bold contention, but for the professionals who spend their careers within such institutions, perhaps not too audacious a claim. Curators, librarians, educators, docents, and guards observe the impact of cultural institutions on visitors on a daily basis. They overhear the conversations, see the awe, watch the interactions, and occasionally have to ask folks not to get too close to the works that are so amazing. They see people come to pursue their passions, find their ancestors, or read the works of Shakespeare or a novelist they've just discovered. Perhaps they simply want to spend an hour or so in the presence of genius—to stand in

1

Figure 1.1.   Raphael. Madonna and Child Enthroned with Saints. Altarpiece, ca. 1504.
Image copyright © The Metropolitan Museum of Art. Image source: Art Resource, NY

front of a work of art where Degas, Botticelli, or O'Keeffe once stood before, to listen to a Stradivarius playing Beethoven, or to imagine that they are
Henry V delivering the Saint Crispin's Day speech. They let the greatness
imbue them, they transform that greatness into their own lives, and in doing
so, they become better people.

The people for whom such transformations take place are not art experts. They are not historians or literary critics; they may not know a whole lot about the works that they encounter. They are firemen, salesclerks, college students, homemakers, lawyers, airline pilots, and schoolteachers. There are no doubt layers upon layers of meaning and depth in the objects they stand in front of that they do not (and may not ever) appreciate. There are, for many works, layers of meaning known only to those who created the works. That is not the issue here. The issue concerns the encounter between an ordinary individual and a great work of art. It is the essence of what art, in its various forms (and I want to define it ultimately as broadly as possible), does when seriously contemplated by an individual. It holds the potential to be transformative. But it may not simply be the case of a person contemplating a single work of art. It may be a bit more complex than that. It may be a person contemplating a series of works of art, dozens, perhaps even hundreds over the course of a museum visit. It may be that it is the cumulative effect of looking at many different works of art, each for a fairly short period of time, that has the power to change how people look at themselves, their interactions with others, and life in general.

I have a wonderful photograph of the young girl from the homeless shelter looking at the Raphael, but sadly no way to get in touch with her to get permission to use it. She loved that painting. So did the tycoon, J. Pierpont Morgan, who bought it in 1901 and gave it to the Metropolitan in his estate. We'll come back to this young girl, but right now, as we are getting started on this journey, let's move halfway around the world, shifting our focus from one of the world's great museums to a small community museum in Waikouaiti, New Zealand, not far from where this book is being written. The Waikouaiti Coast Heritage Centre is only about three rooms large, depending on what you count as a room, and contains objects that reflect the history of this small, ocean-side community (Figure 1.2). It is fascinating in its own right, housing some objects completely foreign to a modern mind, as well as wonderful artifacts like the blueprint for the Lunatic Asylum at Seacliff (which existed for a number of years near Waikouaiti, but is now gone) (Figure 1.3).

In discussing the museum with curator Helen McComb and volunteer Linda Doubleday, a number of stories about the museum emerged. One in particular stood out. Helen was visited by a young Māori man who wanted to look into a family story. Coming from a strong oral tradition among Māori *whānau* (extended families), it seems that generations ago, another young Māori man had walked many kilometers from the south end of the South Island so that he and his betrothed could be married by a preacher who had taken up residence in Waikouaiti. Might the head of the museum have any evidence of such an event, he inquired? Could this young man make a

Figure 1.2.   Waikouaiti Coast Heritage Centre, New Zealand.
Photo by Jeffrey Smith

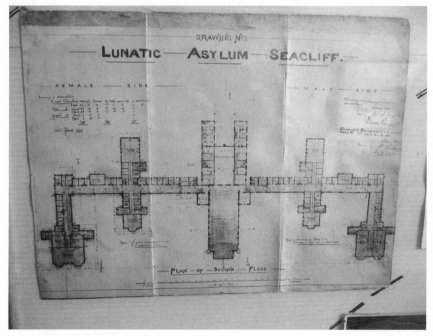

Figure 1.3.   Plans for the Lunatic Asylum at Seacliff.
Photo by Jeffrey Smith

connection with his *whakapapa* (heritage)? Well, indeed there was such a record. His ancestors had been the first couple married by the reverend, and it was there to be seen in the register. His great-great-great-grandfather had stood in front of this register and signed his name. And now, over a hundred years later, another young Māori man stood in front of the same register, at about the same age, and united with that ancestor. And, as it turns out, his great-great-great-grandmother signed in another part of the register, as the first convert to Christianity in the area. So this young man, whose cultural heritage emphasizes oral tradition and lineage, had both of those aspects of his ancestry confirmed because someone decided a registry was important to save and a community believed in creating a museum. It was a good day for him, and for his family, perhaps for generations to come.

Oh, and the Lunatic Asylum at Seacliff? Well, at various times, it housed one of New Zealand's most famous writers, Janet Frame. She tells horrible stories of her time there. What struck me on the day I saw the blueprints, though, was that at the time they were first drawn up, the asylum did not exist, nor did it exist as I stood there looking at it. But in between the time of the drawing and the time of my viewing of the plans, it was built (poorly and on unstable land), had a life of roughly eighty-six years, a terrible fire taking dozens of lives, and then itself, ultimately died. It had wings of equal size for males and females, anticipating, one supposes, an equal gender distribution of lunacy. At times it was a terrible place and at other times a model one. Its director for thirty years was Dr. Truby King, perhaps second only to Sir Edmund Hillary with respect to the regard with which he is held in New Zealand. He started the Plunkett Society, which to this day offers outstanding services to expectant women and new mothers. And so one looks at an interesting set of blueprints on the wall of a community museum and thoughts tentacle out to include a famous and troubled novelist, how we view and treat people with mental illness, social programs to reduce infant mortality and give children a better start at life, and even to scaling Mount Everest. The Lunatic Asylum at Seacliff is now gone, no more in existence than then. It had lived its life as we do, and was now a recollection, as we will be. (I take one more look at the plans for the asylum and note that it also looks a bit like one of the spacecrafts from *Star Wars*. Why the near-perfect symmetry? Why the long extensions and hallways?)

This book is about museums, libraries, and other cultural institutions, and how they affect us and the communities in which we live, especially when we let them. It is something I call the *Museum Effect*. I call it the *Museum Effect* as opposed to the *Museums, Other Cultural Institutions, and Libraries Effect*, for the sake of simplicity. From time to time in this book, I use the term "cultural institutions" to refer to all kinds of organizations collectively. I want to include in the conversation history museums, science museums, arboretums, archives, and public, school, and university libraries. I want to be able to consider the blueprints for the Lunatic Asylum at Seacliff, and the simple signatures of a young man and his betrothed that were kept over the years to be found by a distant descendant. The net is cast wide here, because each of these institutions holds the "promise" to educate, inform, and inspire as my friend and colleague David Carr (2004) says of cultural institutions so much more elegantly than I do here.

Now, having said that I want to talk about all of our cultural institutions and libraries (and perhaps beyond to musical performances, ballet, etc.), the simple fact of the matter is that most of the data I have on the topic is related to my "home institution," the art museum. When people look at art, and when they do so going from one work of art to another as they wander through a museum, or perhaps a special exhibition within a museum, we believe that there is a tendency to use the artworks as a vehicle for personal reflection, a kind of personal mirror. That is, the art causes us to reflect on our own lives. We bring who we are to our interaction with the work, and we often leave a slightly different person than when we were just a few minutes before. Now, might we anticipate the same phenomenon occurring if the objects were historical in nature rather than artistic? What if they were astronomical images rather than works of art? What if they were plants, or might this also work in a library or when in a grand concert hall listening to a symphony? We suspect that the answer to these questions is a qualified "yes," but there is much work that would have to be done to make that "yes" more certain and less qualified. At the end of this book, we look specifically at those questions and invite the reader who works in a history or science museum, an arboretum, or a performing arts venue to join in at looking at such possibilities.

The Museum Effect is simple. It is what happens when we encounter a work of art, book, or event that causes us to reflect upon who we are. We may not even be cognizant that we are doing so. We might simply see a dog in a painting that reminds us of a dog we had as a child, and such a connection might spur thinking about our childhood—maybe friends, maybe family events, and this may then prompt a decision to give a call to a special aunt. On another level, we might see a work that takes our breath away, one that is visually stunning and that has incredible depth and meaning for us. It sets off a very different chain of reactions and musings. A good example of this in my personal experience occurred on a visit to the Philadelphia Museum of Art. My wife and research collaborator, Lisa, were there to talk about conducting a study with the museum, and took the time to see the permanent collection. We turned a corner and encountered Rogier van der Weyden's *The Crucifixion, with the Virgin and Saint John the Evangelist Mourning* (Figure 1.4).

When I first saw this remarkable diptych, I thought it was out of place in the museum. It looked like a modern painting, even somewhat abstract, not

Figure 1.4.   van der Weyden. The Crucifixion, with the Virgin and Saint John the Evangelist Mourning, c. 1450–55.
The Philadelphia Museum of Art / Art Resource, NY

one that was over five hundred years old! It is a large work (almost six feet by six feet), and magnificently presented by the museum. Christ is presented on a cross that is in front of a wall that I had never seen in a crucifixion painting before. A blood-red cloth is hung over the wall behind Christ. Mary and John the Evangelist are presented in a panel to the left. The painting was presented so that one looked up to the work. The panel on the left suggested that this was originally a triptych, and that the third panel was missing. My thoughts jumbled as I took this painting in. I should point out that I am not a religious person, but I was wholly taken aback by this work—at first by its crisp, clean, and startling imagery. It seemed so modern. The next things that struck me were the use of the red in the hanging behind Christ and by the drapery in Mary's dress. Are the drapes symbolic of Christ's blood? Are the folds in Mary's dress indicative of her sorrow? For me they have a sense of one's emotional life being crumpled. Why does Christ's garment appear to be blowing in a wind that does not appear elsewhere in the work? Does this suggest a spirit that will rise on the third day? Were any of these thoughts intended by van der Weyden, or are they my own inventions?

I began to wonder how this work came to be, what was it used for originally? There are a variety of speculations in the scholarship on the work, including that it was indeed a triptych, possibly two of four panels, or perhaps a single work that had been turned into two. In my mind it seems that surely it was a triptych. There is some speculation that the painting might have been donated by the artist to a monastery. But I did not know those things at the time. I just wondered about them. And this led me to wondering about how such incredible skill as possessed by van der Weyden comes to be employed in religious art during the Renaissance. How was religious belief different than from what it is today? What role would a painting like this play in the lives of people who saw it regularly, and in its original context? What were van der Weyden's religious beliefs? Was this merely a commission for him, or was his heart and soul on display here as well as a crucifixion scene? Were the people who saw this painting in van der Weyden's time only the affluent? Or were there people like the peasants who are depicted in Monty Python films viewing this as well—seeing their Lord and Savior in a respite from lives otherwise dreary at best? Did this work alter the courses of people's lives? Did people wonder five hundred years ago what the significance of the wall behind Jesus was? And as I delved into such reveries, about every half minute or so, I would be struck anew with the thought of "Man, this is one stunning painting!"

So why isn't this book called "*The Art Effect*" instead of "*The Museum Effect*"? Because a visit to a cultural institution isn't just one encounter with one object; it is a series of such encounters, and these objects take us on a ride filled with twists and turns, causing us to contemplate not only the art we are viewing, but ourselves as well—*who we are, who we were, and who we might become*—in dozens of different ways. Each stop holds the potential to hold a small mirror up to us, to engage us in a brief dialogue—perhaps with a sculptor who is no longer there, or a poet, or a composer, or the imaginary engineer of a locomotive in a railway museum. It was hard to leave the van der Weyden diptych, as it was simply thrilling. And then, not two minutes after having encountered the van der Weyden diptych, we came across a work of art entitled *Fountain* by Marcel Duchamp (Figure 1.5). Now, I had known about Duchamp from my undergraduate days but had not actually seen this oddly famous work (or more properly this reproduction of the work). It seemed to me to be the "anti–van der Weyden," and yet here it was, presented to me almost immediately after the van der Weyden. What *was* this? How was it a work of art? I left the work without too much more thought other

Figure 1.5.   Fountain, 1950 (replica of 1917 original).
The Philadelphia Museum of Art / Art Resource, NY, Also: © Succession Marcel Duchamp / ADAGP, Paris / Artists Rights Society (ARS), New York 2013

than what an amusing counterpoint it made to the van der Weyden. Whereas the van der Weyden kept eliciting, "Man, this is one stunning painting," the Duchamp elicited, "Yep, that's a urinal."

In writing this chapter, and in looking again at the piece, I saw that it is not in the "proper" alignment. The back of the urinal is lying flat. I noticed this first because I couldn't figure out what the pipe coming out the front was. In my experience, urinals don't have such a front piece. So, what is it? Did Duchamp affix it there himself? No, it is the plumbing used to run the water down to flush the urinal when the urinal is properly aligned. Rotate the image 180 degrees so that the pipe is facing away from you, and then 90 degrees "down" so that the pipe is now pointing toward the top of the page. This would be how a urinal would look when properly aligned. So why was it positioned in the fashion that it is as a work of art? You can see from the "signature" that this positioning is intentional. And then it occurred to me that if one were to actually "use" this work of art with regard to its original intention, that piece of plumbing would cause the urinal to in fact become a fountain! One that would deposit its flow on your shoes. I'm guessing that is the real reason Duchamp called it *Fountain* in the first place. Just a guess on my part—I can't find anything written on this notion, but I'm happy with my conclusion, and I like the piece more than I did before stumbling upon this possibility. I feel a certain kinship with Duchamp because of it. Again, I have no idea if I am right or wrong on this, but if I'm right, then it's funny, and I feel like I have solved a little puzzle that Duchamp posed with this work.

Now contrast that feeling to the ones I described when standing in front of the van der Weyden. Different as night and day. The Duchamp is a treat, a trifle. I have no need to contemplate deeper meanings or look for things in that urinal that might lead to something more profound. The van der Weyden is a work I can go back to time and again. It is filet mignon compared to the Duchamp trifle. I am not arguing for Renaissance art or against conceptual art. In fact, the Duchamp made the perfect counterpoint to the van der Weyden at the time. It took my thinking from one place and turned it around 180 degrees (in a manner of speaking)!

Let's move away from art museums for a minute and consider some other settings. My daughter and I like to go to museums whenever we can get together, and recently the opportunity that presented itself was the National Air and Space Museum Steven F. Udvar-Hazy Center, which is an extension of the Smithsonian Air and Space Museum located near Dulles Airport. We had no idea what we would find there except that friends said it was a pretty cool place. And it was truly amazing. Contained in the enormous hangar-like facility are hundreds of aircraft of all varieties, including a few famous ones, notably the *Enola Gay* and the space shuttle *Discovery* (Figure 1.6).

Unlike the visiting behaviors of most folks to museums (as will be documented in detail later), my daughter and I tend to spend a long time in front of particular objects. (We once spent two hours watching a coopersmith make a bucket at the Museum of America and the Sea in Mystic, Connecticut. After a wonderful two hours, the coopersmith said, "No one has ever watched me make a bucket from beginning to end like you two have.")

While we were looking at the shuttle, we struck up a conversation with a docent who was stationed at the shuttle. My daughter noted that the exterior of the shuttle wasn't smooth as she had anticipated, but rather had a kind of quilted and rough appearance. The docent explained to us that what we were looking at was indeed a kind of a quilt and that it was made of

Figure 1.6.   Space Shuttle Discovery.
Jeffrey Smith

"felted" material. It looked like it was woven or knitted. My daughter is a knitter, and the notion of the space shuttle having this material protecting it from the heat was particularly appealing to her. A conversation about knitting ensued among the three of us, which was soon joined by an Elvis impersonator and his wife. So there were the five of us, brought together by one of the most amazing machines ever devised by human beings, and we were sharing knitting and weaving stories. It occurred to me that the five individuals who found themselves on the Bridge of San Luis Rey were also impacted by weaving (the bridge that collapses had been made of woven material by the Incas), and then I thought about how we were "woven" together at that moment by the space shuttle. I kept both of those thoughts to myself as we had already had plenty of "You're so weird, Dad" moments that day. But the conversation was a lovely one, with each individual bringing to the group some personal tale that could be related to an object that had gone into space and was now resting before us.

One of the fascinating aspects of the Museum Effect is that it does not require expertise on the part of the person experiencing it. The effect may even be more pronounced among those who are not sophisticated with regard to what they are viewing, interacting with, or listening to. If one doesn't know who influenced this artist, or when in the artist's career this painting was made, or what famous person might have owned it, then the ability for the viewer to make a personal connection with the work that is of the person's own making is likely enhanced. A few years ago, the brother of a friend of ours decided to take his wife to Broadway for her birthday, and wondered if going to the Metropolitan Museum of Art might also be a good idea. He was a New York Port Authority police officer, but lived in New Jersey, and had never been to the Met. And, to tell the truth, he was only thinking of going because it would garner him some additional marital bargaining units with his wife on their trip to Broadway, and he would be in the general vicinity anyway. He had actually never been to any kind of art museum. My wife and I were called upon to make recommendations about a visit. The Egyptian galleries is always a good start for those who might be a bit leery of art in general, and the Arms and Armor galleries we thought might resonate with an officer of the law. And then we pushed and suggested European paintings as a kind of branching out of the experience. (We also recommended a nice Italian restaurant near the theater.)

We hoped for a good response but were surprised by how excited this individual was about the Met. He told us all about the trip, asking if we knew this, that, and the other aspect about the museum, and how wonderful the paintings in the European galleries were. He even organized an outing to the museum for his colleagues at the precinct. He was a convert. Does this happen with every first-time visitor to a cultural institution? We have evidence that it does not. But, we also have evidence that it does happen from time to time and that it happens every day at the Met. About one in five visitors to the Metropolitan is a first-time visitor to the museum, and a good number of those tell us that they are certain to return. And some of those tell us that their visit was "wondrous," "incredible," even "life changing." Over almost twenty years at the Met, we've wandered the galleries quite a bit (yes, it *was* a cool job). To be honest, for the most part, we didn't see people who seemed to be in the midst of a life change. We saw people who appeared to be seriously contemplating what they were standing in front of. They would stand there for a while, read the accompanying information, take a parting glance back at the object, and then move on to the next work. But the next work might not even merit a stop. Sometimes the briefest of previews at a work led to the conclusion that time would not be invested there. The emotional reactions one sees can probably best be described as "muted." There are more nods and "hmms" than looks of wonder and "wows"; heads are tilted, eyebrows are raised, and shoulders are shrugged.

We have struggled for years to reconcile these seemingly contradictory messages. We would read comments in comment books and on surveys about how wonderful the museum visit was. We heard the same kinds of evaluations when talking to visitors person to person. We often encountered individuals like our friend the NYC police officer whose enthusiasm for the museum was hard to contain. Still, it was difficult to actually see in situ. It was baffling. It still is to a degree, but we have found a tentative answer to that conundrum that satisfies us, for the moment at any rate. It involves acknowledging the behaviors that we see, the reports that we hear, and data that we analyze as all being accurate reflections of a somewhat complex phenomenon. People go to museums by the millions upon millions. Millions went yesterday and millions more will tomorrow. They do so voluntarily; they see things that reflect genius, accomplishment, uniqueness, natural beauty, and creativity blended with expertise. They will look at a variety, perhaps a very wide variety, of objects while they are at the museum or other cultural institution that they have chosen to attend. They might spend a great deal of time at one object, as my daughter and I are wont to do, but in all honesty, we have fairly strong evidence (presented in following chapters) that typically people do *not* spend a lot of time in front of a particular object. Instead, they spend a relatively short amount of time in front of a lot of objects. Thus, the wonderfulness that they speak of typically does not occur in a peak moment in front of a single object, but rather it accumulates gradually as visitors wander from one object to another. And again, unlike myself with my daughter, the docent, the Elvis impersonator, and his wife, it typically does not happen in a communal and shared activity (although that might be a part of the experience), but with individuals looking at a work alone and contemplating the meaning that that work has for that individual alone. If there is a dialogue, it is with the work, and possibly with its creator, not, typically, with the person one came to the museum with.

If all of this seems a bit odd, it does to me as well at times. But I think it is real. The Museum Effect takes place when individuals take the opportunity to visit an art museum, or perhaps another kind of museum or cultural institution, and they use the opportunity of that visit to let their mind wander constructively—to explore not just the objects, but themselves in relation to those objects, and occasionally just themselves using the objects as springboards or mirrors. They think about who they are as individuals, how they relate to other people and how those people view them, where their life is going, what they are contributing to their friends, their families, or the future. Each new object that they encounter provides them with a new puzzle to solve, a new mirror with which to see themselves, a new opportunity for reflection and contemplation. Some of those objects may be as stunning as the van der Weyden crucifixion or the space shuttle *Discovery*, or as humble as the urinal of Duchamp or the bucket made by the coopersmith at Mystic Seaport. Whenever individuals encounter such works, they bring with them their life histories and interpret the objects with regard to their own experiences, lives, expectations, hopes, and aspirations. The object starts the process for the individual but where that encounter will go, where it will end up, will depend to a great degree on whom the individual is who is looking at it. The Duchamp urinal no doubt has engendered an incredible variety of response over the years, ranging from intense contempt to whimsical amusement. And from such contempt or amusement, what is the next reaction or thought? Where does the viewer go from there? Where does the mind wander to? Now consider the variety of objects that one might encounter in a museum visit and consequently the variety of reflections, emotions, or musings a person might engage in when viewing those objects. The reactions to the objects one at a time don't have to be wondrous or life altering, but they might well accumulate, or accrete, or conglomerate, into an experience that is viewed very positively, and that engenders a return to that institution and the motivation to visit others of the same and of different kinds. It is the Museum Effect.

REFERENCE

Carr, D. W. (2004). *The promise of cultural institutions*. Walnut Creek, CA: Left Coast Press.

2

The Nature of Visits to Cultural Institutions

"**W**here are the dinosaurs?"

I used to like to stand on the balcony of the Great Hall of the Metropolitan Museum of Art and watch people begin their visit. The Great Hall is a magnificent Beaux-Arts room that is larger than many entire museums. There is typically little or no art in the Great Hall (except for the impressive architecture and design of the room itself). It is a place to pay an entrance fee, acquire a map of the museum, and plan one's visit. My wife, Lisa, and I would often stand on the balcony and play "spot the out-of-towners." This was a game where we would try to pick out those folks who were visiting the museum from outside the New York metropolitan region. It wasn't really hard to do. The Great Hall is rather intimidating the first time you enter it. The admissions booths are located well off to the side. These visitors would wander around a bit, look up at the ceiling of the Great Hall, talk to one another, and usually make their way to an information island in the middle of the room. They would engage someone from the Visitor's Services department, and eventually be directed to the admissions booth. Of course, we just assumed they were out-of-towners; they might have been from the East Side of New York City (but we don't think so). And yes, they occasionally would ask about the dinosaurs, which are located on the other side of Central Park at the American Museum of Natural History.

According to the American Alliance of Museums, on any given day, about two and a half million people visit an American museum (American Alliance of Museums, n.d.) or other cultural institution. Another five million or so go to a library (Miller et al., 2011). The corresponding figure for museums in the UK is roughly a third of a million (Museums Association, n.d.). A fair number of these visitors will return to the same museum or visit another over

15

the course of a year: the typical visitor goes to a museum about four times a year. Museums are a regular part of their lives. We know that at the Metropolitan Museum of Art, some people visit monthly, or even more often (some we saw so often we were fairly certain they owned condos somewhere in the building). Some visitors travel from halfway around the world to come to the Met; others come from just up Fifth Avenue. Some individuals have planned their visit for months or even years; others are simply coming in out of an unexpected rain shower. Some know exactly what it is that they want to see; others ask about the dinosaurs.

Each visit is unique—an insight here, a new artist discovered there, a meaningful connection to one's life uncovered or invented. There are millions of stories that might be told about these visits. In this chapter, I describe the nature of the museum visitor from a variety of perspectives (who they are, why they come, what they anticipate, what they do while in the institution). There are numbers and graphs in this chapter, so fair warning to the humanities majors.

FIVE MUSEUM VISITS

But let's begin in a softer focus by looking at some examples we have come upon during our time in museums. These are presented so that we can look back on them later in the chapter (and in subsequent chapters) as exemplars of the trends and statistics that will be presented.

Mario the Airline Captain

Mario was the captain of a Portuguese 747 airliner whom we interviewed as he exited an exhibition of Byzantine art at the Metropolitan Museum of Art (Smith & Carr, 2001) (an example of such art is shown in Figure 2.1, and in Figure 2.2). He wasn't a big art fan in particular, but he always liked to see what the cities that he flew to had to offer, and realizing he knew nothing about Byzantine art, he decided he would take a chance on a visit. He found the exhibition as a whole striking, maybe even a bit baffling. He told us that "the exhibition took me to a place I'd never been before and to experience a culture and people I have never known. Who were these people, what were their lives like? Could I even understand them as a people? I was raised a Catholic, and these people were also Catholic, but they seem very different from my experience. I have many things to think about. This is very different art from any that I have ever really looked at before. You know, my crew is spending the day shopping or seeing the Statue of Liberty. In five years they will have forgotten this day, but I will never forget it."

Figure 2.1. Sardonyx Cameo with the Archangel Michael.
Image copyright © The Metropolitan Museum of Art. Image source: Art Resource, NY

Father Edward

Also at the Byzantine exhibition was Father Edward, an Episcopalian minis-
ter. For him, too, this was a first encounter with Byzantine art. But there was
a resonance for him that differed greatly from what we heard from Mario.
For Edward, this was not simply an art exhibition; it was an exhibition of

religious art. Perhaps it was even a religious exhibition of art. He was not at the Met because he had nothing else to do for a few hours (the case for Mario); he had taken the day to come see religious art that was unfamiliar to him. Father Edward shared a "level of ignorance" with Mario, but he already had a meaningful connection to what he was about to see. These were works of a somewhat different version of his religion and his vocation. He was particularly taken with a beautiful Byzantine censer (incense burner) (Figure 2.2). He told us, "Many of the works were so beautiful, but the one that took me away was the censer. I imagined using it in my church. I could see myself swinging it gently as the smell of the incense wafted through the church. I thought, 'Now that is just being vain,' but I really couldn't help myself. Then I laughed out loud right there in the exhibition." And then he said with a smile, "But I would look really good with that censer!"

The Bride

Shifting away from Byzantine art, in another good example of the sort of thing that can happen in an art museum, we once talked to an elderly woman in an exhibition of Sienese Renaissance art. She had taken up a position in front of a predella piece (part of the base of an altar), *Flight into Egypt* by Giovanni di Paolo, and stood looking at it longingly. It struck me as more of a "nice enough" work of art than something that would merit such loving attention. I approached the woman and asked her how she was enjoying the exhibition. She responded, "Well, it's all beautiful. I've been to Siena several times, but this is the piece that is special to me. It was brought here from Siena for the exhibition, you know. But I first saw it in the city of Siena. Fifty years ago, my husband proposed to me in front of this painting. This is the first time I've seen it since then. He was a wonderful man." We talked a bit more about the works in the exhibition, and I asked how long it had been since her husband passed away. "My husband? He's right over there." Apparently it was only his wonderfulness that had passed; he was still in pretty good shape. But the specialness of the moment of his proposal to her had been recovered by the exhibition. I asked if she knew the painting would be at the exhibition. "No, but I hoped."

The Girl in the Costume Institute

Shortly after we started working at the Met, there was a wonderful exhibition at the Costume Institute called *The Age of Napoleon: Costume from Revolution to Empire, 1789–1815*. We conducted a survey of visitors to the exhibition, and asked what would become one of our favorite survey questions:

Figure 2.2.   Censer with Six Holy Figures. Early Byzantine.
Image copyright © The Metropolitan Museum of Art. Image source: Art Resource, NY

"If the curator for the exhibition were here, what question would you have for her?" This generated hundreds of interesting "questions" and provided food for thought with regard to that exhibition and future ones. A question that arose frequently had to do with the nature of the clothes—"What does ermine feel like?" and "Can I touch that robe?" Well, the answer to the latter question is "No," but the former question is not "out of the question." One couldn't touch the ermine on a particular robe, but providing examples of the material that people could touch would not be unreasonable. It was a great idea and well received by the curator of the exhibition for future shows. But the question that struck us most, and that has become a kind of touchstone for our research was this one:

"What did twelve-year-old girls wear in the age of Napoleon?"

This presumably twelve-year-old girl wanted to know where she fit into this picture. What would she and her friends be wearing? Who would she be here and what would she be looking like? I think we all ask a version of that question from time to time. We see something that sparks our imagination, and we put ourselves in a different place and time, and often a different persona. We never met that girl, but I hope she is still going to museums and wondering where she fits in with what she is seeing.

The Aspiring Genealogists

And finally, for now, a more personal story. On Tuesday evenings after work, I would meet my younger brother, Kevin, in the genealogy room of the New York City Public Library and we would engage in the detective game of searching for our ancestors. Some nights we would pursue the Jamestown colonists and Southern aristocrats from our father's side of the family, and on other nights we would hunt down the horse thieves and Molly Maguire coal-mining anarchists of my mother's side of the family (they were an interesting couple). Some nights we would focus on discovering who our ancestors were and other nights we would focus on their lives. What did they do? Where did they live? Why did they appear in court for stealing horses so often? Could it possibly be that our great-grandfather was a slave owner? Each time we secured evidence of a new ancestor or information about an ancestor that we had established as part of the family tree, it was like discovering an unopened present late on Christmas morning. Each find was a gem to be savored. And equally importantly, we got to work together as a team. We had shared a room together growing up until well into our teens, and it was great fun to be just the two of us again, sitting in a room that was filled with our lineage, daring us to uncover it.

Those are just five visits to cultural institutions. I am certain that if I asked any of the folks whose stories I have just recounted if they could remember the day (or days) of those visits in question, they would respond, "Absolutely." Could they remember the day before that visit or the day after? I seriously doubt it. Those are five stories. There are millions of visits to museums, cultural institutions, and libraries every day. How many of those visits have the impact of the ones I have just described (or of the girl seeing the baby Jesus in the Raphael altarpiece)? Certainly not all, maybe not most, but based on the work we have done in cultural institutions over the years, I am willing to argue at least, "many." And I'll take "many." If just one out of seven, that would mean a million stories like the ones above each and every day. I could give you many more. But I won't, just yet.

What do we learn from stories such as these as a whole? They are heartwarming affirmations of the impact of cultural institutions, but as a social scientist, I'd like to make some possible tentative conclusions about visits like this, draw some threads together if you will. To begin, visits to museums, libraries, and cultural institutions tend to be voluntary. People (adults in particular) *choose* to go to these institutions. The institution has been selected over other options—going shopping, gardening, visiting with a friend, going to a sporting event, watching television, baking a cake, and so forth. People have free time when they visit; they typically are not constrained or on a tight schedule. When we ask folks how long they will visit a museum, their responses are often very open and ill defined, more governed by past experience than by current time constraints. "A couple of hours" is a much more likely response than "Until 3:15." They will "see how it goes." In addition to choosing the idea of going to a museum or a library, they also choose the particular one that they will visit. Now, with libraries, this is often the closest library, but, as was the case with my brother and me, it might be a very specific library.

It is frequently the case, although not always so, that the visit has some degree of purpose to it. "I came to see the Degas exhibition." "I came because I haven't been in a long time." "I need to decompress." "I have an hour free at lunch and I don't want to eat too much." "I am almost out of books to read." "I want to find out how to . . ." "The exhibition is about to close and I didn't want to miss it." "I have to complete an assignment for my art history course." And so on. Now, that purpose might be fairly general, and part of the attraction of the institution is that it offers a lot of possibilities. Once inside, there are a lot of things that might be done or seen. Wandering through the galleries, the stacks, or the paths of an arboretum is part of the allure of cultural institutions. When we are at a cultural institution, we usually are on "Richard time," or "Christopher time," or "Martha time." And that's a good thing.

Visits to cultural institutions are often social events, particularly visits to museums. But they are rather strange social events. People go to museums in groups far more often than as individuals—at the Met, we consistently found that about 75 to 80 percent of visitors were in groups of two or more. But, once inside the museum, they frequently separate (not far) and then come back together again. It is almost as if the group were bounded by a very large rubber band. They drift apart within a room, with one member sometimes getting four or five paintings "ahead" of the other person or persons in the group, then they come back together again, usually before entering the next room or gallery, but occasionally to call one another to look at and discuss a particular work. In a study of how much time people would spend in front of a work of art (Smith & Smith, 2001), we found that of 150 individuals observed in front of six different works of art, 116 were looking at the work alone; 29 were with one other person, and only five were with more than one person. "Visit together—look alone" seems to be something of a rule of thumb in art viewing. People do talk to one another while looking at art, but more often than not they do not. Why is that? Why do people more often than not go to an art museum with one or more other people, but look at the works by themselves? As mentioned in the first chapter, we think the work of art serves as a springboard for personal reflection, and that for most of us, that personal reflection is, well, personal.

Visits to libraries are more likely to be individual visits and more likely to have a specific purpose, even if a "vague" specific purpose such as finding a new novel to read, or looking to see if there is anything interesting on the Civil War. Even if looking for a particular category of book, there is "openness" in a library visit (Carr, 2011). There are worlds that might be explored that are currently not known. Once, on a day that was supposed to be dedicated to working on the literature review for my dissertation, I spent four hours looking at books on "queuing theory" at Regenstein Library at the University of Chicago. Queuing theory happened to be located near the books that I was seeking out. I wasn't looking for a specific book, but rather wanted to see what books there were in the general area of interest I was pursuing. Thus, I was reading the titles of books as I got close to my goal. I came across a title on queuing theory and thought what an odd thing that was. Could there really be a theoretical area of research on how people stood in lines? I am not sure what books I was searching for at the time, but I do remember a lot about queuing theory. And before that day, I only really knew that queue was kind of British for "line" and that people stood in them politely. Now I know all sorts of arcane information about queues, including why elevators in a hotel all tend to come down to the lobby at the same time (you could look it up).

Let us take a wider focus and look at who goes to museums and why they do so. In order to get a comprehensive look at who goes to museums, we can begin with the Survey of Public Participation in the Arts, which is produced every few years by the U.S. National Endowment for the Arts (National Endowment for the Arts, 2009, 2013). We will move from there to looking at some models of types of individuals who visit museums. Some of what follows is drawn from a chapter on art museum visitation that lays out these issues in more detail than can be presented here (Tinio, Smith, & Smith, in press).

WHO GOES TO CULTURAL INSTITUTIONS AND EVENTS, AND WHY?

In 2008, almost four in every five Americans attended a cultural institution or cultural event (museums, historic sites, craft and music fairs, etc.) (National Endowment for the Arts, 2009). The NEA study for 2012 (National Endowment for the Arts, 2013) does not have a comparable aggregation, but Figure 2.3 presents a breakdown of cultural participation for adults by category of activity. It can be seen that almost fifty million adult Americans go to an art museum or gallery each year. Over fifty million go to a historic site. The list goes on with attendance at classical music, jazz, and operatic performances. Attendance at cultural institutions is broad in the United States, but is it widespread as well? Do all sorts of people attend cultural institution and events, or is this primarily the domain of a selected portion of the population? Is it, for example, only (or predominantly) the wealthy who attend such events?

The answer is that attendance is more widespread and diversified than what might be the conventional wisdom on such things. Again using the 2008 data, Figure 2.4 shows a breakdown of attendance at one of the events listed in Figure 2.3 by a number of demographic variables. This presents an elaborate portrait of who attends. We see that men and women attend almost equally, that whites are roughly twice as likely to attend as African Americans or Hispanics, that up to age seventy-five plus, attendance does not vary much by age (attendance drops off for senior citizens seventy-five and older), that income does play a factor in attendance—the wealthy do attend more than less well-off individuals, but that education appears to be most important in determining attendance than wealth. Indeed, in a more sophisticated statistical analysis presented in the same report, it is found that education has a much stronger influence on attendance than income. Figure 2.5 shows the increase in museum attendance by educational level in 2008. Although we see some decline in 2008 from 2002 (recall that 2008 was the beginning of the severe economic difficulties), we still see the strong relationship between education and attendance, with the big jumps coming between having a high school degree and some college, and again between some college and a college degree.

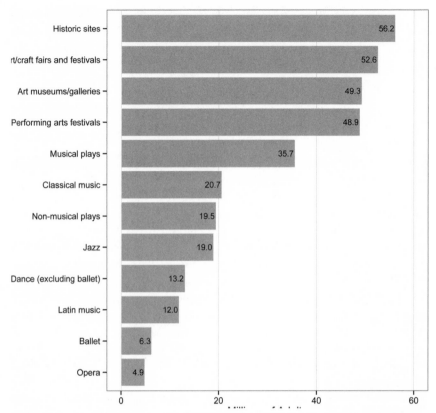

Figure 2.3. Attendance at performing arts and cultural institutions in United States in 2008.
Benjamin Smith

Types of Museum Visitors

The numbers and charts provide a pretty good idea of the breadth of visitors who attend cultural institutions and events, but the question arises as to just who these folks are. We know that there are a lot of them, but what are they like? Are there ways in which we can meaningfully categorize these visitors that are useful to our understanding of their reasons for visiting, motivations, and desires? In fact, there are some places we can go to for help, and we will look at several such efforts here.

Pekarik Typology

Andrew Pekarik and his colleagues (Pekarik, Doering, & Karns, 1999; Pekarik & Schreiber, 2012) at the Smithsonian Institutions have been conducting research on this question since the early 1990s and have a categorization

	US Population (Total)		Individual Attending Any benchmark activity	
	Millions	Percent	Breakdown of attendance in percent	Rate of attendance by group in percent
All adults	224.8	48.3		34.6
Gender				
Male	108.6	51.7	45.0	32.3
Female	116.3	48.3	55.0	36.8
Total	224.8	100	100	100
Race and ethnicity				
Hispanic	30.4	13.5	8.2	21.0
White	154.5	68.7	78.9	39.7
African American	25.6	11.4	7.0	21.5
Other	14.3	6.4	5.9	31.9
Total	224.8	100	100	100
Age				
18-24	28.9	12.8	12.1	32.7
25-34	39.9	17.7	18.5	36.0
35-44	41.8	18.6	20.0	37.2
45-54	43.9	19.5	20.4	36.1
55-64	33.3	14.8	15/8	36.9
65-74	19.9	8.8	8.5	33.4
75 and over	17.1	7/6	4.7	21.3
Total	224.8	100	100	100
Education				
Grade school	11.2	5.0	0.9	6.5
Some high school	22.1	9.8	4.1	14.5
High school grad	68.3	30.4	16.7	19.0
Some college	61.4	27.3	30.1	38.1
College graduate	41.3	18.3	30.4	57.2
Graduate school	20.5	9.1	17.8	67.3
Total	224.8	100	100	100
Income				
Less than $10k	11.6	5.8	2.6	16.1
$10k – $20k	19.3	9.6	4.5	16.8
$20k - $30k	23.4	11.7	6.3	19.3
$30k - $40k	22.6	11.3	8.5	27.0
$40k - $50k	18.8	9.3	8.3	31.8
$50k - $75k	40.7	20.3	20.5	36.2
$75k - $100k	27.2	13.5	17.5	46.2
$110k - $150k	21.4	10.7	16.4	55.0
$150k and over	16.0	8.0	15.2	68.1
Total	224.8	100	100	100

Figure 2.4.   Demographic breakdown of museum visitors.
Jeffrey Smith

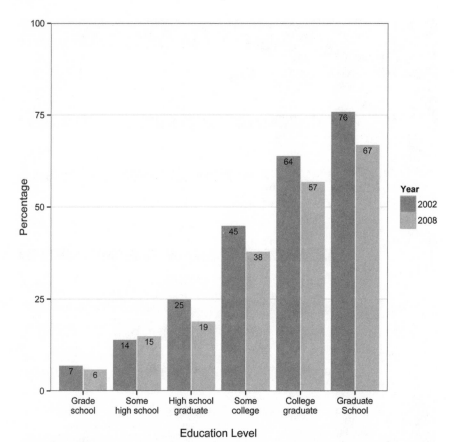

Figure 2.5.   Percentage of adults attending cultural institution or event by educational level.
Benjamin Smith

scheme or typology of museum visitors. This research has been carried out over a number of years and across the wide breadth of the institutions that make up the Smithsonian. The researchers focused on what visitors' expectations were when they were entering the institution, and whether they felt those expectations had been met as they were exiting the institution. They came up with a set of seven types of experiences that visitors were expecting to have during their visit:

Information/Understanding: This is a desire to gain information or enrich one's understanding via observation/interaction with the works in the institution. It's possible, for example, to understand the principles behind a Foucault pendulum, but it is much easier to get a real feel for how one works when watching one swing suspended from the roof of a science museum to the floor thirty or more feet below.

Rare/Real/In Person: This is the desire to see "the real thing" in the institution and not a facsimile of it. There is a difference, for example, between seeing a picture of a space shuttle and standing in front of one. We have conducted research on the differences among various formats in which people might view art (computer, slides, real paintings), and while people do accommodate to seeing a reproduction, which we call "facsimile accommodation," there is also no question that there is nothing like the real thing (Locher, Smith, & Smith, 1999).

Connection: This has to do with making an emotional connection with what is on display. For those readers old enough to have lived through the Kennedy assassination, the Sixth Floor Museum in Dallas, Texas, can take your breath away. If you stand near the window on the sixth floor and view Dealey Plaza from that perspective, or stand on "the grassy knoll," incredible emotional connections to that day come streaming back. I was thirteen when this happened; I visited the Sixth Floor Museum in my fifties and the experience was incredibly powerful.

Beauty: This one is pretty self-explanatory: people like to see beautiful things. A common joke among art museum professionals is that the ideal exhibition would be *"Impressionism in the Age of the Pharaohs,"* given the popularity of these areas of art that both contain beautiful works.

Meaning: Harkening back to the experience of the Episcopalian priest or the woman who was proposed to in front of a predella piece from Siena, works of art and other objects can hold special meaning for people. The young Māori man in the opening chapter got to see his ancestors' signatures, meaningless to almost anyone else, but of critical importance to him.

Feelings: There are lots of items that might fall under the rubric of "meanings," including wanting to experience a sense of awe or wonder, inspiration, sadness, or joy. Think of the young girl sitting in front of the Raphael altarpiece discussed at the introduction of the book. That girl was experiencing awe and wonder in front of that work. Now, when she entered the museum, she wasn't really expecting such an experience, so she wouldn't really fit into this typology. She was maybe anticipating *beauty*, or maybe had no expectations at all. I would imagine that there are more than a few people who enter a museum in a somewhat tabula rasa state of existence. There are, for example, visitors who are "brought" to the museum by a spouse or friend, or are part of a tour group, or the like.

Imagining: This has to do with imagining what it would be like to live in a different time or place, or that you were a different person, perhaps part of a painting you might be viewing. The girl in the Costume Institute who asked, "What did twelve-year-old girls wear in the age of Napoleon?" might be the best exemplar of this expectation.

Falk Categories

John Falk and Lynn Dierking have looked at people visiting a wide variety of museums for decades. Falk (2009) has generated a set of categories that he uses to describe visitors. His breakdown works as follows:

Explorer: These are perhaps the "classic" museum visitors. They want to explore and learn about new things; they are naturally curious and believe that museums hold objects and ideas that will be of interest to them.

Experience Seekers: These are individuals who are looking for new kinds of experiences. They might be going to a museum because it is one that everyone says is a "must-visit." The difference between explorers and experience seekers has to do with what their underlying goals are. Explorers are more oriented toward learning for its own sake—they are intrinsically motivated. Experience seekers want "to have been to the Louvre" rather than being motivated by what they may find there. They are more extrinsically motivated.

Facilitators: These are individuals who are at the museum in order for others to fulfill needs or desires. They might be parents bringing children to the museum, for example, or taking visitors from out of town to see the local museum.

Rechargers: These people are at the museum to get away from their everyday lives and put themselves in a completely different environment. They want to recharge their batteries. Their motivation is more "restorative" in nature than anything else (see, e.g., Kaplan, Bardwell, & Slakter, 1993; Packer & Bond, 2010).

Professionals/Hobbyists: These individuals might be historians, artists, or other professionals who are visiting the museum because of a vocation or avocation. Father Edward at the Byzantium exhibition would be an example of this.

If we step back and look at the data and the typologies, we see several things emerging. First, museum visitors come in all shapes and sizes: young and old, male and female, wealthy and not so wealthy. Museum visitors do tend to be better educated than non–museum visitors, but less well-educated people also visit, just not as often as those with more education. We also see that we might be able to roughly categorize visitors according to their intents when visiting. They want to connect, reflect, recharge, see things of beauty and things that are rare. They want to learn and they want to see the real thing as opposed to a facsimile. They have basically put themselves in the hands of the museum to have an experience, or set of experiences, that differs from their everyday lives. And importantly, they are, in the vast majority, at the museum because they *want* to be at the museum. They have come voluntarily and with the intent to have an experience different from their everyday lives.

WHAT DO PEOPLE DO DURING
THEIR VISIT? WHAT ARE THEIR VISITING PREFERENCES?

We see that visitors to museums vary widely in their demographics, and that they might usefully be categorized broadly in what they are looking for as they enter the museum. But what do they do once inside? How do they behave? What do they experience? What do they want? In a study of visitors to an exhibition on Byzantine art, my colleague David Carr and I (Smith & Carr, 2001) asked a sample of individuals exiting the exhibition a variety of questions, one of which was, "How do you go about visiting an exhibition where the works are new and different from what you are familiar with?" The standard response was, "I have no idea. I just enter. I am in your hands." To a degree, this makes sense, particularly in an exhibition such as one on Byzantine art, where many visitors may not have a good idea of what lies ahead. But what about the situation where the works are more likely to be familiar ones, or perhaps a repeat visit to a museum? How do people approach such situations? We looked at some of these questions in a study we did at the Met in 1995 (Smith & Wolf, 1996). We asked people to indicate where they thought they were in a series of contrasting statements ("I look at many works of art briefly" vs. "I look at a few works in depth"). Participants responded on a six-point scale indicating strength of preference for one statement or the other. The results are presented in Figure 2.6.

What we see in Figure 2.6 is that there is real diversity in what people say about their visiting behaviors and about themselves. We only see any level of agreement on two items in this survey: whether people feel welcome in the museum, and (to a lesser degree) whether they know what they will do at the museum as opposed to not having plans for their visit. Now, on both these items, it should be noted that the Met is a museum that enjoys incredible repeat visitation. Over three out of four people responding to this survey were repeat visitors to the museum, and many had made dozens of previous visits. But let us look at some of the other responses. Thus, we are not surprised that people feel welcome and that they have an idea of what they will do. They are, to a degree, "regulars." Although we have data that suggest that people do not look at works for very long, one-third of the respondents say that this is their preference—more so than say they look at many works briefly. Roughly half (46 percent) say that they like to look at works by themselves as opposed to about one quarter (26 percent) who say that they like to discuss works with others (we are using the extreme two categories in each direction to generate these percentages). People are fairly split between whether they are in the museum to learn or to have fun. The same is true with whether they prefer a linear and orderly organization or a more global and holistic organization. Somewhat

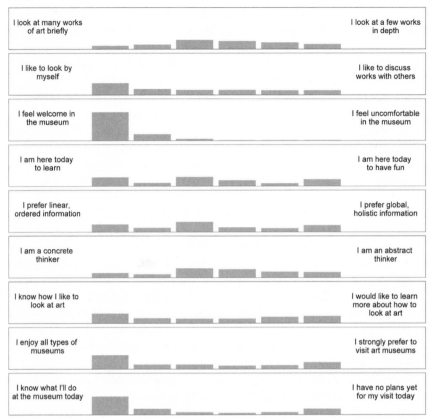

Figure 2.6.   Responses to contrasting statements in study of visitors to the Metropolitan Museum of Art.
Benjamin Smith

surprisingly (to us, at least), there were as many people who thought of themselves as concrete thinkers as opposed to abstract thinkers. Also, and very much of interest to us, over a third of the visitors said that they would like to learn more about how to look at art, almost as many as said that they felt they knew how to look at art. And finally, roughly half (48 percent) of Met visitors said that they enjoy all types of museums as opposed to strongly preferring art museums.

Now, some of these responses may naturally link with one another. For example, concrete thinkers probably enjoy more orderly organizations, and perhaps people who are in the museum to have fun are more likely to want to discuss works with others (who knows?). We might even go so far as to imagine that one of Falk's "experience seekers" is a person who looks at many works briefly, discusses with others, is at the museum to have fun, enjoys all types of museums, and does not have a particular reason for his or her visit. That is to say, the research we have conducted here, even though it shows little in the way of common agreement among museum visitors, might still be quite consistent with the work of Falk and Pekarik in terms of general types of visitors to museums.

This leads us into another categorization scheme to consider, this one based on what people do once they are in the museum, as opposed to what they bring with them in terms of expectations and background when they enter the door. Pitman and Hirzy (2010) developed a typology of visitor behavior while in museums based on research conducted at the Dallas Museum of Art. Their approach has four categories of visitors. Although the categories here are from Pitman and Hirzy, I have put a bit of extrapolation on the interpretation of these categories. My intent here is not to usurp the excellent work of Pitman and Hirzy, but to try to extend it to show how these categories relate to my overall argument of the Museum Effect.

Observers: These are individuals who are, in a sense, not completely engaged in the process of looking at art. They are not sure of themselves or their place in the museum. They feel sometimes like they are on the outside looking in. But they are a very interesting group of people. I sometimes think that they are often the audience that an artist has in mind. Not someone who is going to look at technique, or influences, or provenance, but at the actual work of art. Take a look at the lions from the cave at Chauvet in Figure 2.7. This work is believed to be over thirty thousand years old. It predates the invention of writing by at least twenty-five thousand years. But those lions are as real as today. Those lions could hurt you. And the more you look, the more you see; they are lions juxtaposed on top of other lions. Was this a pride, or simply the best surface to paint on? Are the two lions that are nose-to-nose a mother and cub? And then there are other animals off to the left. What do we see there? The point here is that you don't have to be a sophisticate to be amazed by these works. That they were painted a thousand generations ago and they hit us between the eyes today as something worthy of more than just a passing thought; and that thought can be mulled irrespective of one's background in art or art history.

Participants: The second of Pitman and Hirzy's categories is called "participants." These are people who are "with the program" even if they are not sophisticates. They do not need convincing that an art museum is a good place to be, but they do need some assistance in understanding what it is that they are looking at. They often make sense of art by relating it to other areas of art, such as theater and dance. They are eager to learn more about art and aspire to be able to look at art from a more sophisticated perspective. Often they have had some level of training in the arts.

Figure 2.7.   Lions in the prehistoric paintings in the cave at Chauvet, France.

Independents: The third group are independents. They have a strong back-ground in the arts and, according to Pitman and Hirzy, are more likely to take longer looks at the works they encounter, making personal connections to the works.

Enthusiasts: The final group are enthusiasts; many of them are amateur (or professional) artists and bring a fairly strong knowledge base to their viewing of works. They often relate works of art to their own creative efforts.

Pitman and Hirzy (2010) report that there are roughly equal numbers of individuals in each group, with the independents being slightly smaller than the other groups and the enthusiasts being slightly larger. This is no doubt to a degree a function of the nature of the audience for the Dallas Museum of Art and will be different at other institutions. What differentiates these groups is their knowledge of art and their approach to looking at art, which, one would suspect, is influenced by that knowledge. Two questions concerning this come to mind. First, are these groups really distinctive groups or more modes along a continuum? Is there a bright line between a participant and an independent, or is it more a case of gradual transition, with the categorization serving more as a convenience for understanding visitors than a meaningful shift in how one considers art? The second question has to do with "what all" is associated with one category as opposed to another. That is, one might ask if these differences are primarily differences in what might be called "aesthetic fluency" (Smith & Smith, 2006), or the degree to which people understand art. I ask this not to question the typology, which I think is very useful, but to push the issue of what differentiates individuals in how they approach art, and if these differences are fundamentally caused by an increase in aesthetic fluency, or if such increases and the differences in approach to viewing are coincidental.

TIME AND NUMBER OF WORKS VIEWED

We will consider the issue of time more extensively in the next chapter, but it is worthwhile for purposes of context to get an idea of the issues involved at this juncture. We know from work we've done in a number of museums that people vary in how much time they spend in a museum visit, but that the bulk of visitors spent between about 1.5 to 3 hours. The amount of time varies according to the predilections of the visitor, but also to a degree on the size of the museum. Larger museums with more works to examine naturally stimulate longer visits than smaller museums. But how that time is allocated is rather remarkable. Think about the last time you visited an art museum. And think about the work of art that you looked at for the longest amount of time. How much time was that? How long did you look at the work you looked at the longest? How long do you typically spend in front of a work of art? Now, given that you are reading this book, in all likelihood, you aren't the typical museum visitor. You might look at a work of art for five or even ten minutes. But you would be very unusual if you did. In a study we conducted at the Metropolitan Museum of Art, the median amount of time that individuals spent in front of a work of art was seventeen seconds. The mean was twenty-seven seconds (the mean is higher because a few works got a three-minute look), and the mode (the most frequently observed amount of time) was ten seconds. No one in our sample of 150 viewers looked for as much as five minutes. The longest look was slightly over three minutes. These were not trivial works of art. They included Rembrandt's *Aristotle Contemplating the Bust of Homer*, and Leutze's very large *Washington Crossing the Delaware*.

Now, if you combine the fact that people typically look at a work of art for less than half a minute, and that they spend between 1.5 and 3 hours in an art museum, then they either spend a lot of time *not* looking at art, or more likely, they look at a *lot* of different works during their visit. We are fairly certain that it is the latter situation that is true. The typical museum visitor looks at dozens, perhaps more than a hundred, works of art during a visit. What does that mean? How does one react to so many works of art in a short span of time?

LOCUS OF ATTENTION

We were once asked by the then director of the Met, Philippe de Montebello, if we could do a study to determine if long labels were causing traffic jams in a recently opened exhibition of thirty centuries of Mexican art. He was concerned that people spending a long time reading the labels with works were clogging up the aisles. It was a fun study that we needed to execute quickly (so that the problem could be remedied). We spent the next day standing in front of various sections of the exhibition where we could find two similar works of art, one with a long label, and one without a long label. Fortunately, it was not hard to find about a half dozen such situations. We observed people who approached the work with the long label and people who approached the work with the short label. We timed their stay at the object, and also observed what they were doing.

What we found was fascinating. First, label length did not seem to be the problem. Longer labels weren't causing people to stay longer but were causing them to spend their time differently in front of the works. At a work with a short label, people would approach the object (a large painting, a sculpture, a crucifix), and first make a decision if they were going to invest some time in the work. This would take about three seconds. They either decided to approach or to move on. If they decided to really look at the art, they would first do a quick scan, and then turn to the label accompanying the work. They would read through this and then return to the work. Then they would look at the work for ten to twenty-five seconds, and move on. However, if they found themselves at the work with the longer label, their behavior was a bit different. The initial scan of the work was the same, but then they would spend about ten to twenty-five seconds *reading the label*. After the label was read they would take the briefest of looks back at the work, and then *move on*. That is, the length of the label did not affect the overall time spent at the object so much as what would be done with the ten to twenty-five seconds that the person would spend on the object. Now, not everybody does this, but we have found this behavior time and again in looking at people looking at art in all kinds of settings and works of art. As I was writing this section of the chapter, I got an e-mail from a group of psychology students who had chosen to replicate the Spending Time on Art (Smith & Smith, 2001) study in the Albertina Museum in Vienna as part of a psychology class project (M. Finnan, M. Drabina, M. Felkel, & T. Alfers, personal communication, 2013). They wrote to me to ask a few questions and to compare results. One question they had was whether I had seen the phenomenon described above (reading the label as opposed to spending time looking at the art). We didn't collect the raw data in that study, and had not observed the phenomenon until we did the "traffic jam" study. It was amazing to see a group of individuals independently come upon the same finding!

Whether an individual was reading a label, or looking at the art (or both), they were typically doing it for a fairly brief period of time, somewhere between twenty and thirty seconds for a work that they found interesting. And they do this with dozens or hundreds of works of art in a visit. And as discussed earlier, they often tell us that the visit was "thrilling," "exhilarating," and even "life changing." But one is forced to wonder how can that possibly be the case? How can looking at works of art for less than a minute engender such passionate responses? We think the answer lies in what researchers call "the unit of analysis." The unit of analysis is the thing that you are studying. In the social sciences, that is usually a person, but if you are interested in institutional-level analysis, the unit of analysis might be a school, or a museum, or even a legislature. In the humanities, the unit of analysis might be books, or poets, or whatever it is that the researcher wants to understand better. In an art museum, we believe that the unit of analysis is not a work of art. Instead, we believe that it is the collection of the works of art that a person encounters in a museum visit. It is not *a* work, it is *all* the works. I take this up more extensively in the next chapter, but for now, I think it is important to consider the possibility that the works of art that a visitor views in a museum visit, although individual, and often singular, come together in the experience of the visitor to form a kind of a whole for the visitor.

THE INFLUENCE OF ART-RELATED KNOWLEDGE

In looking at various approaches to categorizing visitors (and we will look at several more later), one factor that enters into the equation again and again is the art-related knowledge that the individual possesses. We look at several approaches to this question in this section.

Aesthetic Fluency

In our own research, we have called art-related knowledge "aesthetic fluency" (Smith & Smith, 2006) and consider it not to be a set of steps or categories so much as a continuum. We liken it to vocabulary development, which is why we have referred to it as fluency. We measure this concept with a fairly straightforward instrument. People are presented with a set of five artists and five art concepts. They are then asked to indicate their level of familiarity with each artist or concept. The list and the response categories are as follows:

- Mary Cassatt
- Isamu Noguchi
- John Singer Sargent
- Alessandro Botticelli
- Gian Lorenzo Bernini
- Fauvism
- Egyptian Funerary Stelae
- Impressionism
- Chinese Scrolls
- Abstract Expressionism

0—I have never heard of this artist or term
1—I have heard of this but don't really know anything about it
2—I have a vague idea of what this is
3—I understand this artist or idea when it is discussed
4—I can talk intelligently about this artist or idea in art

Respondents select one of the five responses for each artist and concept. We have found that this results in a relatively "unidimensional" scale with scores being roughly normally distributed and running the gamut from very low to very high. By "unidimensional," I mean that we found that all ten artists and concepts seem to be measuring the same underlying idea. We also find that scores on this measure are strongly related to both formal training in art or art history, and frequency of museum visitation. They are somewhat less strongly related to age. This approach of listing concepts and asking people their level of familiarity with them has since been used in a variety of other studies in different domains of the arts.

Expert/Novice Differences

Our work on aesthetic fluency looks at this concept as a continuum and questions, to a degree, the notion of discrete categories or levels as perhaps being a bit too deterministic. But no one would question the idea of there being differences between people who were novices in terms of looking at art and people who were experts. The notion of expert/novice differences has a long history in psychology, stemming from the seminal work of Nobel laureate Herbert Simon and his colleagues (see, e.g., Chase & Simon, 1973; Newell & Simon, 1973). There have been a number of studies conducted in this area (see Rawlings, 2003, or Winston & Cupchik, 1992); we will just look at a few that are most pertinent to our purposes here. Cupchik and Gebotys (1988) found that undergraduate students differed from art experts in how they looked for meaning and interpretation in artworks. The undergraduates tended to focus on the content of the works, whereas the experts tended to focus on style and form. Nodine, Locher, and Krupinski (1993) looked at the eye movement of experts and novices looking at the same works of art, finding that experts scanned the works more broadly than novices, looking more at the formal composition of the paintings. On the other hand, novices focused more on individual objects within the works. Experts have been found to make more refined differentiation among artworks (Augustin & Leder, 2006), although they do not necessarily agree with one another on rating the quality of art any more than nonexperts do (Hekkert & van Wieringen, 1996). In an interesting study involving eye movement cameras and measures of skin conductivity, Pihko et al. (2011) found that novices responded more favorably to representational works of art, and looked longer at faces in paintings that included people than did experts. Experts again looked more broadly at the works (e.g., spending more time looking at the periphery of the paintings).

What might we take from this work overall? That there is wide variability in the art knowledge that people bring to bear in looking at works of art, and that, at least at the extreme levels of art knowledge (aesthetic fluency), this is an important factor in how people go about viewing the art. Novices are more focused on the content of the painting, preferring realistic works and focusing on individual objects within the works. Experts are more interested in stylistic concerns and the overall composition of works, showing a stronger preference for abstract works than do novices.

SUMMARY

So what does this all mean? What is the takeaway message from looking at the characteristics of people who visit art museums, or any type of museum for that matter? Well, they are a diverse group, representing all ages, both genders, all ethnicities, all income levels, and all educational levels (but with a distinct proclivity for higher educational levels). But that does not mean that they are just everybody, just a random sample of the general populace. It is important to keep in mind that museum visitation is essentially a leisure time activity and that people *choose* to go to museums, choose to go to a particular kind of museum, and choose (where possible) to go to a particular museum of that kind. Visitors can be usefully categorized into different types, frequently based on their level of aesthetic fluency, but also in terms of other variables. They might be categorized by what they hope to get out of their visit, what they expect to encounter in the museum, what their lives or backgrounds are. Once they are in the institution, their behaviors differ as well.

But there are a few things that we see that are somewhat consistent, at least for a large segment of the museum-visiting audience. There is a tendency for people to look only fairly briefly at works of art, and to look at a lot of them within a single visit. They tend to look at them alone, even if they are visiting with others. They may then discuss the works with others, but not all that often. There is a tendency for people, when provided with a long label that accompanies a work, to allocate their time toward the label rather than toward the work. There is also a tendency for people to view their visit to the museum as the fundamental unit of analysis rather than as a collection of individual works of art. They will say that it wasn't just one work that was special, but the overall effect of their visit as a whole. And they frequently describe that visit to the museum in exceedingly positive terms.

So how do we put these findings together? How can people looking at dozens and dozens of works of art for short periods of time have an experience that is as positive as they tell us it is? Are they just being kind to the interviewers? Are they giving a response that they believe is "socially desirable"; that is, do they not want to seem like a philistine when everyone else is saying how wonderful everything is? If they are having such a remarkably positive experience, why don't they look like that when observed in the galleries? They don't look like their team just won a major game, nor do they resemble the crowd at a rock concert. They look more like people coming out of church. How are these seemingly contradictory findings reconciled? How do we make sense out of what we heard from Mario the pilot, Father Edward, or the visitor to the Costume Institute who wanted to know, "What did twelve-year-old girls wear in the age of Napoleon?"

REFERENCES

American Alliance of Museums. (n.d.). Museum facts. Retrieved from http://www .aam-us.org/about-museums/facts

Augustin, M. D., & Leder, H. (2006). Art expertise: A study of concepts and conceptual spaces. *Psychology Science, 48*, 135–156.

Carr, D. W. (2011). *Open conversations: Public learning in libraries and museums.* Santa Barbara, CA: Libraries Unlimited.

Chase, W. G., & Simon, H. A. (1973). Perception in chess. *Cognitive Psychology*, *4*, 55–81.

Cupchik, G. C., & Gebotys, R. J. (1988). The search for meaning in art: Interpretative styles and judgments of quality. *Visual Arts Research*, *14*, 38–50.

Falk, J. H. (2009). *Identity and the museum visitor experience*. Walnut Creek, CA: Left Coast Press.

Hekkert, P., & van Wieringen, P. C. W. (1996). Beauty in the eye of expert and nonexpert beholders: A study in the appraisal of art. *The American Journal of Psychology*, *109*, 389–407.

Kaplan, S., Bardwell, L. V., & Slakter, D. B. (1993). The museum as a restorative environment. *Environment and Behavior*, *25*, 725–742.

Locher, P., Smith, L. F., & Smith, J. K. (1999). Original paintings versus slide and computer reproductions: A comparison of viewer responses. *Empirical Studies of the Arts*, *17*, 121–129.

Miller, K., Swan, D., Craig, T., Dorinski, S., Freeman, M., Isaac, N., O'Shea, P., Schilling, P., & Scotto, J. (2011). *Public libraries survey: Fiscal year 2009* (IMLS-2011-PLS-02). Washington, DC: Institute of Museum and Library Services. Retrieved April 22, 2014, from http://www.imls.gov/assets/1/News/PLS2009.pdf

Museums Association. (n.d.). Visitors love museums. Retrieved April 22, 2014, from http://www.museumsassociation.org/download?id=165106

National Endowment for the Arts. (2009). *2008 survey of public participation in the arts*. Research report #49. Washington, DC: National Endowment for the Arts. Retrieved November 29, 2012, from http://www.nea.gov/research/2008-sppa.pdf

National Endowment for the Arts. (2013). *How a nation engages with art: Highlights from the 2012 survey of public participation in the arts*. Research report #57. Washington, DC: National Endowment for the Arts. Retrieved December 2, 2012, from http://arts.gov/sites/default/files/highlights-from-2012-SPPA.pdf

Newell, A., & Simon, H. A. (1973). *Human problem solving*. Englewood Cliffs, NJ: Prentice Hall.

Nodine, C. F., Locher, P. J., & Krupinski, E. A. (1993). The role of formal art training on perception and aesthetic judgment of art compositions. *Leonardo*, *26*, 219–227.

Packer, J., & Bond, N. (2010). Museums as restorative environments. *Curator*, *53*, 421–436.

Pekarik, A. J., Doering, Z. D., & Karns, D. A. (1999). Exploring satisfying experiences in museums. *Curator*, *42*, 152–173.

Pekarik, A. J., & Schreiber, J. B. (2012). The power of expectation. *Curator*, *55*, 487–496.

Pihko, E., Virtanen, A., Saarinen, V. M., Pannasch, S., Hirvenkari, L., Tossavainen, T., Haapala, A., & Hari, R. (2011). Experiencing art: The influence of expertise and painting abstraction level. *Frontiers in Human Neuroscience*, *5*, 1–10. doi:10.3389/fnhum.2011.00094

Pitman, B., & Hirzy, E. (2010). *Ignite the power of art: Advancing visitor engagement in museums*. Dallas, TX: Dallas Museum of Art.

Rawlings, D. (2003). Personality correlates of liking for "unpleasant" paintings and photographs. *Personality and Individual Differences*, *34*, 395–410.

Smith, J. K., & Carr, D. W. (2001). In Byzantium. *Curator, 44*(4), 335–354.

Smith, J. K., & Smith, L. F. (2001). Spending time on art. *Empirical Studies of the Arts, 19*(2), 229–236.

Smith, J. K., & Wolf, L. F. (1996). Museum visitor preferences and intentions in constructing aesthetic experience. *Poetics: Journal for Empirical Research in Literature, Media and the Arts, 24*, 219–238.

Smith, L. F., & Smith, J. K. (2006). The nature and growth of aesthetic fluency. In P. Locher, C. Martindale, L. Dorfman, V. Petrov, & D. Leontiev (Eds.), *New directions in aesthetics, creativity, and the psychology of art* (pp. 47–58). Amityville, NY: Baywood.

Tinio, P. P. L., Smith, J. K., & Smith, L. F. (in press). The walls do speak: Psychological aesthetics and the museum experience. In P. P. L. Tinio & J. K. Smith (Eds.), *The Handbook of the Psychology of Aesthetics and the Arts*. Cambridge: Cambridge University Press.

Winston, A. S., & Cupchik, G. C. (1992). The evaluation of high art and popular art by naive and experienced viewers. *Visual Arts Research, 18*, 1–14.

3

Time, Flow, and the Unit of Analysis

"**I** could have painted that."

If you work in an art museum, especially one that exhibits works of a certain type, you most assuredly have heard that phrase. And it grates. I have always found it interesting that nobody reads, "To be or not to be," and concludes, "I could have written that," or hears the first four notes of Beethoven's Fifth and concludes that they could have composed that theme. But they see a Mondrian or a Malevich and they are perplexed. They are not sure what to make of it or how to react.

Even though they sometimes find the works in front of them mystifying, most museum visitors want to grow in their ability to "appreciate art." They truly want to see in the works what experts see; they want to see the genius, the greatness, whatever it is about a work that has caused it to be elevated from other works of art and deemed worthy of hanging on the walls of a museum. They are sometimes baffled by what they see, especially with modern art. We have seen visitors literally stick their head into a gallery, scan the works and move on to the next gallery. They are fairly certain that there is nothing in the room that will hold any interest for them. This seems a harsh judgment, but if one is in a large museum, there is a push to see that art which one thinks will be of interest, because there simply is not enough time to see it all.

Given that most visitors are not going to look at any work of art very long, the work needs to generate a positive response in a viewer fairly quickly, or the moment is lost. There are more works of art calling out to be viewed. I sometimes anthropomorphize artworks a bit, thinking of them as individuals waiting to be appreciated. The works in any particular gallery within a museum engage in a silent competition for the attention and adoration of the visitors. I often wonder if van Gogh could have conceived that he might be in competition with Seurat for the attentions of a young couple on their honeymoon in New York.

This chapter is about three concepts: time, flow, and the unit of analysis. Only "time" is used in its everyday sense here; flow and the unit of analysis will take a bit of explanation. The purpose of this chapter is to look at these concepts as they are critical to understanding the Museum Effect. This is a bit of stage setting for the next chapter. But let's not start with the concepts; let's start with three metaphors for a museum visit.

WHAT IS A MUSEUM LIKE?

Museums are not like most things we encounter. Indeed, they are a fairly modern invention. Although there are some examples of museums from as far back as the fifteenth century, the British Museum was founded in 1753, the Hermitage in 1764, the Louvre in 1793, and the Metropolitan Museum of Art in 1870. Libraries are an older concept than museums, as are universities. If we pose the question, "What is a museum like?" perhaps "library" would be a likely answer. Or university. Hospital? Town hall? Department store? Collection of stuffed animals? In thinking about each of these, one pushes the question toward, "What is the essence of museum-ness in a museum?" Is it an institution? A building? Is it a collection of a certain kind? Is it a place where objects that have some degree of commonality and some degree of unique- ness are kept? Well, we can start with a metaphor that doesn't stray too far from museums themselves—a kind of a jumping-off point.

Museum as Institution

Museums are places. They are buildings. Consider as a starting point two spectacular institutions, one iconic and historic, one startling and bold: the Hermitage (Figure 3.1), and the Guggenheim Bilbao (Figure 3.2).

I chose an interior as an illustration for the Hermitage in part because it is so amazing and in part because it's hard to get a picture of the whole building from the exterior that does justice to the grandeur one senses when standing in front of it.

We did a study at the Met a number of years back where we asked students who were participating in an extended school visitation program to describe the museum. We asked one group of students to do this at the start of their program, and another group at the end of their program. What was interest- ing in the descriptions is that the "preprogram" group typically described the outside of the building. The "postprogram" group described the interior

Figure 3.1.   View inside the Herimitage of San Petersburg.
Scala / Art Resource, NY

Figure 3.2.   The Guggenheim Bilbao.
Album / Art Resource, NY

of the building and the people whom they had met. In other words, the program had the effect of "bringing them inside" the museum. When I think of the Met in general, I never think of the outside of the building. I think of the Great Hall, or the room that holds the Manets, or Arms and Armor, the Egyptian galleries. I spent countless hours in those rooms, and that is what my personal image of the museum is about. On the other hand, when I think of the Philadelphia Museum of Art, I think either of the great room that holds the amazing van der Weyden that was discussed earlier, or, I am somewhat embarrassed to say, I think of the film *Rocky* and the training montage that ends with him running up the steps of the museum. Why? Because although we conducted a number of interesting studies with the great people at the Philadelphia Museum of Art, I did not spend nearly as much time there. So it is a bit more of "an institution" to me. In the nomenclature of my colleague and friend David Carr (2006), in a beautifully written and insightful work on museums and libraries, a museum is "a place."

Museums are institutions. They are places. But now that I live in the south end of the South Island of New Zealand, the Metropolitan Museum of Art is also a website. I view art online far more than in any other mode these days. I have recently become quite enamored of cave paintings, almost none of which I will ever see in person because most are not open to the public. I could see them in books, but mostly I see them online. And although I desperately long to see them in person, they are pretty spectacular online, especially with a good-quality screen. And when I look for possibilities for images for this book, I look online. We conducted a study comparing looking at real art versus on computer and on slide projections (mentioned in the previous chapter). People know that they are not getting the experience online that they would if they could look at the real works in person, but they also know seeing them online is much better than not at all. And I would encourage readers to look up the works reproduced in black and white here. I don't apologize for presenting them in black and white as it lets you know what I'm talking about, but go online to look at them and it will be a clear step-up in your consideration of them.

Museums are places, and those places are distinct. Part of a museum visit is a visit to a place. It is a visit to a museum, to a collection, to the efforts of a group of people to make the collection accessible. The visit begins when you enter and ends as you leave, unless you buy a catalog or other material from the museum shop and take a bit of your visit with you.

Museum as Crossword Puzzle

But we can get more adventuresome with the metaphors. I want to compare art museums to crossword puzzles. If the metaphor of institution is mundane, the metaphor of crossword puzzle is outlandish. But let me make my case. A crossword puzzle is made up of a number of individual items that have to be solved in order to complete the puzzle. If you are a crossword puzzle person, and anything like me, it takes you a while to complete a good, relatively difficult puzzle, say, a *New York Times* Sunday puzzle. A crossword puzzle is a whole entity, but one made up of various parts, each of which has to be addressed. When I go through a puzzle, I sometimes get words right away, and other times I have no idea what the answer is. For some clues, I am intrigued—particularly by the theme clues—and on others I am frustrated. But sometimes, with a little help from a letter or two gotten from solving other clues, I have a bit better idea of what might go in a certain clue, and I "get it." Getting the hard ones is often more rewarding than getting the easier ones. I don't like puzzles that are too easy. Nor do I like ones where I fundamentally don't have a chance of being successful. Much like Goldilocks, I like them in the middle.

I hope the parallels are emerging. I love to visit a new art museum. I enjoy a mix of artists or eras I am familiar with, but I always like seeing works I've never seen before or "discovering" an artist I didn't know. As I approach a work of art, I tend to view it as a bit of a puzzle. What is this work? Are my initial reactions positive or negative? Does it seem like something I might understand if I give it a chance? Does it seem to speak to me in some sense, or is it alien? How does it fit with the work I just saw, or the other works in this room?

One of the things that my wife, Lisa, and I learned early on in our time at the Met was to give art time. If we went through an exhibit and didn't "get it," we went through it again, sometimes immediately afterward, sometimes a few days later. We would read about the works, listen to the audio guides, and work toward trying to get an appreciation of what we were seeing. We sought clues. We readjusted our outlook. We tried to let the work come to us rather than force an understanding. Doing so requires a bit of faith in the institution and the works. You have to believe that "these will be interesting to me and worthwhile to have worked on if I give them a chance." We are almost never let down in that faith. And by the way, I do all those things when working on a particularly difficult crossword puzzle. And when I get a new word completed, it is a real source of gratification and motivation to move on to another. I do have to say that crossword puzzles let me down far more often than art museums.

Art museums are made up of collections of individual works of art. Each work has a history, an artist behind it, a story behind its making, a message or set of messages to be communicated, a challenge to be taken on. A crossword puzzle, then, is a metaphor for the cognitive aspects of a museum visit, puzzling one's way through a collection of challenges, some of them perhaps closely related, thematic, or perhaps not showing much of a relationship at all, as what happens when one leaves one gallery or period of a painter's life, and enters another.

Museum as Baseball Game

The final analogy (for now) is museum as baseball game. I was once discussing soccer with my son and we were speculating on why the game had not really caught on in the United States. He said, "Well I have a theory on this, Dad. My theory is that each society can only tolerate one stultifyingly dull sport, and we already have baseball." Now, we are both big baseball fans, but neither of us likes soccer (sorry, soccer fans). We acknowledge that most of the rest of the world is crazed about soccer, and that this probably is not due to some sort of genetic defect. How could people like a game where so few goals are scored? We fully understand the intricacies and fascinations of a 1–0 baseball game, but cannot fathom why anyone would sit through a 1–0 soccer game (or a 0–0 soccer game, even worse).

Well, we actually do have a theory on why people watch soccer and baseball, and strangely enough, it relates to looking at art. It has to do with what is an event within the game. One might put it this way: "What is the smallest enjoyable unit within the game?" For the neophyte, it is a score. When a team scores, that is something to get excited about. When there is no score, what is there to be enjoyed? If there is only one goal or run scored in a game, does that mean that there is almost nothing worthwhile to watch? Well, if you know any game, you know that subtle things occur that can be enjoyed: a stolen base in baseball, a knocked-down pass in football (American football), a charge taken in basketball, and something really good in soccer (but I honestly don't know what that would be). As one becomes more proficient in his or her knowledge of the sport, more of these possibilities are open to view. And if one played the game as a youth, there are many, many such possibilities. I once went to a baseball game with my daughter on what we used to call "Dad and Leah" trips. We were visiting Toronto together for her birthday and she suggested going to the game because she knew I liked them (thank you again, Leah). What was great about this game in particular was that I was able to show her some of the subtleties that one could appreciate. ("See that guy on first base? He wants to move around and get a big leadoff of first so that the pitcher will become distracted and not concentrate on the hitter. That's why he's bouncing back and forth like that." "Just to be a *nuisance*, Dad?" "Yep." "Cool.")

You might enjoy the game for the pageantry, or the atmosphere, or the hot dogs, but as you get to know the game better, you pick up on things that you might miss otherwise. A really good sport will have levels and levels of meaning. Just as a really good painting will. And a really good sport will present small event after small event that can be appreciated on its own—just as a museum will present work of art after work of art that can be appreciated individually. A baseball game might last a couple of hours or more; the more you know about the game, the more likely you are to stay till the end and enjoy the finer points. The better the teams, the more depth you will find in their play. And when the game has ended, you are as likely to remember somebody being thrown out at home as a single that scored a run. Now compare this to a museum visit. The first thing that might hit you about a museum is the building itself; then you might stay a couple of hours more or so. The better the works of art in the museum, the more likely you are to engage with them and find things in them that resonate with you personally; and what you might remember is the wry smile on a young woman in a Sargent painting, or how the colors struck you in a Jackson Pollock.

So, what is a museum like? It is a place, a challenge, and an event. It is the same museum for everyone and yet each person has a different experience during the visit, and a different experience on each visit. It is not solely *of the art* or *of the individual*, but occurs somewhere in the resonance between what the artists have put before the individual, what the individual brings to the encounter as a human being, and what the museum has done to respect the visitor *and* the collection.

TIME AND MUSEUMS

It is not really a deep observation to note that our lives exist in time. We spend time, use time, lose track of time, make time, time passes, time flies, time heals, time stands still. In the previous chapter I alluded to several studies we have conducted involving time as a variable. I want to reconsider one of them here in a bit more depth, both in terms of its findings, but more importantly in terms of its implications.

One of the ways that we have collected information about visitors to museums is through comment books. In all honesty, they aren't our favorite method of collecting data, but they do come up with some very useful observations at times. Let me provide two examples of useful comments. The first was, "Why don't you say how many works there are going to be at the beginning of the exhibition so I can better gauge my time?" The second was, "Why don't you put fewer works in the first room of an exhibition so that people don't crowd it so much? It's always just the historical copy studies the artist did as a teenager anyway."

What do we learn from these comments? Well, first, that some people anticipate their entire visit even as they enter an exhibition. They understand that there are rooms to follow, but they don't know how many, thus they can't pace themselves. And they want to. They want to see it all. They don't want to miss anything. The same sentiment is found in the second comment. It looks at the exhibition as a whole, not so much as a large collection of individual works, but as something that has a unity to it. Visitors typically only have a rough idea of how much time they will spend in the exhibition, but they want to allocate that time carefully, so as not to be too rushed at the end, and to be able to see everything. Broadly speaking, people treat museum visits as a whole in a similar fashion. They have a rough idea of how much time they have to spend, but it's a bit open. They want to make sure that they see what it is that they want to see, even if they aren't sure what that is. That is, if they are going to a new museum for the first time, and if it is unlikely that they will get back to that museum (say if they are visiting from out of town), then they want to make certain that they see the important pieces that the museum holds. How people spend their time in art museums has always fascinated us, and we have done several studies related to that fascination. Perhaps the simplest, yet the one with the strongest impact, was called "Spending Time on Art."

Spending Time on Art

It is conventional wisdom among "museum people" that visitors do not spend much time in front of any particular work of art. Having an empirical frame of mind and particularly liking the ready quantifiability of time, we decided to test this claim (Smith & Smith, 2001). We selected six works that might be considered "masterpieces" from the Met's collections:

- *Aristotle with a Bust of Homer*, Rembrandt van Rijn
- *The Card Players*, Paul Cezanne
- *Madonna and Child Enthroned, with Saints*, Raphael
- *The Rocky Mountains, Lander's Peak*, Albert Bierstadt
- *Washington Crossing the Delaware*, Emanuel Leutze
- *Approaching Thunderstorm*, Martin Johnson Heade

Washington Crossing the Delaware might not be considered a masterpiece by some, but we decided it was sufficiently iconic that we wanted to include it. *Approaching Thunderstorm* was selected in part because it was relatively small compared to the other works and we wanted to see if the size of the painting mattered in how much time it received. We developed a very simple approach to data collection with one of our superb volunteers, David Rosen.

He was to locate himself near the selected work of art, wait until someone stopped in front of it for at least three seconds, and then time that person's viewing. Twenty-five visitors were observed in front of each work, for a total sample of 150 visitors.

The average amount of time spent in front of these works was 27.2 seconds. The standard deviation (a measure of the amount of variation in the data) was 33.7. The median amount of time spent was seventeen seconds, and the mode was ten seconds. The data showed a distinct positive "skew." What all this means in English is that if you averaged out all the scores, you would get 27.2 seconds. But if you asked what was the most frequently observed amount of time in front of a work, the answer would be ten seconds. And if you asked what was the middle score if you rank ordered viewing times from shortest to longest, the answer would be seventeen seconds. If you looked at a picture of all the scores, it would be bunched up around ten seconds and then spread out to the right (that is "skew"). Only five of 150 visitors looked at a work for more than two minutes, with the longest look being three minutes and forty-eight seconds.

Or, for those readers who like your English without a lot of numbers in it: people don't look for very long. Ten, fifteen seconds, up to half a minute is what the majority of looks consist of. Every once in a while, a work will get a couple of minutes. Now, you might be saying, "Well, sure, that would be true for the average Neanderthal, but I look for much longer." And you may, but you would be very unusual. It is interesting to note in this regard that when we ask people if they looked at one work for at least five minutes during their stay, well over half say, "Yes." And many tell us that their preferred mode of looking is to pick a few works to look at for a long time. But the data seem to be saying otherwise. And that is a bit of a paradox.

But maybe our data are unusual. Maybe the typical New Yorker (or New York visitor as most visitors to the Met are from out of NYC) is a "quicker looker" than most museum visitors. Well, as mentioned in the previous chapter, while working on this book I received an e-mail from a group of students (in particular, Michael Finnan, Magdlena Drabina, Minna Felkel, and Tobias Alfers—to whom I am very grateful for sharing their data) who replicated our study at the Albertina Museum in Vienna. They observed twenty-five to twenty-six visitors each in front of a Monet, a Picasso, a Munch, and a work by Henri Edmond Cross and got average viewing times of eighteen, fourteen, seventeen, and ten seconds, respectively, or an average of just under fifteen seconds overall for their study. So, even though I would like to replicate this at some different kinds of museums, the findings seem robust so far.

Although it is hard to imagine any kind of depth of processing being accomplished in ten seconds or less, it is important to keep in mind that the human brain processes visual information astonishingly quickly. Thorpe, Fize, and Marlot (1996) demonstrated that recognizing whether an image contained a likeness of an animal or not can be accomplished in well under a second (not a minute, a second, and just a fraction of a second at that). Augustin, Leder, Hutzler, and Carbon (2008) showed that artistic style can be processed in something around fifty milliseconds. For discussions of issues of processing speed, one can look at Tinio and Leder (in press) or the Thorpe et al. article. The point of this brief segue is to emphasize that we in fact see things very rapidly.

In looking at the data, and combining that with observations and interviews with visitors over the years, we developed a three-level typology of people looking at art in terms of time. There are people who look for about ten seconds at a work (give or take a few seconds). These people might be thought of as "sampling" or tasting a work. They are looking at the work, but only long enough to satisfy themselves that they had given the work a chance, and perhaps had found it wanting in some respect, not worthy of a longer look. It may be nice, somewhat intriguing, moderately interesting, but in comparison to the potential of other works that lie ahead, it merits no more time than a brief sampling. The visitor moves on. It may seem crass that ten seconds is given to a work that may have taken years to complete. But choices have to be made. Do you look longer at the current work and risk missing one that might be much more intriguing ahead? It is why people would like to know just how many works lie ahead in an exhibition. It is perfectly rational behavior. And if you are not likely to return to the museum you are in, you have a choice between looking longingly at a few works, or for a brief period of time at many. Even though we might like to think we are in the former category, most people are in the latter.

The second level of the typology involves half-minute looks. These might be thought of as works that are "consumed" rather than "sampled." That is, people are spending some real time in front of them. They haven't simply been given a once-over and dismissed. They are being looked at. But what happens in a thirty-second look at a work of art? What can be gained from it? Is it meaningful at all? This is a question that has perplexed us for years, and to a degree, still does, but we think we have begun to see an answer to that question. To begin to answer that question, it might be worthwhile to look at a work of art for thirty seconds. To that end, consider Figure 3.3, a marble from the Parthenon in Greece. Try taking a thirty-second look at it.

What do you see? I think (I hope) that even in thirty seconds, you can respond to the work in a meaningful fashion. It evokes an emotional response.

Figure 3.3.   Figure of Iris from the west pediment of the Parthenon, Acropolis, Athens.

We marvel at the movement in the garment—so fluid. It seems impossible that marble can be turned into something with motion, a motion that has survived over thousands of years. It is fascinating that this motion, this fluidity, has persisted for so long because it is captured in a medium that is absolutely solid. How was this piece made? How was it posed? Was there a live model? Could wind be generated then in a fashion that would allow for careful observation? Are these reactions the same if looking at it for a half hour, or ten minutes, or even two? Almost assuredly not; longer looks are more meaningful looks. So we see that even perhaps in what we are calling a "consuming" look, there is a response to a work of art that is at some level meaningful.

The third group of people (or more properly, "looks" by people) are those that last roughly a minute or so. We refer to these as "savoring" looks by individuals. The notion of being able to savor a work of art in the matter of one minute perhaps grates a bit with a conception of an aesthetic response, but as long as we are using a culinary metaphor, consider what happens when "savoring" a taste of wine. Even the most pedantic oenophile will not have a drink of wine in the mouth for a full minute (or perhaps they would, but I don't want to think about that). But how can we compare a Rembrandt etching to even the rarest of wines? How, indeed? It is a most interesting question, but one for another time. Let us use our empirical approach again, this time with the Cezanne work in Figure 3.4. Take a look at that work for perhaps a minute and a half or two minutes. You might want to time yourself a bit on this, because we find that when people look at a work for this long, they often think they've looked for much longer.

A minute and a half to two minutes is long enough to make some level of real consideration of a work. It is possible in that time to consider style, or how the work was constructed; with this Cezanne, one might want to contrast to other still lifes by Cezanne that the viewer knows. One might notice the fruit in the bowl on the right and wonder about what seems to be an odd stacking of the fruit. Or one might consider how the fruit are laid out on the table. This is not really what one would normally see on a table; these have been arranged. Why in this fashion? The fruit, to me, almost seem like they are people on a busy street, in the kinds of clumps and engaged in interactions one might see in such a scene, or perhaps children in a schoolyard with a stern schoolmarm, one arm akimbo, represented by the jug. Now that is a bit of an off-the-wall interpretation, and probably not at all what you saw in this work. You saw what you saw; it came from you as well as from the work. We will return to that notion in the next chapter.

Different people will look at a work for different amounts of time, but typically not very long. Now let's do a bit of math. If people look at works for twenty-seven seconds on average, and if they spend two hours in a museum,

Figure 3.4.   Cezanne. Curtain, jug and bowl of fruit, 1893–1894.
Erich Lessing / Art Resource, NY

and if we allow maybe ten seconds between works, and perhaps a bit more time to walk from one gallery to the next, then the total number of works that might be viewed in a typical visit would be on the order of 150–200 works. And these would be works that were actually stopped at, not merely passed by. Some of these stops are "sampling" stops where the visitor decides not to invest time, others are "consuming" stops where we believe a certain level of engagement and reaction occurs, and a few are "savoring" stops, where some level of real contemplation is realized. As we will see in the next chapter, people engage works in a meaningful fashion, and part of that engagement involves what the person brings to the interaction. In the models that we will look at, the viewer's background, knowledge, prior experience, and current state of mind are all important factors. In considering what the viewer brings to a particular work of art, we would like to suggest adding the experience that the viewer had at the previous work of art. Is the viewer a bit melancholy, excited, wistful, fondly remembering a past love, or inspired to accomplish great things? If a work of art has triggered memories, reactions, contemplations, and so forth, then these do not simply vanish in the stroll to the next work. They linger, perhaps become infused in the response to the subsequent work, form a confluence of thoughts and emotions, or perhaps they run on parallel tracks, switching over to a new routing by seeing a new work. Whatever happens to a particular individual, we believe that it happens cumulatively over the course of encountering 150–200 works of art, not just a single one. The Museum Effect builds.

Reconsidering the Crossword Puzzle Analogy

It might be useful to harken back to one of the metaphors introduced at the beginning of the chapter: the crossword puzzle analogy. Here the similarity is primarily a structural one. If you do crossword puzzles, you know that there are clues that you look at and almost immediately say, "Nope, cannot do this without more information." And then there are ones that you look at for a few seconds, and wonder, "Do I really know whether the answer I've just come up with is really the answer here?" And finally, there are ones that you realize are going to make you think harder about them. You say to yourself, "I don't think the maker of this puzzle means the common meaning of this phrase; I think there is a twist in here that I need to consider." When you "get" an answer, especially one that required some creativity to solve on your part, you feel good about it, and to a small degree, about yourself. That one was a success. But sometimes you have to leave the clue to come back later. It was not a success. Maybe you are a bit frustrated by your encounter with it. As with all metaphors, if one considers them closely enough, they start to fray at the edges. If the linkages were perfect, it wouldn't be a metaphor for the thing; it'd be the thing itself.

A crossword puzzle is similar to a museum visit in that it is comprised of a series of pieces that bear a relationship to one another—stronger in some instances and weaker in others. Each piece presents a challenge to the participant: crossword puzzles that are too easy are not enjoyable, nor are ones that are too difficult. Crossword puzzles that can be solved with real effort, or ones that are not quite solvable with real effort, are the ones that are essentially the most engaging. The series of challenges, interrelated, forming a coherent whole, is the essential nature of a crossword puzzle, as is a museum visit. But there are differences as well. Crossword puzzles are essentially cognitive activities by nature, and although there are certainly cognitive aspects to a museum visit, there are strong emotional ones as well. Also, crossword puzzles are very much "bounded" events. The number of words to be solved and the structure of them are the same for everyone. Museums, on the other hand, are relatively unbounded. There are almost always more works than one could see in a single visit, and the ones that will be "taken up" by visitors will vary on an individual basis. The museum visit ends when the visitor decides that it has ended; there is no notion of having solved the museum or having failed to do so.

Finally, even though people visit museums typically in a group, they tend to look at art alone. If there is a dialogue going on, it is one between the individual viewer of a work and an artist who is no longer present, certainly not in the museum, and perhaps hundreds of years removed from being anywhere on earth. Conversations among visitors do take place and are often useful conversations, but they are not as common as one might think. Like most crossword puzzle expeditions, they are essentially solitary activities.

To sum up thinking about time in museums, we see that people enter the museum with a somewhat open-ended view of their visit, that they allocate their time to individual works of art according to whether those works intrigue them or not, and that they look at dozens, perhaps hundreds, of works on a given visit, each for a relatively short period of time. Now we move on to beginning to look at the question of what happens when people look at art.

EXPERIENCING FLOW IN MUSEUMS

Any theoretical notion has precursors, both proximal and distal. The ideas presented in this book are no exception. If the notion is related to the social science, as this one is, then John Dewey is almost certainly one of those precursors on the distal side. The great philosopher and psychologist wrote expressively and extensively about the psychology of art. His classic work, *Art as Experience* (Dewey, 1934, published in 1958) contains enough intriguing ideas about art, aesthetics, and society that one could write an entire book about them. In fact, someone did (Jackson, 1998). And so, if sufficiently enticed, one might consider perusing Jackson's excellent analysis of Dewey, or go to the original source. What is important for what we are looking at here with regard to Dewey's contribution was his emphasis on the human nature of experiencing art. Aesthetics is about the reception of art. As Dewey points out, the work of art is to be perceived, just as a chef prepares food to be eaten, and teachers teach in order for someone to learn. There is an element of reciprocity here, of parallelism. Pablo Tinio (2013) has recently examined the relationship of the maker to the viewer in art, as will be discussed in the next chapter. For Dewey, aesthetic reception of a work of art depends on the knowledge and skill, and perhaps the disposition of the viewer in receiving it. He points out that any of us can enjoy a beautiful flower, but to understand it requires some comprehension of the underlying botanical principles. He argues that an epicure's enjoyment of dinner is different in kind and not simply magnitude from one "who merely 'likes' his food as he eats it" (Dewey, 1958, p. 49).

But ultimately, what does this mean for us? Does it segment off aesthetics to the province of those who are trained in art history, or in studio arts? Perhaps it does. Perhaps the proper study of aesthetics should be focused on the appreciation of fine works of art by those who have a strong background in the art that they are perceiving. I say that not in a contrarian fashion: there is without question a good argument to be made for excellence or exceptionality in the perception of fine art. It does not have to be a democratic endeavor. It is why people want to know more, want to learn more, and consistently tell us that they are at a museum to enjoy *and* to learn. Almost every person we have ever interviewed in a museum setting (if asked) has told us that they would like to know more about what they are viewing and how to view it (be it a Picasso or how to make a bucket out of wooden staves). No one has ever said that they would like to know less or be less sophisticated about what they are viewing.

At the same time, we know that most people who visit the museum tell us that they are not particularly sophisticated with regard to their knowledge of art. When we ask people to rate their knowledge of art on a scale of one to ten with one being "no knowledge" and ten being "a true expert," the median response at the Metropolitan was in the five-to-six range. In a joint study we did with the Pushkin Museum of Fine Arts in Moscow (Smith, Wolf, & Starodubtsev, 1994), their mean on this scale was a four, with only 7 percent giving a rating above a six. In the same study, we asked people to choose among four options as to what their primary reason for visiting the museum was: education, inspiration, relaxation, socialization. Education was the highest rating, followed by relaxation, socialization, and inspiration. Visitors to art museums are typically not connoisseurs; they aspire to be connoisseurs, or to get closer to being so, but they are better characterized as intelligent, well-educated individuals with some background in art and a strong interest in it. That is, of course, too broad a generalization, as there are also connoisseurs in museums as well as people who have very little background in art. They are Mario the airline captain from the previous chapter, or the retired woman looking at a work of art she was standing in front of when her husband proposed to her. They are Pekarik's individual looking to see something rare, or to better understand what he or she is looking at; they are Falk's explorers or experience seekers, or maybe they are facilitators, at the museum today because they are bringing out-of-town visitors. They are Pitman and Hirzy's (2010) observers and participants; their aesthetic fluency is of a middling level. These are the individuals who populate museums.

If museums have a profound effect on the lives of individuals, as I am arguing they do, then this effect should be observed not just on art experts, but also on the police officer, the priest, and the girl who believed she was looking at the baby Jesus. The question I am focused on here is somewhat different from what Dewey was contemplating, or what many scholars who look at aesthetics from a philosophical perspective contemplate. I am not focused on a person looking at a single work of art, nor am I focused on a sophisticated viewer of art (although I will spend some time on such viewers). I am interested in the effects of a museum visit as a whole on an individual who enjoys looking at art, but whose sophistication and background in what he or she is looking at is, perhaps, only of a middling level. Why? Because that is who looks at art and how they look at art.

The Idea of Flow

"Flow" is a psychological notion (idea, concept, theory) developed by Mihaly Csikszentmihalyi (1982). It has become one of the most widely used and studied phenomena in psychology over the past thirty years, and has been adapted to an incredibly broad range of subfields within and outside of psychology. My wife and I had the pleasure of having dinner with Csikszentmihalyi one evening as he was presenting an address to the Met on the next day. We talked about many exciting ideas and possibilities for research. The part of the conversation that I remember best, however, was the following exchange:

> Me: If you don't mind me being so crass, how do you pronounce your name?
>
> Csikszentmihalyi: It is simple. Four words in English: Chick Sent Me Hi.
>
> Me: That *is* simple. How about your first name?
>
> Csikszentmihalyi: Mike.

I liked him immediately. The fundamental idea behind flow is that there are things that we do in our lives that cause us pleasure in the doing of them, not for any reward, be it extrinsic or intrinsic. We play bridge, read crime novels, hike, surf, paint, do crossword puzzles, or visit museums because they are things we like to do for their own sake; they are *autotelic*. In a flow situation, the individual is solely focused on a particular activity of interest, tends to lose track of time, and loses oneself in the activity.

In his work *The Art of Seeing*, Csikszentmihalyi (1990) takes the idea of flow and applies it to art experts (art historians, museum professionals) as they look at art. He compares the flow experience to Beardsley's (1982) criteria for the aesthetic experience. Beardsley argues that aesthetic experiences are characterized by (1) a focus on the object—the work of art, (2) freedom from concerns about other issues, (3) a detached sense of affect, (4) active mental engagement with an effort to understand the object, and (5) a sense of wholeness or integration with the object/experience. Csikszentmihalyi shows how these are related to the criteria of the "flow experience" and indeed, there is a strong parallelism. Since the "flow experience" is critical to the ideas underlying the Museum Effect, we take some time here to look at them more carefully. To that end, the following set of criteria comes directly from *The Art of Seeing* (p. 8):

1. Merging of Action and Awareness: Attention centered on activity
2. Limitation of Stimulus Field: No awareness of past and future
3. Loss of Ego: Loss of self-consciousness and transcendence of ego boundaries
4. Control of Action: Skills adequate to overcome challenges
5. Clear Goals, Clear Feedback
6. Autotelic Nature: Does not need external rewards, intrinsically satisfying

There are some differences between Beardsley's aesthetic experience and Csikszentmihalyi's flow experience, but the commonalities are remarkable. Looking at art clearly requires a focus on the work of art. What are we seeing here? What is the whole, what are the parts? Is there a single central impact that resonates, or are we being told a story? What emotions and cognitions are evoked? The second criterion is quite similar as well. When we are focused on a work of art, we tend not to be thinking of other things. We are not worrying about the time or where we parked our car. One of the major goals of going to an art museum is to escape the humdrum realities of our everyday lives and put ourselves in front of genius for a while. The third criterion seems to diverge a bit, for me at any rate. Beardsley's notion of detached affect is a complex one, and to a degree, fits with Csikszentmihalyi's notion of loss of self-consciousness. But there is also the notion in "detached affect" that the affect that one experiences when looking at art is different from normal affect. We can experience a melancholy or sadness when listening to a piece of music, looking at a sculpture, or reading a book, but it is a different kind of melancholy or sadness that occurs when events in our real lives engender them. Aesthetic affect is a kind of sympathetic affect. As such, it affords opportunities and entails limitations that personal, or real, affect might not. For example, we can explore the emotions that a painting brings out in us secure in the knowledge that we can leave them when and as we choose. We can push ourselves more deeply into the emotion and then retreat from it. At the same time, we are always conscious of the fact that the situation is an empathetic one, not real, and therefore the emotion, too, has something of a lack of reality to it. I think this is an important component in Beardsley's conceptualization and in work that followed on from him. Perhaps Csikszentmihalyi meant this as well, but I don't quite see it in flow. This isn't intended to be a criticism of flow, just perhaps, a distinction.

The fourth criterion is a critical and fascinating one for the perspective on art viewing in museums that we are to take on here. What is the role of knowledge, skill, or expertise in the aesthetic experience, and in flow? I have suggested that a model of aesthetics that does not consider what happens to the vast majority of people within an art museum has some severe limitations. It might be an appropriate model under some notions of what aesthetics should be about, but it doesn't help much with understanding what happens to those people who lack the cognitive background to be connoisseurs, and because of that limitation, it doesn't really explain why millions of people go to art museums, or what happens to them while they are there. So for me, although such a theory explains questions that I am inherently interested in, it doesn't explain the bulk of what I have observed in museums for the past quarter of a century. It is those people and their behavior that I want to understand. And I think the crux of the issue comes with criterion number four. What is the role of knowledge, skill, and expertise in appreciating art? I reiterate that no one we have ever spoken to wants less of them, and most people are expressly in the museum in part to gain more of them. The art educator and philosopher Ralph A. Smith (1999) expressed the importance of this elegantly:

> The personal benefit derived from having learned to experience things aesthetically is an expansion of the self that may include energized perception, enlarged powers of imagination, and insights gained into the nature of things. As such a disposition does not emerge without tuition, it becomes the task of aesthetic education to develop the skills and knowledge needed to shape it. In other words, knowing how—that is, knowing how to deploy the skills and knowledge learned—is intimately related to knowing within. (p. 21)

For us, the power of knowledge, of simply knowing more about objects, often came through wonderful interactions with curators at the Met and other museums. Two stories might help to illustrate this. We were going to do a study on a special exhibition in the Egyptian galleries at the Met, and were fortunate enough to have the now retired curator of the Egyptian galleries, the delightful Dorothea Arnold, give us a tour of the galleries to get a better sense of a curatorial perspective on the galleries and what we could learn about the people viewing them. Two things stand out in particular from that tour. The first was the room where the statues of the female pharaoh, Hatshetsup, are displayed. Dorothea told us of the amazing story of Hatshetsup—her twenty-year reign as pharaoh—a story filled with intrigue and mystery, and then she explained the statuary in the room. One interesting aspect of the statues is that they exist in a number of states of repair. Usually the phrase "states of repair" means that some things are repaired and others are not, or that things aren't really repaired at all. But in this case, they are all repaired (restored), but are in various states. The statues of Hatshetsup were mostly destroyed after her death (another mystery). Dorothea explained that they basically represent different approaches to conservation over the decades, ranging from attempts to completely bring works back to what they had looked like originally to works that are held together with wire armature with empty spaces where original material from the smashed statues had not been found. So this room, which had always been a bit fascinating because the statues seemed so different from one another, now became a must-stop when we gave tours to friends from out of town, and resulted in fairly extensive reading on the female pharaoh.

The second story is shorter and more amusing. Within the Egyptian galleries is a wonderful side gallery that contains the materials from the tomb of an Egyptian named Meketre. It holds the objects that were buried with him so that he would be comfortable in the afterlife, and basically tells the story of the burial of this individual. It is intriguing in the kind of completeness of the works on display. Dorothea explained this to us and then focused our attention on one work in the middle of the main room. It is called *Statue of an Offering Bearer* (Figure 3.5) and in fact, it was one of our favorite pieces in the Egyptian collections.

Dorothea told us that it was one of the finest pieces in the collection, which made us feel good, as we had always liked it. But we didn't know that it was an exceptional piece and inquired as to why that was the case. The question caused her to laugh out loud. "Well," she said, "it is wonderful because it is rare for a statue carved in wood to be so incredibly well preserved, and the way she is depicted, the movement, the way her dress clings to her body. But if you really want to know why she is so amazing, you have to come around and look at her from the other side! Now, just look at those buttocks. They are in motion! You can see them underneath that dress!" It was true. I didn't mention it to Lisa, but in fact, it was something that I had observed before but had never really linked to a notion of "greatness" in the statuette.

In these two examples, we see the effect of knowledge on appreciation. Knowing that the different restorations of the statues of Hatshetsup represent different philosophical approaches to what restoration and/or presentation should be allows the viewer to compare and contrast those approaches, and to better understand what goes on behind the scenes in museums. In having our attention directed to the way the offering bearer's dress clings to her body and reveals that body, we learn to trust our instincts a bit more when considering the quality of a work of art.

So, to return to the original issue here, how does having the skills and knowledge to meet the challenges of the activity play out in thinking about flow and visitors to an art museum? As we have seen, the knowledge and skills

Figure 3.5.   Statue of an Offering Bearer. Egyptian; ca. 1981–1975 BCE.
Image copyright © The Metropolitan Museum of Art. Image source: Art Resource, NY

that visitors bring to the task vary widely, from true novices to true experts. Surely the novice does not have the skill to address the issues that the expert is considering! Our New York City policeman from chapter 1 enjoyed the Egyptian galleries, as most visitors to the Met do, but he could not come close to the Egyptology expertise that an Egyptologist possesses. And yet, when we talk to people after a museum visit, many tell us of the wonderfulness of the experience. They are not art experts, but it would be hard to deny that they have engaged in a flow experience. Great art speaks to people at a variety of levels. Renaissance religious art was often commissioned in part to provide illustrations of Bible stories and events that could be appreciated by the faithful who were not literate (that is, not literate in that they could not read, not that they were unsophisticated in appreciating art). The audience, in part, for such works, were people whose faith was strong but whose knowledge of art was weak. Raphael spoke to those people five hundred years ago as he does today.

How can this be? I think it is because people have different expectations for looking at art. They set different challenges for themselves. Great art speaks at a wide range of levels; that is why it is possible to come back to great art time and again, and see new and different things, and have a deeper understanding on a second, third, or fourth look at a work. Art can speak directly to the individual. One's appreciation of a work can be naïve and still be profound.

So, we see parallels in how Csikszentmihalyi conceptualized the idea of flow, and how Beardsley conceptualized the aesthetic encounter. And in both of their works, we can see parallels with Dewey's description of the aesthetic experience. There is the object and the individual; there is content, form, and style to be considered; there are challenges to be set and met or not met; there is a loss of a sense of place and time; and there is a feeling of wholeness or integration as a result of the experience. These ideas are central to the notion of the Museum Effect, but we need to build in one more component to complete our preliminary work here: the unit of analysis.

THE UNIT OF ANALYSIS IN LOOKING AT ART

When we visit a museum, we do not look at a work of art. We look at *lots* of works of art. These works may differ greatly in style, type, and design. We might look at some Impressionist paintings, and then at some trompe l'oeil works, and then at reliquaries, and then at a reconstructed room from Pompeii. Or we might spend all our time in an exhibition and see many works by a single artist. If we look at the field of aesthetics, either from a philosophical or a psychological perspective, we are usually considering what happens when *a* person encounters *a* work of art: one person, one work of art. But if we look how people look at art in an art museum visit, we know this occurs for multiple works of art for brief periods of time. And fundamentally, people think of their visit as a complete event. They have in fact looked at many individual works of art, but they have *visited* the Louvre, or the Getty, or any of thousands of smaller museums. The visit is the thing. As introduced in the previous chapter, in considering the Museum Effect, it is the visit that is *the unit of analysis*, not the work of art.

In arguing that the museum visit is the appropriate unit of analysis, I am saying that if one wants to understand how museums affect us in our lives, we should look at the museum visit as a whole. Now, that might raise some hackles and ruffle some feathers here and there, so let me try to smooth those out a bit. One person looking at one work of art is the essence of aesthetics. There is no question about that in my mind. That is why the models of aesthetic interaction that are presented in the next chapter are so important to consider. It is the essential building block of all of aesthetics, and it is rightly the focus of the vast majority of work in the psychology of aesthetics. But, if we are thinking about what happens in museums, and in particular art museums, then, I would argue, we have to consider the visit as a whole. And furthermore, there is something that occurs with the choice to visit, the disposition that people bring with them as they enter a museum, and how they actually go about looking at works that all argue for the museum as the proper unit of analysis, as opposed to one person/one work.

When we shift from a focus on objects to a focus on the museum as a whole, a number of things change. Stops in front of objects are now pieces of a whole. What has happened at one object may well influence what happens at the next stop, or perhaps even determines where the next stop will be. What we are considering changes from something that occurs over the course of about a half minute to something that occurs over the course of several hours. In thinking about the museum visit as the unit of analysis, we can return to our metaphors to help in shaping some considerations. First, there is the notion of *museum as institution*, or place. Going to the Hermitage, or the Getty in Bilbao, or the Frick Collection inherently involves the place of the museum as well as its collection.

Perhaps the most obvious example of the institution itself being a critical component of the visit is the Solomon R. Guggenheim Museum in New York City. The building is an iconographic piece of art and part of the city. One cannot escape its influence while viewing the art there. But perhaps the Guggenheim is too facile for our purposes here. Let us consider instead the old Barnes Foundation when the collection was housed in Lower Merion, Pennsylvania. It isn't necessary to go into the controversy and history of the Barnes Foundation here, but a tour of the collection when it was in Merion was a treat for many reasons, not the least of which was the enduring influence of its founder, the remarkable Albert C. Barnes. While looking at an amazing collection of Cezannes, Renoirs, Matisses, and Picassos, the influence of Barnes continually intruded on the visit. The pictures were hung according to his preferences, and the audio tour insisted upon a particular approach to looking at the works. Interestingly, Barnes was friendly with, and influenced by, John Dewey. Dewey refers to Barnes several times in *Art as Experience*. The nature of the collection and Barnes himself can be garnered through an excellent piece in *Philanthropy* magazine by James Panero (2011). Of particular interest is this quote of Barnes on how he acquired much of his collection:

> "Particularly during the Depression," Barnes said, "my specialty was robbing the suckers who had invested all their money in flimsy securities and then had to sell their priceless paintings to keep a roof over their heads."

One might wonder if this is really the person whose views on art are the ones one wants to focus on. And yet he is inescapable, or at least was, in the presentation in Lower Merion.

If one considers viewing an individual work of art not as an event in and of itself, but as part of an overall visit with lots of looks at art, then the metaphor of the crossword puzzle is clear. The metaphor is enhanced, I would argue, by taking the concept of flow into account. A really good crossword puzzle can be engaging for hours, and ultimately, if one is successful, an experience that brings about a real sense of satisfaction of having bested an intellectual challenge. The individual clues, and the associated challenges they pose, come together as an integrated whole. The works of art in a museum are typically more diverse than clues in a crossword puzzle (unless one is viewing say, a biographical exhibition), but what one does with the works bears a level of similarity from one work to another. That is, although we may react very differently from one work to another, we are in "art response" or "aesthetic" mode when we do so. And we stay in that mode throughout the visit. That mode will no doubt differ from one person to the next, and from one visit to the next within individuals, but there is a commonality in our mental experience of the works that allows us to form a whole out of the parts.

And the baseball game can be seen as a good metaphor now as well. Around eighty or so batters will come to bat in a baseball game, roughly the same order of magnitude as the works of art viewed in a museum visit. Each of these "at bats" holds the potential to be engaging. Each at bat will have its own components and pieces. Some will turn out to be exciting, others less so. And a story line of the game will develop. It might be a duel between two excellent pitchers, or perhaps a very high scoring game. A fight might break out, or a brilliant play made in the field. A casual fan or first-time visitor to a live game might find enjoyment in the home team winning, or the quality of the food that is served, or the atmosphere of the ballpark. A more serious fan might view the game in terms of the strategic decisions that are made by the managers or the boldness in the base running of one of the teams. Baseball can be enjoyed at a variety of levels of expertise because different people come with different expectations and levels of knowledge (harken back, if you will, to the different kinds of visitors in terms of background and expectations that we saw in the previous chapter). Or baseball can be not enjoyed at all. Some people simply don't like baseball just as others don't like soccer, and still others don't like museums. But it is an event just as a museum visit is an event, something to be looked back upon as a coherent whole made up of interesting pieces.

SETTING THE STAGE

We are ready now to look seriously at the notion of the Museum Effect. The stage has been set. We are in a position to take what we know, and put pieces into place that will argue for the fundamental proposition of the Museum Effect: that museums make us better people and civilize society. It is a bold claim to be certain but one that I believe can be substantiated.

REFERENCES

Augustin, M. D., Leder, H., Hutzler, F., & Carbon, C. C. (2008). Style follows content: On the microgenesis of art appreciation. *Perception, 128*, 127–138.

Beardsley, M. C. (1982). Some persistent issues in aesthetics. In M. J. Wreen & D. M. Callen (Eds.), *The Aesthetic Point of View*. Ithaca, NY: Cornell University Press.

Carr, D. W. (2006). *A place not a place: Reflection and possibility in museums and libraries*. Oxford: AltaMira Press.

Csikszentmihalyi, M. (1982). Toward a psychology of optimal experience. In L. Wheeler (Ed.), *Review of personality and social psychology* (Vol. 2). Beverly Hills, CA: Sage.

Csikszentmihalyi, M. (1990). *The art of seeing*. Los Angeles, CA: Getty Publications.

Dewey, J. (1958). *Art as experience*. New York: Capricorn Books.

Jackson, P. W. (1998). *John Dewey and the lessons of art*. New Haven, CT: Yale University Press.

Panero, J. (2011). Outsmarting Albert Barnes. *Philanthropy*. Retrieved June 24, 2013, from http://www.philanthropyroundtable.org/topic/donor_intent/outsmarting_albert_barnes.

Pitman, B., and Hirzy, E. (2010). *Ignite the power of art: Advancing visitor engagement in museums*. Dallas, TX: Dallas Museum of Art.

Smith, R. A. (1999). Justifying aesthetic education: Getting it right. *Journal of Aesthetic Education, 33*(4), 17–28.

Smith, J. K., & Smith, L. F. (2001). Spending time on art. *Empirical Studies of the Arts*, *19*(2), 229–236.

Smith, J. K., Wolf, L. F., and Starodubtsev, S. P. (1994). Cross-cultural learning in two art museums: The Poushkin and the Metropolitan. *Current Trends in Audience Research and Evaluation*, *8*, 75–78.

Thorpe, S., Fize, D., & Marlot, C. (1996). Speed of processing in the human visual system. *Nature*, *381*(6), 520–522.

Tinio, P. P. L., & Leder, H. (in press). The means to art's end: Styles, creative devices, and the challenge of art. In A. S. Bristol, J. C. Kaufman, & O. Vartanian (Eds.), *The Neuroscience of Creativity*. Cambridge, MA: MIT Press.

Tinio, P. P. L. (2013). From artistic creation to aesthetic reception: The mirror model of art. *Psychology of Aesthetics, Creativity, and the Arts*, *7*(3), 265–275.

4

Defining the Museum Effect

$\mathbf{A}$ conversation with my then fourteen-year-old son as we exited an exhibition of Jusepe de Ribera at the Met:

"How did you like the exhibition?"

"Exhibition was good. But they should have had a different title."

"What would you have named it?"

"'*Bad Days in the Lives of the Saints.*' And one other thing, Dad."

"Yeah?"

"Those little chubby flying guys."

"Yeah."

"I don't like them."

When we look at a work of art, what we see, how we see it, and how we react to it depend on us as individuals—who we are and what we bring to the interaction with the work. The differences among people, and within a person on two different occasions, are the sources of the variation in how a work of art is viewed. The context in which the work is presented will have some effect on the interaction—an exceptionally interesting label or audio commentary can influence perception—but the fundamental differences are the ones that are precipitated by differences among viewers.

We vary; the work is constant.

No two people have the exact experience with a work of art. If we hold the work constant, the only thing that can cause variation in the experience resides within the individual. The St. Sebastian painting by Ribera (Figure 4.1) is the same for all viewers, and has been for almost five hundred years. Of course, the context has changed, probably fairly substantially over time, and that is a factor to take into consideration, but the work itself is the same. In a museum context, there aren't just a number of visitors looking at one painting; there is also the notion of one visitor looking at a number of paintings. So we need to consider both the variability in the individuals who are viewing works, and the variability in the works as one individual makes his or her way through the museum. That is one of the basic ways in which the Museum Effect differs from other approaches to aesthetics: it explicitly takes into account the idea that the individual will have multiple, relatively short, interactions with works of art during a museum visit.

My son's reactions to Ribera were actually a little bit surprising to me. He tends to be a bit on the squeamish side when it comes to things like blood and body parts (taking after his father), and I was a bit reluctant to take him to the Ribera exhibition. There was no question that his general reaction to things anatomical would color his reactions to the works. Ribera was a master of mixing the corporeal with the spiritual and putting both right in the face of the viewer. I was also surprised that he seemed more off-put by the putti

Figure 4.1.   Ribera. St. Sebastian; 1621.
Album / Art Resource, NY

than by the gore. My reactions to the exhibition differed markedly from his. I was focused on whom Ribera was making these works for. Apparently Ribera was not a particularly nice individual, and was much concerned with his personal prosperity; were these works intended to uplift the faithful, or were they intended to appeal to patrons? How does one portray the intense religious devotion of the martyrdom of saints if one is primarily motivated by financial benefit? Thus, the two of us viewed the exact same exhibition, mostly standing side by side as we did, occasionally discussing the works that we viewed, and came away with very different experiences.

This chapter lays out the basic argument of the Museum Effect and its workings. It is a model of what happens when people visit an art museum and partake of the offerings therein. It does not say *how* one should look at art but rather focuses on trying to understand the effects that are obtained when people *do* look at art. The argument for the model rests on a number of theoretical and empirical studies that have been conducted over the past forty years, and combines that with what we have found in our work for a quarter of a century studying people in museum settings. I examine the models that form the supporting basis for the Museum Effect first, and then present several studies that speak to and test the model.

HOW *SHOULD* WE LOOK AT
ART VERSUS HOW *DO* WE LOOK AT ART

There are many things that one could say about the painting of St. Sebastian presented in Figure 4.1, or about Ribera, his time and fellow artists, or about how people have viewed his work over the past five hundred years. They are fascinating questions and I enjoy reading about them and others in the history of art, but I have no particular background or expertise for discussing them myself. I am a psychologist, not an art historian. And as a psychologist, I am more interested in *what is* than *what ought to be*. I want to understand what happens to individuals when they look at a Ribera, or a Matisse, more so than in what they might be able to see if they were more sophisticated, had a sharper sense of discrimination, or knew more about Ribera's life and times. But because my interest is different than the questions that arise from such a perspective, please do not conclude that I do not revere them. I love art and art history. I don't believe that everyone's views on a work of art are as valid and worthy of our consideration as anyone else's views. Experts are experts for a reason.

Thus, I pay attention to experts if I want to know about art. But if I want to know about how art affects people, people in museums, then I need to go to the source. I need to look at people looking at art, aesthetic warts and all. And thus, if fourteen-year-old boys are part of what my population of interest includes, then I need such opinions under advisement. We aren't really all that interested in fourteen-year-old boys here (we are going to concentrate on adults), but we *might* have been. We are interested in the millions of people who go to art museums every day (and by extension to people who go to other cultural institutions as well), and how those institutions affect their visitors. If I want to learn about that St. Sebastian painting and about Ribera, I know where to go. I know the scholarship to consult and even individuals I might ask questions of. But my actual interest here is not in the art itself, but in the interaction between the art and the individuals who view it, individuals who come in all levels of sophistication, interest, and background. I am interested in people with keen eyes and dull, because outside the walls of the museum, they are all participants in society, and thus are all worthy of consideration in seeing how cultural institutions affect them.

A BRIEF TOUR OF MODEL CITY

In the previous chapter, we looked at the work of Csikszentmihalyi, whose notion of flow provides a basis for looking at the Museum Effect. But there are other bases as well, and over the next several pages, we will look at a selection of other models that relate to the Museum Effect directly. In the social sciences, models are presented in a variety of different ways depending upon what one is trying to explain or understand. If we look at the Housen and Parsons models (presented below), or those of Falk or Pekarik from chapter 2, we see that they are a set of categories or stages. The basic theoretical work is coming up with those groupings, and defending their nature (and their existence) through prior work, empirical data, and argumentation. These might be contrasted with the models of Chatterjee, Leder, Locher, or Tinio (also presented below), which are models of processes. In these models, a series of steps or processes are argued to be explanatory of some particular phenomenon. Again, the argument is made through logic, prior work, and empirical justification. Now, in some cases, the empirical work has just begun, or perhaps does not exist at all, but is called for, in which case the theoretical and logical work needs to be stronger to make the case. In some work in physics, for example, it can take decades for empirical justification of theoretical ideas. A third type of model that one sees in the social sciences has to do with how variables are related to one another—a set of variables are posited to influence (or to actually cause) other variables. For example, in education, one might argue that parental levels of education and quality of instruction together influence (or cause) the educational achievement of children. There are no stages or groupings here, nor is the nature of the process explained; the argument rather, is that variables A and B influence variable C.

This is actually probably the most commonly seen form of theoretical work in the social sciences.

The Museum Effect is not of the type of the Housen or Parsons model, but I rely on their work in making the argument here. The Museum Effect is basically a process model, although the testing of the model relies more on the variable A influencing variable B approach. The argument is that interaction with works of art causes people to engage in personal reflection that leads them to think more positively about themselves and their future, their relationships with others, and how they view the world. But before we get too far down that road, let us look at some theoretical work that provides an underpinning for the Museum Effect.

Developmental Models of How People Look at Art

Two scholars, Abigail Housen and Michael Parsons, have developed developmental models of aesthetics. In the models, they argue that as people get more sophisticated in their art viewing, they take on a different kind of viewing, or one might say a different stage of viewing than was the case previously. The models aren't strictly developmental in nature, but they resemble Piaget's stage theoretic work in looking at how we grow as human beings.

Housen's Model of Aesthetic Development

The 1970s were in some respects, the high point of the popularity of Jean Piaget's work in developmental psychology, in particular as it related to educational issues. Although his work is not as highly esteemed today as it was then, it is still important among educators and psychologists, and his contributions to developmental psychology are still highly regarded. Piaget's work was extended into a variety of fields, most notably moral development by Kohlberg (1971), and into aesthetics by Housen (1999). Housen and her team interviewed thousands of individuals in many different countries as they looked at art, and analyzed the transcripts from those interviews to construct a developmental model of aesthetics (this can be seen best in Housen [1999], but the work was conducted before then). She has presented a very clear description of her model on the website for her Visual Thinking Strategies program: www.vtshome.org. Her model has five stages: accountive, constructive, classifying, interpretive, and re-creative.

In the *accountive* stage, individuals are basically recounting what they saw. They describe the events in the work, or if abstract, the features of the work. In this stage, people might say, "There are many shapes, and the shapes are different colors," or "The people on the left side of the painting all look like they are taking a nap." In the *constructive* stage, viewers use their knowledge, background, and values to build an understanding of the work of art. They use their knowledge of what really exists in the world to view the works before them. They are likely to be much more receptive to realism than abstraction. At this stage, people might say, "Well the person's face is all broken up. I guess that is to show different angles, but it looks weird to me." The third stage is called the *classifying* stage. Here the viewer is looking at the work from the perspective of where it stands in the history of art. "Is it an early Picasso, or foreshadowing the blue period?" Viewers at this stage are enamored of their art history knowledge and want to learn more about art. The fourth stage is the *interpretive* stage. In this stage, viewers combine their knowledge of art history with their emotional and personal reactions to a work of art. They trust their feelings more in looking at the works. A viewer at the interpretive stage may say, "I think that Davis's assemblage of images presents a childlike approach to the work, but at the same time, for me, says, 'This is the feeling of this time and place—this is how to feel about it.' I think that is what he's trying to do here." The fifth and final stage Housen calls the *re-creative* stage. In this stage, the viewer can take a history of looking at art, and perhaps a number of encounters with a particular work of art, and view it in a new and different light, finding in it what he or she has never seen before. In Housen's words, "The viewer gives himself permission to encounter the artwork with a childlike openness. A trained eye, critical stance, and responsive attitude are his lenses as the multifaceted experience of the artwork guides his viewing." (Housen, 2007, p. 175) The re-creative stage reminds me of a conversation I once had with trombonist Jonathan Harker. I asked him if he felt as if he is being creative when he plays, particularly in an orchestra. He responded, "I don't create. The composer created. I re-create." I think Jonathan's view reflects the spirit of the re-creative stage in Housen's model.

What can be seen here is that Housen's model runs a range from very rudimentary viewing to highly sophisticated viewing. She doesn't assign age ranges to her stages, but argues that the progression through the stages is necessary to reach higher levels of response. For our purposes, what is of particular interest is not the argument for the developmental nature of the progression, or even of the progression itself, but for the insight it presents into how people are looking at art and how they are responding to it. We see that for much of what occurs when people look at art, there is a natural tendency to blend what one sees with what one brings as a person to the work. Look in particular at Housen's fourth and fifth stages. In each of these stages, she argues that there is a strong influence of one's personal and emotional reactions to works. The viewer brings him- or herself into the very nature of the viewing and the interpretation. We also see this to a degree in Housen's second stage.

Parsons's Model of Aesthetic Development

Contemporaneously to Housen, Michael J. Parsons (1987) developed a model of aesthetic development that he presented in *How We Understand Art*. Parsons argues that his stages should not be regarded as a strict hierarchy. He, too, has five stages in his model, but they don't align precisely with Housen's approach. His model begins with what he calls *favoritism*. In this stage, viewers talk about what they basically like or don't like. This stage is typically associated with children, as Parsons did a lot of work with young viewers. Stage two is *beauty and realism*. Here the viewer is looking for realistic depictions and pictures that are visually appealing. The similarities between the first two stages of Housen and of Parsons are clear, although Parsons's stage one emphasizes what is liked and Housen seems a bit more focused on a telling of what the viewer sees in the work. The third stage for Parsons is called *expressiveness*, and is focused on what is expressed by the work of art as opposed to a more realistic analysis of what the painting is about. Viewers at this stage are looking for themes and ideas in the works of art that they are viewing. This contrasts with Housen's third stage where the focus is more on a rudimentary notion of classification according to art historical notions. In Parsons's fourth stage, *style and form*, the relationship of the work of art to other works, to styles and genres, and so forth, is emphasized (similar to Housen's third stage). The final stage for Parsons is *autonomy*. In this stage the viewer can make a sophisticated assessment of a work of art, broadly encompassing a variety of factors and a strong background in art history.

The differences and similarities in the Parsons and Housen approaches can be seen in Figure 4.2. Generally speaking, Parsons has a more art historical focus in his model, where Housen includes personal factors to a much greater degree. Parsons, it seems to me, is more focused on the art and how people go about understanding it, whether they are getting it "right" or not, whereas Housen is more focused on people's reactions to works and understanding differences in how they react to works. Parsons asked his participants questions such as: "Describe the painting to me." "What feelings do you see in the painting?" "What about the colors? Are they good choices?" (Parsons, 1987, p. 19). Housen, on the other hand, simply asked people to talk about what they were viewing, without using specific questions.

The two different models, of what might seemingly be thought to be addressing the same issue, give rise to an intriguing set of questions. It is a bit of a digression, but perhaps worth consideration. How does a true expert look at a work of art? Who would that true expert be? Does the approach of a true art expert represent the pinnacle of art appreciation, of aesthetics? To me, there is no question of the sophistication of the viewing of the art expert—that more is brought to the game than for any other viewer, but sometimes I wonder if

	Parsons	Housen
Stage 1	Favoritism: This stage is associated with young children; paintings exist for pleasure.	Accountive: The viewer creates a narrative of the art. Evaluation is based on what the viewer likes.
Stage 2	Beauty and Realism: Paintings exist to represent things and should be attractive.	Constructive: Personal judgments of whether works of art look like they are supposed to.
Stage 3	Expressiveness: The expressiveness of the painting as it is personally understood is more important than beauty.	Classifying: Works described in art historical terms, using a school, genre, or period as a basis.
Stage 4	Style and Form: Medium, style, and form are important. The work of art exists in public and in an artistic tradition.	Interpretative: Personal feelings and meanings guide interpretation of the work.
Stage 5	Autonomy: The individual can transcend traditional and cultural limitations on interpretation of the work.	Re-Creative: Personal meaning combines with broader understandings and concerns.

Figure 4.2.   Comparison of Parsons and Housen Models.
Jeffrey Smith

that view represents the fullest expression of the relationship between the artist and the viewer. Does a seventeen-year-old aspiring "tagging" artist have a stronger appreciation of a Basquiat painting than a curator of modern art? Does a fellow cave dweller better appreciate the work at Lascaux than an expert on art and archaeology? And who is to decide? But, these questions get me dangerously close to the "how should" side of how people look at art and away from the "how do" people look at art, so I will leave this issue and return to more familiar ground. For now, the important point of looking at the Housen and Parsons models is to get an idea of the types of things that people talk about, think about, when they look at art.

Cognitive Models of How People Look at Art

In recent years, the field of psychology has seen a strong trend toward work in cognitive (and neurological) perspectives. Consonant with those trends, we have seen cognitive models being offered on how people look at art, most notably by Helmut Leder and his colleagues; Paul Locher, Kees Overbeeke, and Stephan Wensveen; Anjan Chatterjee; and most recently, Pablo Tinio. It is particularly instructive to see how these cognitive models contrast with one another, and also how they contrast with the developmental models described above.

Chatterjee's Framework for Visual Aesthetics

Anjan Chatterjee has developed a rough framework for considering how we look at art based on a cognitive and neurological perspective (Chatterjee, 2004, 2010). To a degree, his model might be thought to be a bit too focused on what occurs in the visual system and the brain to be of direct relevance here, but there are some aspects of his work that are particularly interesting. I have roughly reproduced his 2004 model in Figure 4.3 below.

As Chatterjee describes the work, we start with the stimulus, a work of art that is first viewed rather quickly for general features such as shape and color. There is then an intermediate vision that groups together the elements in the initial viewing and begins to make sense out of a work (in a rudimentary notion of the word "sense"). As the viewer spends more time looking at the object, issues such as understanding the work and making emotional (or cognitive) judgments about the work come into play. These different types of viewing are consonant with what we have found in looking at how individuals look at art in museums. Some works are merely glanced at and passed over. Only a very basic view of them has taken place. Others are looked at for a few seconds or so, but no serious time is invested in them. They are not deemed worthy of real consideration. And then there are works where the viewer spends a half minute or so looking, taking the time to process what is before the viewer, and making judgments about the work.

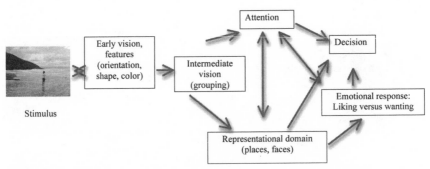

Figure 4.3. Chatterjee's "General framework for the neural underpinnings of visual aesthetics guided by visual neuroscience."
Anjan Chatterjee

Locher, Overbeeke, and Wensveen's Aesthetic Interaction Model

Paul Locher, Kees Overbeeke, and Stephan Wensveen (Locher, Overbeeke, & Wensveen, 2010) developed a model for looking at artifacts that have an aesthetic component. Their model is primarily concerned with products whose design includes aspects intended to make them attractive or pleasurable, but the ideas presented in their model also seem appropriate for looking at the interaction of individuals with works of art. The schematic representation of their approach is presented in Figure 4.4. The applicability of the Locher et al. model to the Museum Effect is apparent from a first look at the model. These scholars have conceptualized what they call an ongoing interaction space, that is, the conceptual location of the interaction between the person and the object. They use the cognitive psychology model of top-down and bottom-up processing to look at how individuals perceive, use, and come to appreciate an artifact. The artifact presents its characteristics to the user within the context of the situation that the user encounters it in. This is the bottom-up component of the model. The user brings to the interaction a host of characteristics: cognitive, emotional, cultural, and so forth. This is the top-down component of the model.

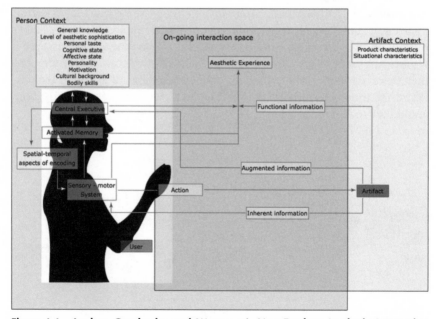

Figure 4.4. Locher, Overbeeke, and Wensveen's User-Product Aesthetic Interaction Model.
Paul Locher

The interaction takes place when the top-down and bottom-up components interact. The authors argue that the aesthetic experience occurs during the interaction of the person with the product. They also point out that there is an initial perception of the artifact where an overall impression or "gist" of the object is determined, and that this parallels what happens when looking at a work of art (as discussed above). There is then a working back and forth between the characteristics of the object and the characteristics and behaviors of the individual that forms the basis of the aesthetic interaction. We see here that the Locher et al. model is more concerned with the interaction of the person with the object, and with what the person brings to this interaction, than we saw in the Chatterjee model (whose focus was on other issues).

Leder, Belke, Oeberst, and Augustin's Model of Aesthetic Appreciation and Aesthetic Judgment

Helmut Leder and his colleagues at the University of Vienna (Leder, Belke, Oeberst, & Augustin, 2004) have developed a model of aesthetic appreciation and judgment that sets out to address a very fundamental and straightforward question: Why are people attracted by art? They take an information-processing perspective on the issue, and pay special attention to the problem of the perception and appreciation of modern art. They see the interaction of a viewer with a work of art (again, think a piece of modern art) as an intellectual challenge, and that the perceived "mastery" of such an interaction provides intrinsic motivation to take up the challenge with a new work. The relationship of this work to the work of Csikszentmihalyi and Beardsley from the previous chapter is clear in this conceptualization. Also, to a degree, is the relationship to the metaphor of the crossword puzzle discussed in previous chapters. A successfully solved crossword clue provides motivation to take on the challenge of the next clue. Leder et al. point out that as one engages in a series of successfully "solved" interactions, one builds the ability to process works of a given style.

The Leder et al. model has five stages (see Figure 4.5). The first stage is *perceptual analysis*, which involves the intake of the work. Issues of complexity, symmetry, form, color, and grouping occur during a rapid and relatively automatic initial perceptual analysis of the work. The second stage is *implicit memory integration*, which refers to the familiarity or prototypicality of a work of art. For example, is this work a Nevelson or Nevelson-like work? Have I seen this work before, maybe in a book or online? Do I recognize this work in some sense of the notion of recognition? The authors argue that this stage, too, is automatic, and leads to a sense of preference for a work that has a degree of familiarity.

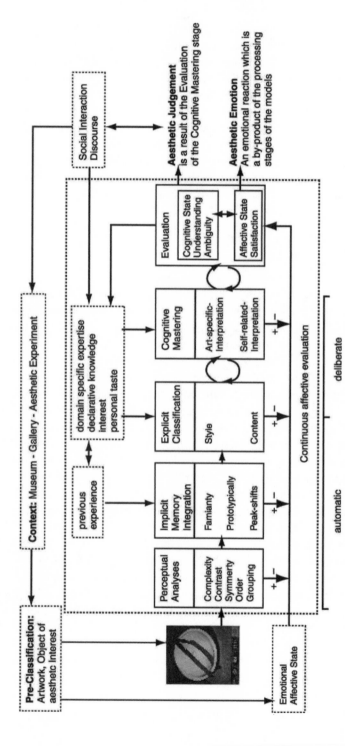

Figure 4.5. Leder et al. Model of Aesthetic Appreciation and Aesthetic Judgments.
Helmut Leder

The third stage of the model is *explicit classification*, which has to do with the ability to classify work with regard to content and style. For highly experienced and knowledgeable viewers of art, explicit classification is probably automatic, but it may be more deliberate for those with less knowledge. The fourth and fifth stages of the model work together in an ongoing feedback loop. They are *cognitive mastering* and *evaluation*. One might think of this as problem solving and evaluation, and again the crossword puzzle analogy serves well here. One might think of a six-letter word for "trip" as "outing," but then think that maybe "outing" doesn't really capture the word "trip" very well. After some additional thought, "voyage" comes to mind and seems much more satisfactory. The same kind of cognitive mastering and evaluation, albeit at a much more sophisticated level, takes place in an interaction with a work of art. You have a sense that "you get it" with a work, or you don't. Again, at a much more sophisticated level, but the notion here is to communicate the underlying idea of the model.

Leder et al. argue that naïve viewers might well use their personal situations to make connections with works of art, letting the subject matter (or style) cause them to reflect upon a personal memory or association in developing their appreciation of a work. The authors point out that modern art is particularly challenging on a number of fronts with regard to its successful perception. They also note that when one is successful in perceiving art, one's repertoire for doing so builds, and the new level of sophistication that one enjoys allows for a deeper appreciation of works. Although, as alluded to in the previous chapter, Parsons argues, at least implicitly, for some sort of ideal or optimal way of viewing art, Leder et al. counter by promoting the notion that there are various levels or solutions to looking at art. I sometimes wonder if it is possible, perhaps, to read more into a work than what was intended by the artist—that it is possible that the optimal level of appreciation is not necessarily the most refined analysis.

The Leder et al. model sees the five stages of aesthetic processing leading to outputs of two types: aesthetic emotion and aesthetic judgments. Aesthetic emotion has to do with how one feels at the end of the aesthetic interaction, and aesthetic judgment has to do with one's evaluation of the work of art. Leder et al. speculate that the model holds potential for understanding listening to music and reading as well. The Leder et al. model and the Museum Effect are, in my view, nearly completely compatible approaches to thinking about the viewing of art. As will be seen shortly, I take a slightly different tack on the issue of viewer response and its nature, but the fundamental structural elements of the Museum Effect are very similar to the Leder et al. approach. One more model to go before we move on to an explication of the Museum Effect.

Tinio's Mirror Model of Art

The final stop on our tour of model city is the mirror model of art developed by Pablo Tinio (2013) (Figure 4.6). The mirror model looks at the artistic production side of art and the aesthetic reception side of art as mirror images of one another.

Tinio's model involves three stages of the art-making process and three (mirror image) stages of the art-viewing process. The symmetry in the model is what reveals the underlying ideas and power of Tinio's thinking here. Starting with the art-making process, the first stage is *initialization*. In this stage, the initial ideas about a work are generated, reviewed, sketched out, examined, and an idea/framework/set of ideas is decided upon for execution. The second stage is *expansion and adaption*. This is where the initial conceptualization is developed and expressed more fully. Works are reworked and reworked again. Relationships that were not apparent initially become apparent, and ideas that seemed strong initially may prove to only be catalysts to new or refined ideas. The third stage in the process is *finalizing* the work. According to Tinio, finalizing occurs when the major structural elements have been completed and the artist is now working on fine-tuning and executing highlights and final processes such as varnishes. As a work progresses from initial conceptual work to the final product, layers and constructions are developed that allow the final work its complexity and depth.

Tinio then turns to the other side of the equation, the aesthetic experience of a work of art. In looking at perception, Tinio relies on the work of the Chatterjee, Locher, and Leder models discussed previously in this chapter. It begins with the notion of *early, automatic processing*. This is detailed in

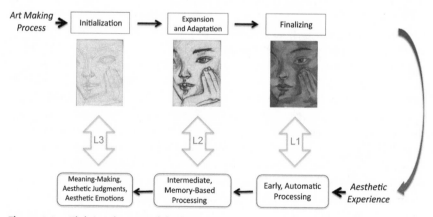

Figure 4.6.   Tinio's Mirror Model of Art.
Pablo Tinio

the discussion of the work above, particularly Leder et al., but what I think is important to point out here is that the finished product from the artistic product is the beginning point for the aesthetic process. The viewer begins with what the artist has left to the viewer. Imagine, if you will, an artist, nearing completion of a work, asking, "Is this it? Do I finally have it here? Is this the image, the set of ideas, the conceptualization that I want this work of art to be?" And the viewer picks that up with, "What am I looking at here? What are these shapes, colors, and forms as they initially strike my eye?" The things that occur in the final stages of the art-making process are picked up on at the beginning of the art-perceiving process. The artist ends; the viewer begins. As with Leder's model, Tinio views this initial processing as a relatively automatic process.

Working from the initial stage, the viewer moves to *intermediate, memory-based processing*. At this stage, different things happen for different kinds of viewers. Here is where the initial visual strike of colors and forms gives way to seeing the objects, figures, and relationships among them. The viewer is looking to see what the work is about. The viewer might be seeing the work as being by a particular artist or from a particular school, and is reading the surface features of the work. The third stage of perception for Tinio is *meaning-making, aesthetic judgments, aesthetic emotions*. Tinio's notion is very similar to Leder's at this point in his model. But what Tinio brings to the table here is an exploration of the kinds of mental activities the viewer is engaging in at this point and comparing them to where the artist was at the beginning of the artistic process. And this is very interesting. Is the message being received by the viewer related to the conceptualization that the artist had in mind in the first place? Does that matter? Tinio goes on to wonder what effect auxiliary information about the work or the artist might have in influencing the viewer's perception. What I find particularly intriguing about Tinio's conceptualization of the production/reception process here is that it is inclusive of the process as a whole. It relates perception to production, calling out the importance of some notion of relationship between the two.

That concludes our tour of model city. As can be seen, the work that has been developed in thinking about aesthetics is impressive, even if only briefly described in these pages. The Housen and Parsons developmental models look at how we grow in our ability to look at art. They focus on how this ability develops and how people differ according to what stage in the process they are at. On the other hand, the Chatterjee, Locher, Leder, and Tinio models focus more on what happens when an individual looks at a work of art (or interacts with an object in a fundamentally aesthetic fashion). The model of the Museum Effect draws heavily on this research, along with the work of Csikszentmihalyi discussed in the previous chapter. It differs from all of those models in important respects, one of which has to do with the unit of analysis that is under consideration.

The Museum Effect is concerned with how individuals look at a work of art, but only in the context of looking at that work *along with* a number of other works. When individuals visit museums, they spend typically several hours at the museum and look at dozens, perhaps hundreds of works. We have seen in the cognitive models discussed here that the conceptualizations of how people look at art fit fairly well with what we have seen in terms of the amount of time spent looking at the works. And so, in part, we might conceptualize the Museum Effect as a process that involves a cycling through of the process described by Leder or Tinio, and then going through that cycle again and again over a two-hour block of time. And in the end, it is that entire visit that we are concerned with. What happens during, and as a result of, the visit as a whole?

WHAT (ALL) HAPPENS WHEN WE LOOK AT ART?

What happens when people look at art? To a degree, the models presented here so far have all tried to address that question. They have taken different perspectives on it, but underlying that research was a desire to better understand the art-viewing process. The Museum Effect takes that question and places it unabashedly in the context of a museum visit. What happens when people look at art in a museum setting, when one looks at many works of art? What is the effect of seeing the models of Chatterjee, Locher, Leder, and Tinio cycled through many times over? I think the effect is straightforward: people think. That seems simple enough. They think about things that are stimulated by what is in front of them. They are prompted, engendered, encouraged, and persuaded to think about things that they might not otherwise be thinking. At this point in the book it would be great to say, "Go visit an art museum and come back after you have done so and pick up your reading again here." That would be impractical to say the least, and I think it wouldn't be so useful to ask you as a reader to recall your thoughts the last time you were in a museum. So instead, what I'm going to do is to present three reproductions and ask you to look at them as if you were viewing them in a museum. Take as much time as you normally would. Let your reactions/thoughts/perceptions take place as they might in a museum, but as you have these thoughts, pay attention to them. What are you thinking about as you view these works? Here they are in Figures 4.7–4.9. I recognize that they are in a book and not a museum, and in black and white at that, but do your best!

Figure 4.7.   Goya. Josefa Castilla Portugal de Garcini y Wanasbrok. 1804.
Image copyright © The Metropolitan Museum of Art. Image source: Art Resource, NY

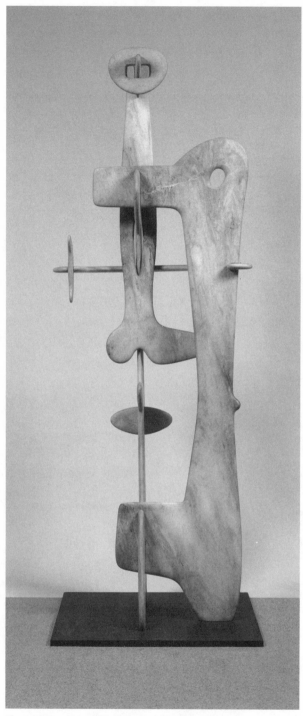

Figure 4.8. Noguchi. Kouros 1944–45.
Image copyright © The Metropolitan Museum of Art. Image source: Art
Resource, NY, Also: © 2013 The Isamu Noguchi Foundation and Garden
Museum, New York / Artists Rights Society (ARS), New York

Figure 4.9.   Charles Sheeler (1883–1965). *River Rouge Plant*, **1932. Oil and pencil on canvas, 20 3/8 x 24 5/16 in. (51.8 x 61.8 cm). Whitney Museum of American Art, New York; purchase 32.43.**
Whitney Museum of American Art

Welcome back from the miniature museum tour. I tried to mix the images up a bit in terms of content, and I tried to pick works that you might not have been familiar with. Let me also mix up things a bit in terms of posing a question or two about your viewing. How much of what you thought about while looking at these works was fundamentally about you as a person? The Goya portrait, did it remind you of someone you know? Did it cause you to think about who the sitter was, was she pregnant (there is speculation that she might have been at the time of the portrait), what kind of status did she hold at the time? Is that a smile or a sense of anxiety on her face? How much time did you spend looking at the work?! Did you leave it with a sense of satisfaction and success, or with some level of disappointment? This is probably my favorite Goya. It's from the Met, and it reminds me of my daughter. I love the expression on her face and reflect on my relationship with my daughter every time I see it.

Moving on to the *Kouros* sculpture by Noguchi, what were your reactions there? How long did you look, and did you leave with a sense of satisfaction or disappointment? Now, to a degree, this work is truly not fairly shown as it is a sculpture, so not only is the size and coloring lost, so is the real sense of three-dimensionality. But did you think about those things as you were viewing the work, or were you more focused on the work itself? Did you accommodate your viewing of the image to the limitations just mentioned? In some work that we did with our colleague, Paul Locher, we examined just this issue (Locher, Smith, & Smith, 2001). We found that when people are looking at reproductions of works (in our study, comparing computer images and traditional slides with the original works in the museum), they adjust to the fact that they aren't seeing the real thing, a phenomenon we labeled "facsimile accommodation." There is no question that people prefer the original, but when looking on a computer or on a slide, and giving their reactions to the work, it is clear that it is *the work* they are focused on. I picked this kouros work for a variety of reasons, including the fact that I wasn't very familiar with it. I know a bit about kouroi and looked to see if this work conveyed my sense of what a kouros is. And it did, to a degree, but I have to say that even though I enjoyed the kind of "assemblage" nature of the work, it left me a bit cold. The title of the work, to me, makes it more engaging (I would never have picked it to be a kouros without the title), but I think I would need to know more about what was going on with it to get a positive engagement with the work.

As you looked at the Noguchi work, do you have a sense of what your emotions were going into it? How had the Goya affected your perception of the Noguchi? For me, I was leaving a warm sense of paternal affection as I viewed the Noguchi. Thus it hit me initially as hard and cold. It caused me to feel a need for a real shift in gears in terms of my viewing. Now, it is not usually the case within a museum that you go from a Goya directly to a Noguchi to a Sheeler. The transitions from one work to another are usually smoother unless you are moving from one collection of the museum to a completely different one (as I did when I went from viewing the van der Weyden diptych to the Duchamp urinal at the Philadelphia Museum of Art, described in the introductory chapter).

And the third work was the Charles Sheeler painting, *River Rouge Plant.* This is a painting I have spent a fair amount of time in front of and reading about. How did it strike you? What did it cause you to think about? How long did you spend looking at it? For me, the painting (which is in earth tones and almost monochromatic in a kind of brownish yellow) has a warmth and a glow to it. When I first saw it, at the Whitney where there are no descriptive labels, I thought it was an attempt by the artist (whom I did not know at the time) to show the humanity of production—that an auto plant could be a good thing, a home almost. Then I read, several years later, that Sheeler was not exactly a fan of industrialization, so I had to think about the work again. And then, many years later, I read that he wasn't too concerned about what people read into his works. Once he was done with them, he kind of turned them over to the viewer. So I figured that Sheeler and I were OK with me interpreting the work the way I wanted to.

Having looked at three works of art, how might you characterize your over-all approach? Well, I hope that there are a large number of museum special-ists among the readers of this work, so to a degree, I would imagine that most of you are toward the higher end of either Housen's or Parsons's stage mod-els, or toward the top of the aesthetic fluency scale that we have developed. You may have viewed these primarily from an art historical perspective. But I hope that somewhere in there, you brought yourself into that picture—that you viewed the works as a simple human being reacting to them on a personal and emotional level, that they caused you to *reflect* on something in your life. It is that sense of personal reflection that we see in comment books, in interviews with individuals in museums, and in discussions with groups of individuals about museum visiting. It is the sort of thing we often overhear when gently eavesdropping on conversations within the museum walls.

ART AS MIRROR

What I am arguing for here is that people who are viewing art are frequently using that art as a mirror in which to see themselves. As people view great works of art, their backgrounds, their dispositions, their experiences, their hopes and aspirations reside within them. What they see in a work of art is largely determined by who they are, and, I would argue, by how they are feeling about the objects that they have seen before this work, and what they anticipate lies ahead. This potential resides within all of us as we approach a work of art. The work prompts certain reactions in us. My reflection will differ from your reflection. And that can be meant in the two very different uses of the word "reflection." First, literally, if you see something pertinent to your life in a work (reflection as mirror image), it will likely be different from what my reflection in that work is. And as you ponder the work and your life (reflection as cognitive process), that, too, will differ from mine.

We see color, form, lines, and then these form objects and the objects have relationships to one another. But then we move past that surface processing if we choose to stay with a work. We don't move on to the next object to view; we stay with this one for a bit more time. We look more deeply, and I would argue, as we do so, we begin to see something of ourselves. Our hopes, dreams, memories, and aspirations push themselves to the foreground. They insist upon themselves. They demand to be heard. "That dog is like our dog." "Those colors are soothing to me." "This work is offensive to me." "This looks like something that would be done by a person I wouldn't like." Art is a mirror in that it encourages us to see aspects of ourselves in the works. And since we differ, different reactions will occur to the same work.

At the same time, to be sure, there are other concepts coming to the fore as we view a work as well. They might be art historical concepts, style con-cepts, or comparisons with other works by the same artist that we have seen and know well. And the disposition to think of those concepts is a part of us as well. If one is not in possession of a particularly strong art background as it relates to the work under consideration, other factors come into play, and other readings are made. No two individuals will view a work in the same way; no two works will be viewed by an individual in the same way. And no one work will be viewed in the same way by a given person on two different occasions. The work of art reflects who we are in that moment as it relates to the work. Thus two different works are going to give us different images of ourselves. Consider the uniqueness of the responses of people in front of works of art that we have discussed so far. They are everyday people having an extraordinary reaction to a work of art. They are the lady who was looking at the work of art in front of which her husband proposed to her. They are the priest who could envision himself using the incense burner in a service. They are the girl who was seeing the baby Jesus. They are the girl who wanted to know, "What did twelve-year-old girls wear in the age of Napoleon?"

How does this work? Why do we see art this way? Well, to put this bluntly, *who we are is all we have.* What I mean by that might be exemplified by the fact that the Goya portrait reminds me of my daughter. It probably does not remind you of your daughter. You might see the privilege of the court in that painting, or you might see it as an exemplar of Goya's approach to portraiture. Or maybe you simply struggled with having a reaction to that work as I did with the Noguchi sculpture. And that struggle is a good thing to be occurring. If it were always easy, it wouldn't be a challenge. And so our reaction to a work of art, anyone's reaction to a work of art, is as an individual, inspired by the work and guided by the personal circumstances of the individual. I would like to say that this is my idea, but it was at least Dewey's well before me (and perhaps someone's before him):

> For to perceive, a beholder must create his own experience. And his creation must include relations comparable to those which the original producer underwent. They are not the same in any literal sense. But with the perceiver, as with the artist, there must be an ordering of the elements of the whole that is in form, although not in details, the same as the process of organization the creator of the work consciously experienced. Without an act of recreation the object is not perceived as a work of art. (Dewey, 1969, p. 54)

I think, at this point, we have to avoid veering off in one direction or another with this line of reasoning. In part, this is why I am enamored of Pablo Tinio's work here. Although my focus is on the viewer and the viewer's reaction to the work, I don't want to lose sight of the work. The work is not a potted plant. Works don't mean just anything, and they don't mean whatever anybody wants them to mean (except to that person). Thus, a work of art is not any old mirror. It is a special mirror, distorted if you will. It holds up to the viewer a potentiality. It is an opportunity to engage. To reflect. To consider possibilities. To leave here and now and go elsewhere and elsewhen for a time. To let the work of art provoke us, maybe to bring out old parts of ourselves and try them out a bit. To consider a lost love, a path chosen well or poorly, or perhaps to make us consider where we are in our lives and where we want to be. One might look into a historical painting and ask, "Who would I be in that painting? Would I be royalty or storming the prison walls to bring the monarchy down?" "Do I do my job as well as this artist did hers?"

Now, that is a lot to think of in thirty seconds, which is part of why I think the process is fundamentally a cumulative one. I think it begins at one work and carries on to the next. And at each stop, one has the possibility of a successful and engaging encounter, solving the problem of the work (as in Leder) or not, and continuing the flow experience of losing oneself a bit in the museum to spend time in one's childhood, current relationship with a significant other, or in one's future. That is what viewing works of art in a museum can do. It can cause us to reflect on who we are, who we were, and who we might become.

THE MODEL OF THE MUSEUM EFFECT

The Museum Effect concerns how looking at art in museums, and perhaps engaging in related activities in other cultural institutions, causes us to be better people. It is a bit of an audacious claim, so I will try to present it as carefully and as clearly as possible. The Museum Effect is a process model, more akin to the Leder and Tinio approaches than to the Housen or Parsons approach. I will walk through the components of the model and then present a visual representation of how I believe it works. This will be a little bit repetitive, I'm afraid, as I need to go over some ground that I hope is now familiar in order to bring the pieces together in a coherent whole.

Coming to the Museum: The Better Angels of our Nature

As we have seen in chapter 2, people come to museums for a variety of reasons. Pekarik (Pekarik, Doering, & Karns, 1999), Falk (2009), and Pitman and Hirzy (2010) have all described different categories of visitors to museums. But if we look at those categories, and consider museum visitors in general, there are certain aspects and characteristics of visitors that if not held in common by all visitors, are at least widespread among visitors. Simply put, a visit to a museum puts one in a different state of mind than engaging in other activities. People come to museums with a desire to learn, to see rare things, to enjoy themselves, to engage in activities with friends and family, to have a new experience, to put themselves in front of objects that reflect talent, genius, creativity, originality. They want to restore and recharge themselves. They come to the museum for a host of reasons, but most of those reasons have to do with "the better angels of our nature." When we come to a museum, we tend to do so with an open mind and with a positive anticipation for what our experience is going to be. We are typically ready to receive what the museum has to present to us.

We bring with us not only family and friends, but also who we are. We bring in our preferences and dislikes, our history—both recent and distant, our knowledge of art—in general and of specific works that the museum might hold. Both the Leder and Locher models talk about the characteristics of the individual encountering a work of art or object with aesthetic value. Locher in particular mentions: "general knowledge, level of aesthetic sophistication, personal taste, cognitive state, affective state, personality, motivation, cultural background, and bodily skills" (Locher, Overbeeke, & Wensveen, 2010, p. 73). These characteristics form a background confluence that is brought to bear on the interaction of the individual with the work of art. And that is why no two interactions are ever quite the same, and can be strikingly different. For example, I have never wondered what it would be like to use an incense burner in a religious ceremony. On the other hand, I did propose to my wife in Westminster Abbey, right where the royals get married, so I share some sense of appreciation for the woman who wanted to see the Sienese Renaissance painting in front of which her husband proposed to her.

We enter a museum with a certain sense of common purpose and anticipation, but with dramatically different backgrounds and life experiences that cause us to experience the works of art that await us in remarkably different and interesting fashions.

How We Look at Works

As described above, when we look at art, we engage in a process that has certain similarities from one person to another, and from one work of art to another within individuals. But in considering the models of looking at art that have been presented here, we see two somewhat different pictures. The approaches taken by Housen and Parsons emphasize how people at different stages of aesthetic perception ability look at works differently (Pekarik and Falk do this for looking at differences among people in their motivations to visit). On the other hand, Chatterjee, Locher, Leder, and Tinio look not at how people differ, but at how the process is the same for individuals within a broad conceptualization of the art-viewing process. The approach taken here follows on from the Locher, Leder, and Tinio approaches, and indeed, is informed by them to a large degree. It is probably most similar to the Leder model but differs in several important aspects. One of those aspects is that although one might consider the form of the interaction to be similar from one person to the next, the content of that interaction will vary because of the different people that we are.

The interaction of a viewer to a work of art might be conceptualized as a challenge, an opportunity, an invitation, a problem to solve, a prompt, even a dare in some instances. As we have described in our work, and has been described in the models, there is an initial intake of the work, a brief overview of what one is looking at. This might last for three seconds, or in some cases, perhaps even less than a second. There is a world of art that can be seen at most museums, so one of the problems that one has to solve is which art to "see" and which art to only glance at and pass by. This seems to be a harsh description of the situation, but it is one that we are all famil- iar with: a visit to an art museum involves a large number of choices, and hence, decisions. What to see, what to pass by. It would be interesting to study that, to develop a model of how people make those choices. There is a vein of research in psychology about making rapid decisions versus more contemplative decisions, with the catchy title of *Thinking, Fast and Slow* (Kahneman, 2011). This work would probably be interesting to explore here, but it is simply beyond the focus of this work. Besides, the Museum Effect is concerned with works that people stop and look at, not the ones that are passed by.

As we look at a work, we are cognitively engaged in processing what we see. After the initial intake, we look to see what this work is about, whom it is by, what school of art or era it is from. Usually, we are looking within a room that has similar works; hence, many of those questions are answered fairly quickly. For some works, if there is a substantial label that goes with the work, we may invest time in reading the label to learn more about what we are looking at. To say that we are "cognitively engaged" is actually a bit limiting. It suggests that we are exclusively in some sort of problem-solving, "right or wrong" mode of thinking, and actually, probably nothing could be further from the truth. I would argue that looking at a work of art, particularly a great work of art, is more of a liberating experience than a constraining one. That is not to say that the experience does not have constraints, and those constraints are important, but we are not looking at a right/wrong dichotomy or even one that is better or worse. It might be more accurate to say that we are mentally engaged in viewing the work. Not only is cognition involved, but emotion as well, and reflection.

Following Tinio, a work of art may be based on an idea or set of ideas that the artist wanted to communicate. Those ideas may have been about the struggle for liberty (think of Delacroix's *Liberty Leading the People*), the love of a mother and a daughter (much of the work of Mary Cassatt), or nightlife in New York City (Mondrian's *Broadway Boogie Woogie*). Or the idea may have been more visual in nature and difficult to translate into words. In fact, the notion of being able to describe in words what is essentially a visual communication has always been baffling to me. If Jackson Pollock had wanted to talk about his ideas, he would have been a poet or a novelist. Dewey (1969) put this same sentiment rather well when he wrote about poetry, "There is always something stupid about turning poetry into a prose that is supposed to explain the meaning of the poetry" (p. 165). Now, once that image has been offered, we might think of the artist as being "out of the picture." At a conference on literature, I walked by a presentation to hear the speaker say, "Poets are not communicative cripples who need high school English teachers to explain what they meant." But upon perception of a work of art, we may not know what the artist intended. We might even get it exactly wrong. The artist may be long dead, or even long dead and unknown. I don't know who painted those images of lions on the walls of the cave at Chauvet (Figure 4.10). No one does, nor do we know why they were put there. Everything at this point is speculative.

But once that work has been presented, whatever the ideas that spurred it into existence, and whatever the history and provenance of the work is, what the viewer makes of it is up to the viewer, within the constraints of the image. That is, one will not react to those cave paintings of lions in the same way as a Renoir painting of a young girl. The interaction between the person and the work of art is constrained by what the artist has done, along with the context and materials in which the work is presented. Thus, the cave lions and the Renoir girl are going to set the viewer on different paths. Cave lions are unlikely to remind you of the girl down the street that you had a crush on, and a Renoir painting of a young girl is not going to cause you to wonder if you would have been a good hunter with a spear. The crucifixion scene by van der Weyden commands attention of a completely different nature than the urinal by Duchamp. It causes different reactions, different connections to be made. Chatterjee would tell us that different areas of the brain might light up in an MRI. And at the same time, the reaction is going to be different for a highly religious person than for an atheist; it will be different for a young person than for a person who is in his twilight years.

And so, how should we conceptualize this meeting of a richly complex human being and a richly complex work of art? What would the good metaphor be here? Are they two armies, ready to do battle over interaction and interpretation? Is this a dance, and if so, what kind and who leads? Or perhaps the gastronomical metaphor we used in talking about time spent is appropriate. The viewer consumes the work, assimilating it into one's being and making the necessary accommodations of one's understandings of art as a result of having done so. (This language is drawn from the theory of developmental psychology of Jean Piaget. See, e.g., Piaget & Inhelder, 1969.)

I prefer a simpler metaphor, the mirror. Ultimately, we see ourselves when we look at art. How is that possible if the Renoir painting of a young girl is so different from the cave lions at Chauvet? Or the kouros by Noguchi shown above? As Dewey pointed out in the quote from earlier in the chapter, the viewer *creates* the experience. Actually, to be a bit more precise, Dewey said that the "beholder" creates the experience. I like "beholder." It connotes that the work is literally held in the eye. This is *my* work of art right now. I possess it. I stand in front of (for example) the marvelous *Juan de Pareja* by Velazquez at the Metropolitan Museum of Art, and I am the only person in the world seeing it right now (Figure 4.11).

Figure 4.10.   Lions in the prehistoric paintings in the cave at Chauvet, France.

It is me, Velazquez, and Pareja. I stand as close to the painting as Velazquez did when he painted it (making the guards a bit nervous), and the subject of this remarkable portrait would be directly in front of me, Velazquez's man-servant and an artist in his own right. He was a slave who Velazquez freed shortly after this painting was made. But Pareja stayed with his mentor and friend until Velazquez died. Apparently they were close friends. Do I need to know those things in order for my interaction to be a positive one, even a dramatic one? No. Does knowing those things change how I see this work

Figure 4.11.   Velazquez. Juan de Pareja.
Image copyright © The Metropolitan Museum of Art. Image source: Art Resource, NY

and react to it? Yes. I look at Pareja and I wonder if I am seeing pride in those eyes, or perhaps anxiety? I can go either way on it. Did Velazquez intend that ambiguity? I wonder about the relationship between the two friends. I wonder about Pareja as a painter. I've never seen any of his works. I smile as I think about the fact that my son looks like Pareja, including the hair and Vandyke beard. I think about the relationships that I have with my former students; people who refer to me as "Dad" and with whom I still frequently conduct research and write. I wonder about the notion of "slave" here, which is how Pareja is often referred to (sometimes "manservant" but often "slave"). What did that mean in that time and place? I think about the mastery of Velazquez as a painter: one of the greatest painters of all time. I go back into the painting. What was that collar like? That cloak? The neck of the collar seems a bit large to me. Was that the style of the time? Were those Pareja's clothes, or ones used for the painting? Is that why they seem a bit big to me? Was Pareja trying to look as noble as he could in them?

This is an easy painting to get lost in. To me, the portrait is amazing. I never tire of looking at it. Sometimes I like to look at it from my (limited) knowledge of art and art history. Other times I simply let it spin me off into whatever thoughts come my way. It lets me explore me for a while. Can I be better at what I do? Can I be a better father, husband, brother, friend? Being a professor has been a good career in large part because of the people I have been a mentor to, and the people I have taught in classes. There is a bit of a legacy there, and that is a comforting thought. But look at the legacy of Velazquez! It is 450 years since his death, and he is still admired, debated, studied today.

I hope you'll forgive me my ruminations on this portrait. I lay them out here as an exemplar of the kind of interaction that an individual can have with a work of art. One can move from just taking the image in and marveling at the expertise to losing oneself in the image itself to having the image serve as a springboard for thoughts that are personal and reflective. Information about the painter and the subject of the painting can enhance that process. Now, this painting in particular engenders certain reactions in me. It is a portrait, so there may be a focus on personal types of reactions. It is from centuries ago, so that will stimulate reactions as well. It is by a very famous artist and there are reactions prompted by that reality. And so, when I think of my reactions to this work, I see that they are obviously greatly influenced by the work, *and* that they are greatly influenced by me, by who I am. This work holds up a certain kind of mirror to me. It allows me to see myself with regard to certain aspects of who I am and what my life is about. So it functions as a mirror, but a rather particular and perhaps peculiar mirror. It pushes certain buttons and not others. I do not react to it the same way I do to Sheeler's *River Rouge*

Plant, or Duchamp's *Fountain*. Each work presents a mirror, an opportunity, a challenge to think about art, but also to think about myself, my relationships to others, and broader issues of society, the future, the world.

It might be useful to step back for a second and see where we are. I am arguing first that museum visits are deliberate. People choose to come to museums and they do so for a variety of reasons. Thus, persons entering a museum are ready to see art. They are not just entering any building; they are not going to a movie, a ball game; they are not shopping or balancing their checkbook; they have deliberately chosen to spend an afternoon putting themselves in front of creative genius.

The second point is that the visitors to an art museum bring with them fundamentally the entirety of their lives. That is saying less than it seems; we pretty much carry that around with us wherever we go. But the point here is that the museum visitor enters the encounters with the works of art from a unique perspective. One person views from a different perspective, psychologically as well as physically, than the person standing next to her. They have different life histories, emotions, cognitions, motivations, experiences with art, approaches to viewing, and all these influence their interaction with the work of art that they are approaching.

The third point is that the work of art has a history, a unique communication, a reason for being that might only be known to the artist, or might have been the focus of a dozen PhD theses. A landscape is not a portrait is not a history painting. The life histories of works of art are fascinating things in and of themselves. Just to provide a flavor of how works of art might differ, consider that Picasso produced tens of thousands of works, and Vermeer probably fewer than a hundred (only about forty known today). Accompanying a work of art might be simply what my wife and I refer to as a "name, rank, and serial number" label, while others may go into great and fascinating detail about a work. The context in which it is presented will also influence how it is seen. Is it given prominence in the room, or off in a corner? Is it in a huge room or one that is more intimate?

One of the most depressingly displayed works that I have ever seen is the *Mona Lisa*. For completely justifiable reasons, it is behind a double-glass partition. On the day I got to see it, tourists kept taking flash photographs of it, with the light from the flash bouncing off the glass. So just as I would get a bit of a reverie going, there would be another flash of light. I have always been baffled by people taking pictures of works. The *actual work* is right there. Look at it! If you want a reproduction, you can buy one fairly cheaply that has been done by people who make their living making such images, or you can see it online. And yet . . . *another flash!* (I'm not blaming the Louvre here, just lamenting a sad situation.)

Depicting the Museum Effect Model

At this point, we have the individual, the work, and to a lesser degree, the context. The visitor approaches the work and either decides to give it a preliminary view or move to the next work. That view may last only a few seconds, or it may be a half minute, or even a minute's viewing (and occasionally more). We might think of this as having three levels of viewing:

1. Saw it and am passing it by
2. Looking at it, but after a few seconds have decided I've seen enough
3. Looking at it long enough to give it some thought and reflection

In the first two situations, for one reason or another, the work has been dismissed as not worth more extensive viewing. This represents, to some degree, a failure in the challenge. If an object is passed by with little or no consideration, then this is less of a negative interaction, but a ten-second look followed by a decision to pass the work by is clearly something less than a successful interaction. If one consistently passed works up hoping for better ones to consider, the net effect would be a very unsatisfying visit.

But that is not typically the case. Instead, the visitor finds a work that is worth some additional time and he or she takes up the challenge or invitation of the work. For some works, a challenge more or less presents itself. This might be true of a Jackson Pollock or a Kazimir Malevich work. They put themselves in front of a viewer and say, "Figure this out." In other instances, it is the viewer who creates the challenge. The viewer says, "How do I want to see this work?" "How do I want to react?" And with great works of art, challenges or invitations exist at a variety of levels. You can go back to them again and again and ask new questions of them, or of yourself as you view them.

As has been discussed, for many visitors, for many works, this contemplation includes consideration that is self-reflective. Prompted by the image in front of them, visitors think about themselves as individuals, their relationships with those who are close to them, and about society and the future. In part, I think, this is a direct effect of the individual and the work of art. But as pointed out earlier, it is also because of several other factors related to the situation. First, the visitor is there intentionally; he or she wants to engage the institution and immerse himself or herself in what the institution represents and offers. Second, there is the institution itself. Even the most humble of museums possess a certain sense of nobility of purpose. People who are in museums are in institutions that represent what we feel is good about our society; they house those things we deem to be of exceptional value to us. Third, there is the quality and importance of the works themselves. It is not possible to stand in front of a Giotto, or a Masaccio, or a Rembrandt without thinking, "Hey, this is a Giotto. . . ." It simply commands more respect and attention than a work of art in a hotel room or a movie poster or a subway advertisement. It is important. It causes us to think.

Perhaps we try to perceive the communicative intent of the artist, or to locate it within an artistic trend or tradition, or to judge the quality of the craftsmanship of the execution of the work, but perhaps we also think about ourselves. We reflect, extend, fantasize, return to the work, see something new, and cycle through the process again. Then, the interaction reaches a conclusion. At some point, we decide to move on. We make something of a conclusion or summary assessment of the work and of our interaction with it. We may judge the work aesthetically, may have decided that the interaction was a good one in some sense, may have enjoyed thinking about the work from a personal perspective, may feel that we had been successful with the work in some fashion, and may have engendered a bit of what Csikszentmihalyi calls flow. This is not to say that all these things happen with each interaction with a work. But they represent the range of possibilities. Visitors leave one work and approach another, taking with them the glow, the residue, the buzz from viewing the previous work. Or they may leave feeling unsatisfied, feeling that they did not make a connection with the work. The challenge was taken on but was not successful. This is the start of the Museum Effect. It is what happens as a visitor to an art museum looks at a single work of art. What we have here is depicted in Figure 4.12. There are basically three phases represented in the diagram. Just start on the left, work your way down to the bottom of the first third ("Approach") and then on to the second third, and so forth. This might be likened to what Leder or Locher have presented, but with a focus on the person and what the person might be thinking about while viewing. But it is only the start of the process. It is one interaction of many such interactions. It is one cycle of the Museum Effect.

This is an interaction that takes a half minute to a minute, only occasionally longer. And then the next work is encountered and the process is repeated. And then again and again. There are dozens if not hundreds of works to be seen, contemplated, reflected upon. That is what happens in a museum visit. Even though I would readily acknowledge that any work a person encounters in a museum visit might be worth a half hour's contemplation (and then repeated visits following an initial viewing), it is simply not how it works. What happens is that visitors go from one work to the next; they encounter or pose for themselves multiple challenges. They are less successful or more so in these challenges. Some works they find very pleasing or provocative; others less so. As this process, this series of encounters and challenges continues, successes and failures, the visitor becomes more and more invested in the

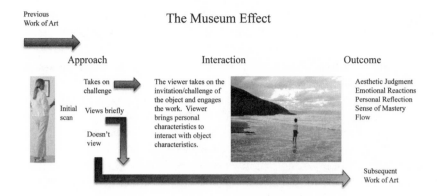

Figure 4.12.   **The Museum Effect.**
Jeffrey Smith

activity, less concerned about time and place, and enters into the kind of flow state that Csikszentmihalyi discusses.

To get a feel for this phenomenon, consider a person who has just completed a successful interaction with a work in a museum. That person has just finished a pleasurable, thought-provoking, emotion-provoking activity. This doesn't have to be an intense experience, but one where the visitor believes that he or she has seen an excellent work of art, or believes that he or she has gotten the message that the artist was conveying, or has engaged in a bit of personal reflection or reverie that is pleasing, or has stepped into an emotional experience in empathy with what is portrayed in the image. This visitor leaves that work with an overall sense of "That was good" in some fashion, and is now seeking the next work that might provide a positive interaction, perhaps similar, perhaps quite different. The visitor leaves the work with a feeling of accomplishment, positive emotion, and so forth, and is now looking forward to the next challenge or invitation. The individual also may have a set of reflections, musings, or anticipations that have been activated. One may be thinking about oneself in one's job, or as a parent, or a sibling. He or she might be thinking, "I should call Mom tonight" or "I should get out my guitar." The next work might be a ten-second "pass-by" or even a three-second tasting. It may take three or four more works before that visitor is ready to invest some time again. But then that next intriguing work is found and the process begins anew. "What am I seeing here?" "What is the story/the deal/the idea with this work of art?" "How am I reacting to this work?" "How should I react?" "Here I am standing in front of this incredible work by this amazing artist. What should I make of it?" The game is joined again.

This process continues on throughout a museum visit (see Figure 4.13). Visitors encounter works, interact with them, and then move to the next work, having been affected in a variety of ways from their encounter with the previous work. This process builds throughout the visit, resulting in what might be thought of as a kind of aesthetic version of Csikszentmihalyi's flow experience, the kind of interaction that Beardsley described. During this experience, the individual has the opportunity to encounter a variety of "mirrors" that result in the kinds of reflection mentioned above. As a result of this process, visitors spend time thinking about who they are as individuals (who, perhaps, they would like to be), how they relate to their family and friends (and how they might do that better), and what they think about society, the planet, the future (and what they might do to contribute to that). Looking at art in museums makes us better people. The viewing of these works of art is not just a concatenation of one-off events; they wind together into a thread, a narrative. The visit becomes a coherent whole forming a pleasurable and

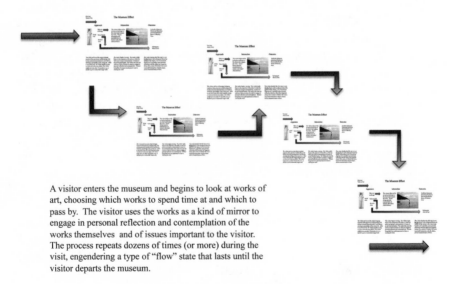

A visitor enters the museum and begins to look at works of art, choosing which works to spend time at and which to pass by. The visitor uses the works as a kind of mirror to engage in personal reflection and contemplation of the works themselves and of issues important to the visitor. The process repeats dozens of times (or more) during the visit, engendering a type of "flow" state that lasts until the visitor departs the museum.

The Museum Effect Across Multiple Works

Figure 4.13. The Museum Effect across multiple works.
Jeffrey Smith

meaningful experience. The viewer has encountered works of exceptional talent and expertise, and sometimes incredible creativity and even genius. At the same time, the visitor to the museum has engaged in a creative enterprise himself or herself. The visitor has posed and/or faced challenges, interpreted works with respect to his or her own life, and contemplated what is important to that person. One might think of there being parallel tracks in the museum experience, one related to the visual delight of artistic virtuosity, and a second, personal creative enterprise of reflection and contemplation that I am calling the Museum Effect.

We go to the museum because we want to be inspired, entertained, to learn, to grow, to socialize with others, to place ourselves in the presence of genius. And while we are there we think about things that are important, that are even noble. We are invited by brilliant works of creative artistry to see ourselves in these objects, and in doing so, we become better people.

INVESTIGATING THE MUSEUM EFFECT

That is the argument of the Museum Effect. I hope you find it compelling to some degree. But as a social scientist, I am interested not just in ideas, I am also committed to the notion that one has a responsibility to back those ideas up, buttressing arguments with prior research and with data collected to directly test the arguments. To begin, I hope you will agree that the basic components of the model have been established on fairly good grounding from prior work. We know that people come to museums for specific purposes. We know that they come to learn, to be inspired, to put themselves in front of great works of art. We know that they spend relatively little time viewing any particular work, and that they view many works while they are in the museum. We know that they tell us that their visits are exciting, thrilling, even life altering. We know that they engage in personal reflection and bring their own lives into their viewing of works. We know that they see challenges in the works that they see, and that they try to solve these challenges, or problems. We believe that they engage with art in a fashion that is similar to the flow experience. But, at the end of the day, do we have any real evidence that people are thinking better thoughts, that the museum visit makes them better people? Indeed, in discussing the Museum Effect once with a museum director, he observed, "If this were true, art historians would be the most wonderful people in the world, and we have evidence to the contrary." More on that later, but for now, the question remains as to actual evidence that this phenomenon is real.

The concept of the Museum Effect was developed in an effort to make sense out of a wide variety of research findings, some of them seemingly contradictory. But once the model is established, one needs to set up conditions to see if the Museum Effect is realized when people visit museums. Smith & Waszkielewicz (2007) have examined the Museum Effect directly in museum settings. This research was based on the PhD dissertation research of Izabella Waszkielewicz (2006). The study took place in the Whitney Museum of American Art in New York City and the James A. Michener Museum in Doylestown, Pennsylvania. A pilot study was conducted in the Metropolitan Museum of Art. The basic argument of the study was that if, indeed, the Museum Effect were taking place, then people who had been looking at works of art in a museum should show some signs of the effect. What would those signs be? Well, the argument is that the effect causes people to think about themselves, their relationships with others, and the world in general. We had a questionnaire, that covered those issues, developed by Barber, Higgins, Smith, and Ballou (1996), who were looking at issues of citizenship. There were twenty-six statements on the questionnaire, and participants were asked to rate themselves on a scale of one to ten "with respect to how well you do each of these as compared to most people." The anchors for the one to ten scale were "Not as good = 1," "About the same = 5," and "Much better = 10." Examples of the statements are:

- Think about the future
- Strive toward personal growth
- Relate well to others
- Able to compromise
- Contemplate ways to make a difference in society
- Believe that people are inherently good

People taking this survey rated themselves on twenty-six items as to whether they thought they were not as good as, about the same as, or much better than most people with regard to ideas such as "think about the future" or "able to compromise." The items were organized around three central themes: Intrapersonal considerations (such as "strive toward personal growth"), Interpersonal considerations (such as "relate well to others"), and Societal considerations (such as "contemplate ways to make a difference in society"). If people were being reflective, thinking better thoughts, contemplating important issues in a positive fashion, then we should see higher scores on these three themes (called "scales") from people who had been looking at art for a while than for people who are just entering the museum. We created three scales from the citizenship survey based on the work of Barber et al.

(1996) and based on our factor analyses of the data gathered for this study. (Factor analysis is a statistical technique for determining common themes, or "factors," across a number of variables in a data set.) Internal consistency reliability coefficients (coefficient alpha) for the three scales were in the .80 to .90 range, indicating that the items in the scales were strongly related to one another.

We conducted a pilot study at the Metropolitan Museum of Art. We had initially anticipated that visitors leaving the museum would have the highest scores on the three variables. At the Met, all visitors were surveyed in the Great Hall, which serves as the entry and exit point for most visitors. It is also a thoroughfare from one major area of the museum to another. Thus, in surveying people in the Great Hall, we could not assume where people were in their visit and had to ask people where they were as part of the survey. They could respond that they were at the beginning of their visit, in the middle of their visit, or at the end of their visit. Surprisingly, we found that people who were *midvisit* scored the highest on our measure (which differed from the one described above, but got at the same kinds of issues). At first, we thought this might simply be a chance finding, but as a result of the pilot, we deliberately included a midvisit sample for the Whitney and Michener parts of the study. In each of these museums, we collected between 54 and 109 questionnaires at each of three locations in the museum: where people entered, somewhere inside the museum that allowed us to get a "midvisit" sample, and where people exited the museum. On the questionnaire, we asked people where they were in their visit to ensure that we didn't put anyone into the wrong grouping.

To summarize the design, we argued that people who had been viewing art would show higher scores on the three scales of the questionnaire (Intrapersonal, Interpersonal, and Societal) than people who were at the beginning of their visit. We had initially anticipated that people at the end of the visit would show the highest scores, but the Metropolitan pilot study results caused us to consider the possibility that midvisit scores would be highest. We gathered a sample of visitors to the Whitney and to the Michener at each of three locations: entry, midvisit, and exit. The visitors in each location were different people. That is, we did not follow the same people through the museum and survey them three times; the samples were different. This approach runs the risk that maybe they were just different kinds of people, but since we took all samples at similar times of day and days of the week, we felt this risk was minimal, and that the approach was superior to convincing people to take our questionnaire three separate times. Thus, we had two museums, and a before/mid/after sample from each museum.

This design led to a statistical analysis called a multivariate analysis of variance. I am a research methodologist by training. The reduction of complex, multifaceted, and distinctive individuals into a series of mind-numbingly reductionist quantitative abstractions is just about my favorite thing to do. I realize that few readers share this interest. Thus, I will present the quantitative results in an abbreviated fashion, and then say what they mean in English. The basic findings (the means and standard deviations for each group) are presented in Figure 4.14.

The results from the analysis by place in visit confirmed the results from the pilot study. At the Whitney, differences by place in visit were statistically significant at $p < .001$, with effect sizes (Hedges's g) ranging from .23 to .61. For all three scales (Intrapersonal, Interpersonal, and Societal), the midvisit mean was significantly higher than the entry or exit mean. At the Michener, the results were basically similar for both the Intrapersonal and Interpersonal means (with significance levels $p < .01$). But for the Societal mean, a different result was obtained. In this case, the exit mean was much higher than either the entry or midvisit mean ($p < .001$, $ES = .71$). Simply, the Whitney results are fundamentally the same as the pilot study at the Met, and the Michener results are similar except for the Societal means, where the exit scores are the highest. It might be easier to see the results rather than to describe them. They are presented in Figures 4.15–4.17.

What is clear here is that as people are looking at art, their responses to the questionnaire increase on all three scales. On the Intrapersonal and Interpersonal scales, the same kind of result found in the Met pilot study was obtained for both museums. The effect appears to peak midvisit, and then wane. For the Societal scale, the same finding was seen in the Whitney, but not at the Michener. At the Michener, the mean on the Societal scale shoots up for the visitors at the end of their visit. We believe this is a bit of an artifact, but informative nonetheless. At the Michener, visitors were surveyed for the midvisit sample just before entering an exhibition of African American artist Romare Bearden. Bearden's work in part focuses on issues of the struggle against slavery and for civil rights and is very moving. Many visitors exited the museum after seeing the exhibition (the Michener is not a large museum). Thus, the exit survey caught many people just after they were leaving the exhibition, so the results might be interpreted as being close to midvisit as well.

Overall, we see two basic findings here: first, visitors increase in their responses to these scales from previsit to midvisit, and second, the effect tends to wane as people are exiting the museum. The one exception here is the post-Societal scores for the Michener sample, where Societal scores increased

	Whitney Museum of American Art			James A. Michener Art Museum		
	Period of Observation					
Scale	Beginning	Middle	End	Beginning	Middle	End
	n = 101	*n* = 66	*n* = 109	*n* = 67	*n* = 79	*n* = 54
Intrapersonal	57.5 (10.6)	60.5 (7.4)	57.0 (10.0)	58.0 (10.1)	63.8 (7.5)	60.4 (9.8)
Interpersonal	65.5 (10.8)	67.8 (8.4)	65.0 (12.2)	66.9 (13.0)	69.9 (8.9)	69.6 (11.5)
Societal	53.5 (11.5)	54.9 (10.8)	52.8 (12.8)	52.9 (13.5)	53.9 (10.4)	59.3 (10.4)

NOTE: Numbers in parentheses are Standard Deviations
(Taken from Waszkielewicz, 2006).

Figure 4.14. Means by Museum and Time in Visit.
Benjamin Smith

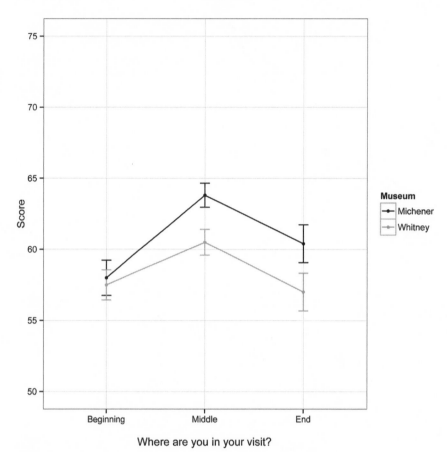

Figure 4.15.   Results of Intrapersonal Scale Means.
Benjamin Smith

primarily, we believe, due to people exiting the Bearden exhibition and then shortly thereafter completing the questionnaire.

In considering these results, it is important to keep in mind the nature of the study. We asked separate groups of people entering, midvisit, and exiting the museums what they thought about Intrapersonal, Interpersonal, and Societal issues. The visitors were not cued as to whether to respond more favorably midvisit or not; they simply told us where they thought they stood on these issues compared to others. When asked to do so, people in midvisit at a museum gave statistically significantly higher responses than those at the beginning of the visit. And then we saw evidence that the effect wanes as one

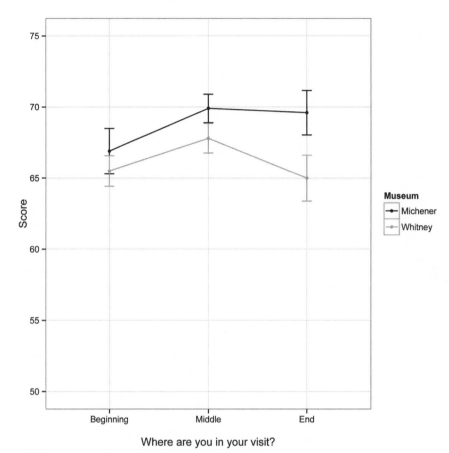

Figure 4.16.   Results of Interpersonal Scale Means.
Benjamin Smith

concludes the visit. The one exception was a much higher postvisit mean at
one museum (as detailed above). Thus, the conclusion that it was the effect
of having been in the museum viewing the art that led to the increased scores
is one that is strongly supported by the data. Whether this finding can be at-
tributed to the exact nature of the Museum Effect as it has been presented here
requires more of an inference, clearly. However, the Museum Effect basically
argues that what was found here is what one would expect to find. As is always the case, one can imagine alternative explanations, but the workings of
the Museum Effect as conceptualized here, and the findings from this study
align fairly well.

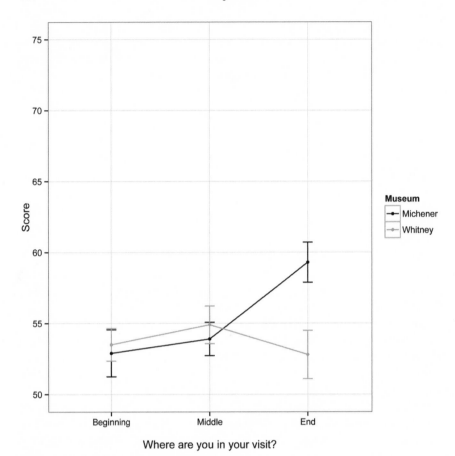

Figure 4.17.   Results of Societal Scale Means.
Benjamin Smith

WHAT TO MAKE OF ALL THIS?

One might be tempted to conclude from the research just presented something along the lines of "OK, the Museum Effect exists, but it is ephemeral." And that would not be an unreasonable conclusion to draw. At some level, it is almost certainly the case, and it would explain why art historians aren't the most wonderful people in the world (although there are some historians who are exceptionally good human beings). What happens here, I think, is that people in their visit are engaged in the activities described in the model above: they are finding challenges or setting them for themselves; they are engaging in active self-reflection; they are in the flow of the museum visit. During the museum visit, they quite simply spend some time in a conceptually better place, think better thoughts, and are better people. And then the visit comes to an end and with it, the effect wanes. Thoughts move from self-reflection to "Where did I park the car?" "What will the drive home be like?" "Should I stop for groceries?" Our lives return to us as the visit ends. That which is exhilarating leaves and that which is mundane returns.

It is important to note that we actually only have three times sampled here. We know that the scores are typically lower at the beginning and the end, and higher somewhere in the middle. Now, we have placed "the middle" halfway between the beginning and the end, and this seems as logical a location as any. But does the effect really go up to a midpoint in a linear fashion, and then decline in a similarly linear fashion? It is hard to believe that it does. Perhaps it goes up linearly, but does so all the way through the visit until the end, and then comes back down sharply as the visit concludes. Or perhaps it goes up rapidly at the beginning and then tails off throughout the rest of the visit. Without additional data points, we simply don't know. There are many reasonable curves that would fit these data. Our suspicion is that there is a general accumulation to a certain level, that this level is maintained through the visit, and then there is a fairly steep decline at the end of the visit. Such a set of events would be logically appealing, but this is simply speculation.

Whatever the case, and this is key, the museum visitors have spent a few hours on an elevated plane. They have contemplated those better angels of our nature. They can return to those thoughts perhaps on the drive home, perhaps in some other quiet hour. We don't spend *our entire lives* thinking great thoughts and contemplating how we can become better people. But it is important that we do so at least some of the time. To do so is a fundamentally uplifting experience.

We know from other work that we have done that visitors like to "emotionally amortize" their visits. That is, they want to take the experience with them. That is why catalogs of exhibitions are so popular. It is why the typical visitor to the Metropolitan returns roughly four times each year. It is why the Metropolitan gets fifty million visits to its website per year. The museum offers respite, restoration, the opportunity to view that which is extraordinary about humankind. It gives us the chance to see ourselves, our relationships, and our society in a better, more hopeful light. Even if the look is only fleeting, it is wondrous. It is why millions of people visit museums every day. They go to experience the Museum Effect.

REFERENCES

Barber, B. R., Higgins, R. R., Smith, J. K., & Ballou, J. (1996). *Measuring citizenship: Assessing the impact of service learning on America's youth: A four-part project report on the Walt Whitman Center's Whitman Center Measure (WCM).* Presented at the 1996 American Political Science Association Meeting, San Francisco, CA.

Chatterjee, A. (2004). Prospects for a cognitive neuroscience of visual aesthetics. *Bulletin of the Psychology of the Arts, 4,* 55–60.

Chatterjee, A. (2010). Neuroaesthetics: A coming of age story. *Journal of Cognitive Neuroscience, 23*(1), 53–62.

Dewey, J. (1969). *Art as experience.* New York: Minton, Balch.

Falk, J. H. (2009). *Identity and the museum visitor experience.* Walnut Creek, CA: Left Coast Press.

Housen, A. (1999). *Eye of the beholder: Research, theory and practice.* Paper presented at the conference of Aesthetic and Art Education: A Transdisciplinary Approach, Lisbon, Portugal. Retrieved July 5, 2013, from http://www.vtshome.org/research/articles-other-readings

Housen, A. (2007). Art viewing and aesthetic development: Designing for the viewer. *From periphery to center: Art museum education in the 21st century,* 172–179.

Kahneman, D. (2011). *Thinking, fast and slow.* New York: Macmillan.

Kohlberg, L. (1971). Stages of moral development as a basis for moral education. In C. M. Beck, B. S. Crittenden, & E. V. Sullivan (Eds.), *Moral education: Interdisciplinary approaches* (pp. 23–92). Toronto: University of Toronto Press.

Leder, H., Belke, B., Oeberst, A., and Augustin, D. (2004). A model of aesthetic appreciation and aesthetic judgments. *British Journal of Psychology, 95*(4), 489–508.

Locher, P., Overbeeke, K., & Wensveen, S. (2010). Aesthetic interaction: A framework. *Design Issues, 26*(2), 70–79.

Locher, P. J., Smith, J. K., & Smith, L. F. (2001). The influence of presentation format and viewer training in the visual arts on the perception of pictorial and aesthetic qualities of paintings. *Perception, 30*(4), 449–466.

Parsons, M. J. (1987). *How we understand art.* New York: Cambridge University Press.

Pekarik, A. J., Doering, Z. D., & Karns, D. A. (1999). Exploring satisfying experiences in museums. *Curator, 42,* 152–173.

Piaget, J., & Inhelder, B. (1969). *The psychology of the child.* New York: Basic Books.

Pitman, B., & Hirzy, E. (2010). *Ignite the power of art: Advancing visitor engagement in museums.* Dallas, TX: Dallas Museum of Art.

Smith, J. K., & Waszkielewicz, I. (2007). The civilizing influence of art museum visitation. Paper presented at annual meeting of the American Psychological Association, San Francisco, CA.

Tinio, P. P. L. (2013). From artistic creation to aesthetic reception: The mirror model of art. *Psychology of Aesthetics, Creativity, and the Arts, 7*(3), 265–275.

Waszkielewicz, I. (2006). *Encounters with art: The Psychological impact of art museum visitation.* (Unpublished doctoral dissertation). Rutgers, The State University, New Brunswick, NJ.

5

Expanding the Museum Effect to Other Cultural Institutions and Events

"It *has* to be cowboys."

These are the words of a friend who had just retired and had recently discovered the joys of reading. He had never read books before; he was a home builder and never had an inclination toward reading. We wanted to encourage this newfound passion and were about to recommend a series of works that we thought he might enjoy. After two suggestions, he looked at us with a bit of a frown and said, "It *has* to be cowboys." We are unique as individuals and our preferences and desires are our own.

We have looked at the Museum Effect and how it works in art museums. I have also suggested that the Museum Effect probably generalizes to a variety of other cultural institutions. In this chapter, I want to explore that possibility, and consider the prospect that what we see in art museums we will also see in natural history museums, science museums, libraries, historical sites, and other cultural institutions. To begin, we have evidence of how art museums encourage individuals to reflect on their own lives, their relationships with others, and their place in society. We believe that we understand how this process takes place within the confines of the art museum. But might this same phenomenon occur in a history museum, a botanical park, a library, or a symphony performance? Each of these other institutions edges us away from some of the fundamental arguments of the Museum Effect. A history museum has objects that are important in their own right, but are not works of art. They may be unique objects, but were they objects of genius, or rather of great historical importance? Do they have the same effect on us as does art? What about a science museum (where often the works are created for the museum and have no inherent value), or a botanical garden whose wonders are created by nature? And then what about a library, where a visitor might only encounter a few works, or a symphony, where there is one work made up of many pieces? In this chapter, we explore these possibilities with regard to the fundamental arguments of the Museum Effect.

WHAT IS ESSENTIAL ABOUT THE MUSEUM EFFECT?

The underlying argument for the Museum Effect is that what people do in an art museum causes them to engage in a kind of flow state where they reflect on important issues in their lives. This occurs as they move from one work of art to the next, trying to solve the puzzle or challenge that is presented by the work. Thus, as Csikszentmihalyi (1990; Csikszentmihalyi & Robinson, 1990) argues, the effect builds as the visitor works through a series of challenges in the visit. Part of the argument is that the works of art serve as a kind of mirror for us as we view them; perhaps we see ourselves as a participant or the subject of a work, and at other times we might empathize with the artist, or are simply stirred by what we see and react to it accordingly.

So, if that is what happens when we view art in a museum setting, what about other cultural institutions? Do we experience the same, or similar, reactions in other kinds of museums, historical sites, libraries, or when attending a concert? The short answer for this is that I do not have empirical evidence to make such a claim, but I believe it is so. It may not work in exactly the same fashion in all these institutions, nor necessarily to the same degree, but I believe we can see it and that there is logic behind why it should be seen. In this chapter I want to explore that argument, and look at a number of possibilities.

Let's start by considering what is absolutely essential for the Museum Effect to take place. I believe that the *sine qua non* of the Museum Effect is reflection upon one's life and life in general. When we go to an art museum, we may go for different purposes, as seen in the beginning chapters of the book, but we typically go to see art, to ponder it, to stand in awe of it, and perhaps to learn more about it. Sometimes this is a bit of a social event, but we note that most people typically are looking at works alone. I think that when we make the decision to go to an art museum, we anticipate being in a contemplative state of mind. We are ready to think, to receive visual input that is stimulating, perhaps beautiful, or provocative, or emotional, and we are ready to react to that on a personal level both with our cognition and our affect. We do this for a couple of hours, and during that time we receive dozens of different aesthetic stimuli to react to. That is the nature of an art museum visit. It may also include taking care of children, or interacting with a spouse or friend, having lunch, shopping in the museum store, and so forth, but the heart of the issue is responding to great works of art as an individual.

In this state of mind, we encounter art, and as has been pointed out in previous chapters, usually a fair number of works of art. We argue that these works present a series of challenges to us as we view them, and to an extent, they might also be conceptualized as mirrors that allow us to reflect upon ourselves and our lives. A great work of art can do this repeatedly, allowing us to see different things and engage in different reveries on subsequent visits.

So, how does that translate to looking at historical artifacts, or scientific displays, or plants, or listening to music, or reading in a library? And are there other things that we do in our lives that might fall outside the range of cultural institutions, but might also have the same effect (there is one in particular I want to consider). Do these institutions and activities hold the same power to cause us to be reflective, contemplative, inspired? Indeed, if we leave the art museum, what other cultural institution is closest to it? A history museum? An arboretum? A concert?

WHAT IS SIMILAR AND DIFFERENT ABOUT VARIOUS CULTURAL INSTITUTIONS?

If we think about what we do in art museums and try to extend that to other institutions, a host of interesting questions and comparisons arises. How is a history museum like an art museum—and how is it different? How is an object of historical significance different from one of artistic significance?

The British Museum

We will start by taking a small step to a great institution. Consider the British Museum. It holds great works of art in its collection. But it also holds a wealth of other objects of wonder to us, whose historical interest exceeds their artistic interest. There are many objects that come to mind when one considers the British Museum, but let me focus on three here: the Parthenon Marbles (a.k.a. the Elgin Marbles), the Rosetta Stone, and a stone chopping tool from Olduvai in East Africa that is estimated to be 1.8 million years old (Figures 5.1–5.3). These are clearly three rather different objects.

How do these objects relate to what we might see in an art museum? Well, the figure of Iris, which we first considered in chapter 3, is unquestionably a great work of art. In fact, the Parthenon Marbles could just as easily be in an art museum, as they are great works of art. But when we view them, it is hard to take them out of their original context as ornamental to one of the greatest buildings in the history of mankind, or the current controversy over efforts from Greece to have them returned. So their appeal to us is not only a function of their beauty but also of their historical and political significance.

Figure 5.1.   Figure of Iris from the west pediment of the Parthenon, Acropolis, Athens.
© The Trustees of the British Museum / Art Resource, NY

Figure 5.2. The Rosetta Stone.
Erich Lessing / Art Resource, NY

What do they mean to us in terms of what Greece means to us: philosophy, democracy, science, and art? The Parthenon, and the marbles that adorned it, are really iconographic when it comes to thinking about all these things. We are pulled to that reality whenever we see or think about them. But there are other issues to contemplate as well. Where do these objects rightfully belong? What exactly were the circumstances that brought them to the British Museum? What condition would they be in today if they had been left in Greece?

Figure 5.3.   Prehistoric chopping tool, Olduvai Gorge, Tanzania.
The Art Archive at Art Resource, NY

We move from the Parthenon Marbles to the Rosetta Stone, again, an incredibly famous and important object (Figure 5.2). But why? To be a bit hard on the Rosetta Stone, it has no aesthetic value in and of itself. It is a text written (carved) in two different scripts of Egyptian, demotic and hieroglyphs, and in ancient Greek on a granitelike stone called granodiorite. It is clearly an object of awe and wonder. But the awe and wonder here are pretty much exclusively because of its historical import. It is the object that opened up the history of ancient Egypt. The story behind the deciphering of the Rosetta Stone is a fascinating one, and it is without question one of the most important historical objects ever. And just the words "Rosetta Stone" are eponymous for unraveling and understanding that which is unknown. If one had to name the half dozen most important objects in the history of humankind, the Rosetta Stone would certainly be on most educated people's list.

This in turn, brings us to the chopping tool in Figure 5.3. It's a tool for chopping bones, plants, and wood according to the information provided by the British Museum website. I've got tools for those purposes in my kitchen and garage. Nicer ones. But this tool is 1.8 million years old! A bit of googling will show you that this tool was made by an individual who did not look much like you or me. It was well over a million years before Homo sapiens would appear. This is not a beautiful thing, nor is it one that is important in the history of humankind—except that we have it. It lets us know when early versions of ourselves were using tools, and in that sense, the very fact that this clearly *is* a tool is remarkably important. We can look upon something that comes from our genus, but from before our species. It comes from us, but before us. What must life have been like for the person who used this tool? What was it like to make it? Was it better than others of its kind? It is not artistic like the Parthenon Marble, nor revealing like the Rosetta Stone, and yet it holds a very real fascination for us, and can produce all manner of ruminations and reflections.

So, with the British Museum, we see an institution that holds objects of art, many of the most famous of such objects in the world, but that also holds objects that tell of the history of humankind. It is broader in scope than a typical art museum, combining art with natural history. If we think about the arguments that underlie the Museum Effect, it is hard to imagine that they would not apply equally well to the British Museum. But how far does that take us in our journey of extending the Museum Effect to other institutions? Not so far, I think, but a useful beginning in that we have extended what we are considering to include objects of strong historical significance as well as historical objects that, while not important in their impact on human history, are representative of important milestones in human evolution and history. That is, they, too, cause us to reflect on who we are, who we were, who we might become. But we deliberately have only moved a very small step away from an art museum here. Now we move to consider cultural institutions that differ from art museums in important ways.

Looking at Differences among Institutions

In thinking about how the Museum Effect might extend beyond art museums, it is important to consider the wealth of other kinds of institutions that exist, and how they differ from an art museum. The simple fact is that there are too many different kinds to do justice to them all, but we can begin by looking at the range of possibilities. We'll do this in a simple list and then in a figure that attempts to display the relationships among cultural institutions and their relationships to one another, and to art museums. First, a list:

- Science museums and centers
  - Aerospace museums
  - Museums for invention
  - Computer museums
- History museums and historic sites
  - Natural history museums
  - Museums of eras and of places
  - Historic sites including historic homes

- Institutions with living objects
  - Zoos
  - Aviaries
  - Aquariums
  - Botanic gardens
- Art-related museums
  - Museums of decorative art
  - Fashion museums
  - Craft museums
  - Glass museums
- Thematic museums
  - Agricultural museums
  - Community museums
  - Sports museums
  - Music museums
- Libraries
  - Public libraries
  - Academic libraries
  - Specialized libraries

It would be very easy to put several levels of subcategory beneath what is present here, and there are no doubt areas that I've missed, but the notion that there are many, many different kinds of institutions is clear. For all these institutions, we can assume that they are visited primarily voluntarily by people with a few hours of leisure time. The possible exception to that is libraries, but let us cycle back on that a bit later.

Science Museums and Centers

Let us push this a bit and consider a science museum. There are different kinds of science museums, but let's look at the Boston Museum of Science as an example of a science museum. We took a visit to the Boston Museum of Science recently to see the Dead Sea Scrolls and to look at how the nature of a science museum differs from an art museum. If you visit the Museum of Science in Boston, what you see a lot of is: kids (Figure 5.4). The kids are with adults to be sure, but there are lots and lots of kids. They are interacting with exhibits that have been constructed to instruct. They are didactic in nature and intent. And this is good. Most science museums and centers have as their mission to instruct about science; they want to amaze, entice, inform, and communicate the wonders of science. Adults are welcome to come along for the ride, but if you look hard at most science centers, there is clearly a

Figure 5.4.   Kids at Boston Museum of Science.
Jeffrey Smith

focus on the young and the young at heart. Science museums are often bright, colorful, hectic, noisy places, full of children and parents shepherding them.

But if we are concerned with the Museum Effect, and primarily concerned about adults and the Museum Effect, how does this all play out? There are some very interesting differences here. If I look at a work of art, I am looking at something that was deliberately created to be a work of art, with all that that entails. A human being, in most cases a specific human being who is a known entity, made that work for a specific purpose. As I look upon it, it elicits emotions, cognition, reflection, and recollection. It presents a challenge to me to interpret that work in some fashion that I find meaningful. The artist may be long dead, perhaps have no notion of modern times, or even a conception of such a thing as a museum where the work now resides. It is a singular work, and is perhaps presented with other works by that same artist, or of the same era. It may have an elaborate label that accompanies it, or perhaps just a "name, rank, and serial number" approach. I might feel that I understand the work or have had a successful encounter with it, or not.

And then compare that to an exhibit in a science museum. To begin, it is usually the case that the objects themselves have no intrinsic value beyond their replacement value. That is, if part of a science center burned down or were damaged in an earthquake, it could be put back together again, probably better than it was before (as the replacement could take advantage of technological improvements as well as an understanding of what was working well or less well in the initial exhibit). If a Foucault pendulum is presented as part of an exhibition, unless it had some particular tie to Foucault himself, or some other historical linkage, it is simply a heavy ball at the end of a line that demonstrates the rotation of the earth in a fashion that I only vaguely understand. (The original Foucault pendulum sadly snapped and was badly damaged in 2010.)

Art museums contain objects that were created as works of art, and eventually ended up in an art museum being organized, preserved, interpreted, and presented by the museum. Science museums and centers primarily contain objects and exhibitions that have been put together specifically for the purposes of being perceived by the visitors to the museum. If they aren't functioning as desired, they often can be improved to better communicate the underlying scientific principles. Art museums are curated; science museums are created.

How does this relate to the Museum Effect? I'm afraid I have to say I'm not sure. In part, this is because science museums vary quite a bit. The Museum of Science and Industry in Chicago, for example, contains many objects of historic and scientific significance. On the other hand, most science museums are constructed to present the scientific concepts that they choose to highlight. So let's stay with that notion and explore how it might relate to the Museum Effect. If one is learning about photosynthesis in a walk-through diorama-like display of a greatly enlarged plant cell, will that engender the kinds of reflection that might be comparable to viewing *Juan de Pareja*, or *Guernica*? Most likely the answer here is no, but I think the answer depends very much on the nature of the science museum and who it sees as its primary audience. For museums that have a more adult orientation, and where the exhibitions and displays present scientific concepts at a level of complexity, there may be something of the Museum Effect going on. But even here, the nature of the communication from the display/object/exhibition is usually didactic and usually cognitive as well. Does this result in contemplation about one's life and the world? Perhaps, but science museums, which I love to visit, seem to me to, in the main, to be more oriented toward learning and engendering interest in scientific issues than personal reflection. Having said that, while at the Boston Museum of Science, I happened upon a large wall full of biographies of famous mathematicians. I was drawn to the smaller entries, mathematicians famous enough to be on the wall, but not so famous as to occupy a large portion. I came upon an entry for Evariste Galois. It was very small compared to others, and fairly soon the reason became apparent: he died at age twenty. In a duel. It almost demanded further investigation, which I took up with my nephew who is an astrophysicist. He told me that Galois was so certain that he would lose the duel that he spent the last night of his life writing up some of his mathematical ideas. Further reading on Galois revealed a truly amazing character, a life full of arrests, romance, drama, as well as mathematics. And so, the science museum perhaps does have the potential for substantial reflection and personal growth.

History Museums and Historic Sites

History museums and historical sites are considered together here, but there are many important differences between these categories. We begin by looking at history museums, and in particular, natural history museums. Some of the research that my wife, Lisa, and I have done over the years has been in natural history museums. We have spent many hours at the American Museum of Natural History in New York City, looking at who visits, what their interests are, and what they get out of their visit. Natural history museums contain artifacts that reflect the history of our planet. There are minerals and meteorites, fossils and amphibians, depictions of early humankind, and dinosaurs. They are typically organized thematically, and vary in terms of the depth and richness of the collection. If one substitutes the objects found for works of art, it might be reasonable to see a direct parallel between the kinds of things that go on in natural history museums and art museums. The difference has to do with the nature of the objects that one encounters.

Take a dinosaur, for example. You might see a fossilized bone from a dinosaur, or an entire reconstruction of a dinosaur that includes some real bones and some that have been supplied by the museum, along with an armature that allows the skeleton to be presented whole. I love the dinosaur in the Roosevelt Rotunda of the American Museum of Natural History. I always think of it as a brontosaurus, but it isn't. Even if it were, it wouldn't be, as the proper name for a brontosaurus is an apatosaurus. And this one isn't either of those; it's a barosaurus. There are some interesting stories about confusions among these creatures and a tendency to get the bones mixed up, but as interesting as that is, it isn't part of the story here.

The story here has to do with our reactions to seeing such a thing. It is so big and its neck is so long. It is truly an object of wonder and awe. An important part of that wonder and awe is that those animals are no longer with us. Indeed, if they were, we might not be here! For me, it is hard to look at a dinosaur, or a meteorite, or a reconstruction of a moa bird in New Zealand, and not contemplate the grand order of things. Are we contributing to the extinction of species at an alarming rate, or are those estimates overblown? As a person who works with statistics a lot, I wonder how such things are estimated and what assumptions underlie the estimations. At the heart of the issue, though, is how do people react to the objects that they see in natural history museums? Most of the objects are not man made, although some might be. Is there really a direct parallel between a fossil and a Fauvist painting? What do people think as they look at the objects in a natural history museum? Are they similar to art museums?

Before leaving history museums, it would be important to look at history museums other than natural history museums, and at historic sites. In London, one can find history museums dedicated to the heritage of anesthesia, Lord Baden-Powell and scouting, the Arsenal Football Club, and fans (those things we use to cool ourselves on a warm day). Of course, while in London, one might also take in Westminster Abbey, the Tower of London, and the Victoria and Albert Museum. And it is not far to go to Stonehenge or Stratford-upon-Avon. All of these museums and historic sites differ from a natural history museum in that they are dedicated to things that people have made. In the case of Baden-Powell or Shakespeare, it is a single individual and what that person accomplished. For Westminster Abbey, there is of course the building itself, but there is also the history of what took place there, and whose remains remain there today. For the history of anesthesia, things get a bit specialized. What is one likely to find there? But in each case, one encounters artifacts made by human beings. Some are amazing; others may be more mundane. One can consider the astonishing individual achievement of Shakespeare, or the life of Baden-Powell and his efforts at creating the Scouts. Or one can contemplate the comparatively anonymous yet stunning construction called Stonehenge. In each of these situations, one is forced to think about who these people were, what they contributed, how it affects us today, and perhaps how life might be different without their contribution.

In a history or natural history museum, the parallelism to an art museum is clear. There is an institution, there are objects, the objects hold interest for the viewer, and many objects may be encountered by the visitor during the time spent in the institution. The question is: Does the nature of the visit and the contemplation of the objects engender the same kinds of personal reflection that we believe occur in art museums? I think a strong case can be made that in most instances, the answer would be yes. If I look at a daguerreotype of a Civil War soldier such as the one found in Figure 5.5, I am hard pressed not to think of that individual.

What was his life like? Did he survive the war? My great-grandfather was a surgeon in the Confederacy, and we have his letters home during the war. My father told me stories of his conversations with him when my father was a young boy. He lived a full life after the Civil War and was not defined by

Figure 5.5.   Union soldier from Civil War.
Library of Congress

it. My great-great-great uncle, however, died at the battle of Savage's Station, Virginia, at the age of nineteen. I have the Bible he had with him that day. Who might I have been had I lived at the time? If I had lived in the South, would I really have fought for a cause that seems so anathema to me today? And yet I know my great-grandfather did, even though his brother voted against secession in the Mississippi legislature. The American Civil War, so recent in historical terms, but so distant from current sensibilities, brings home for Americans an uncomfortable reminder of our history.

There is a strong parallelism between history museums and art museums on a number of variables: who comes to such museums and what their purposes are, the layout of the museum, and the notion that it is a collection of objects that usually have some level of intrinsic value. The major difference we see is in the nature of the objects themselves, although we see, as in the case of the British Museum, some overlap between the two. But generally speaking, does an object of historical significance, but not artistic significance, have the same or similar effect on an individual as an object of artistic significance, but not historical significance? Do we react in a similar fashion to the two?

Institutions with Living Objects

Zoos, aquariums, botanical gardens, aviaries, and game parks are all examples of cultural institutions that contain living things. Although they do not speak directly of things that are made by humans, nor of places of human history, they are who (and what) we share the planet with, and societies that believe that we should understand them better are typically societies that have a richer and fuller view of who we are and where we are headed. So much for the soapbox, the hard question is, "Does looking at a meerkat cause you to think better thoughts about yourself, your relationships with others, and the future of the planet?" (Figure 5.6).

I mention meerkats here as opposed to lions or tigers or bears, because their faces have expressions that look so human. In other words, for me, if meerkats don't cause you to think about humanity, boa constrictors are highly unlikely to. A trip to see wildlife certainly holds the potential for causing us to think about issues such as biodiversity, climate change, and habitat, but does it cause us to think about where we are going in our lives? What about a visit to a botanical garden? I have to say that it seems to me that this "pushes the envelope" about as far as I am willing to go in the absence of any hard data.

Libraries

Those of us who work in libraries or in museums tend to think of one another as kindred spirits, I think. We exist to serve and enlighten the public;

Figure 5.6. Meerkats.
Courtesy of Michael Elliott and FreeDigitalPhotos.net

we collect great works and make them accessible to individuals, and people tend to not speak loudly in our institutions. But there are many differences as well. Although most people come to visit a library voluntarily, others are there perhaps because of work, or school assignments. People don't go to a library with the anticipation of looking briefly at dozens of different objects. Actually, people go to libraries for a host of different reasons, sometimes very specific reasons. Sometimes it is to find one's next set of reading materials. Other times it may be to do some work with reference materials for some specific personal or work-related task. Or it may be to look for books that one typically cannot find in a bookstore. And then, it might not be for books at all. One might be looking for periodicals, movies, or to read a newspaper. People come to browse in a leisurely fashion, and often to sit and read what they have found.

Upon coming to New Zealand, we discovered that there were things called "toy libraries." We had never heard of them before, although they exist in other countries as well. We didn't know quite what they were or what they did, and I allowed for the possibility that they were very little libraries where children could pretend to be librarians. But in fact you can play with, and check out toys. What a brilliant idea! New Zealand also has a fairly active mobile library program (what in the United States we would call "bookmobiles"). As books are rather expensive to purchase in New Zealand, we have found that libraries are popular institutions, as is the habit of lending books to one another.

In order to consider libraries seriously with regard to the Museum Effect, let us make some simplifying assumptions about a library visit. Let us imagine a person who is coming to the library with a general idea of what he or she wants to look for, and has something of a goal to leave with two or three books that might be read over the next few weeks. If this person is familiar with the library, he or she might go directly to a given area, or a few, or might look in a "recently arrived" area of the library. Or that person might begin by striking up a conversation with a librarian friend, or maybe just go up and ask a librarian for help or recommendations.

So this is a person who enters a library open to a new experience. That is, this person wants to read, to explore new ideas and thoughts, or new characters and adventures. Perhaps the person has fairly specific tastes. With an idea, broad or narrow, the visitor goes to see what is available. She might pick up five, or maybe up to twenty books to take a look at. She might only pick up those books whose titles seem intriguing, and then might flip through them or read a paragraph or two. If she is methodical, she will winnow the selection down by comparison and by what the works offer up in terms of style or content. She may limit her search by genre or by author. And when she has completed her task, she will take several books up to the checkout counter to take them home. How long will she have been at the library?

In comparing a library and a museum visit, there are several areas where clear differences appear. To begin, the library visit is typically more purposeful. People come to the library with a goal in mind: they want to get a book to read, look at a newspaper or magazine, do some reference work. Any of these activities might include, either purposefully, or through happenstance, some degree of browsing, meandering, or considering possibilities. But at some level, that browsing is not the purpose of the visit. It is more a means to an end. People do not spend three minutes looking at a possible book to check out because looking at a book for three minutes was their goal. They spend that time in order to decide whether to take that book home to read: that is the goal here. They typically are not going to spend two hours going from book to book as they might spend in a museum going from object to object. If they do spend an extended amount of time in the library, it is much more likely to be because they are actively reading material that they have secured.

The library visitor comes to the library expressly to take a book home to read. It is true that some visitors will take the opportunity to read while in the library, others will read other kinds of materials there, and still others will do reference work, or be at the library for an event. But at its heart, libraries are about finding books that are typically not at the bookstore, are free, and can be taken home to read. So while the library is an absolutely key cultural institution, it is entirely possible that the Museum Effect, as has been described here, does not really have a library parallel.

Except. Except that what libraries do is give their users (visitors, patrons) access to brilliance in writing (and some mediocrity as well, but let us not focus on that for now). Any visitor to a library can immerse himself or herself in Shakespeare, Joyce, Oates, Lagerkvist, Bronte, other Brontes, Morrison, Voltaire, Twain, Hemingway, or Whitman. While at the library, they can discuss options with people who are trained at helping them make choices. They can join book clubs, attend readings, and see what the news is from their hometown. And it is all for free. Libraries are an amazing invention, and sit at the heart of democratic societies.

But I wonder if what I am thinking of as the Museum Effect occurs in them very often. The library is the repository for the books as museums are the repository for objects, but the unit of analysis issue here becomes of interest. Is the unit of analysis the visit to "the library" as I have argued that it is for the museum visit? Is it the library itself that is the attraction, or is it what can be accomplished by going there? If I go to the library, but don't find anything to read, or maybe take home something that seems more a concession than something that is exciting, has that visit failed? I won't really know until I am well into the book. Lisa and I once took a vacation to Iceland (great fun) and my good friend from the Met, Kent Lydecker, insisted that if I were going to go to Iceland, I first had to read *Njal's Saga* in order to be in the proper frame of mind, and was kind enough to buy it for me as a gift. Well, I took his advice, as well as his gift, and read much of it on the plane to Reykjavik. I absolutely loved it. I could not put it down, nor could I stop from reading sections to Lisa, who pretty much thought I was crazed. I connected with the book, the characters, the style of saga writing, everything about it. I might have gotten that book from a library. Most decent-sized libraries are likely to have a copy. If I had gotten it from a library, it would have only necessitated a five-minute visit. But the experience of reading *Njal's Saga* was incredible. It still puts a smile on my face thinking back on it (yes, I found it tremendously amusing). So how do I relate my reading of the book to its acquisition? In this case, a lovely act of friendship, but it just as easily could have been a library loan. Reading *Njal's Saga* expanded my horizons, enhanced my vacation, gave me an appreciation of looking at the law and at one's responsibility to the family (two major themes in the saga) in a new light. That book sits in libraries all over the world, holding immense potential for enriching the lives of readers. And although the author(s) of the work are responsible for its existence, just as Picasso painted his paintings, it is the library that makes it accessible to all.

And so, I see the library as an absolutely critical vehicle for making us better people, but I think the process happens in a fundamentally different way. But it is a bit speculative. I would love to explore it.

Music

Music presents a particular challenge for thinking about the extension of the Museum Effect. In considering music, it is necessary to consider both attending a concert and listening to music in one's home (or other venue, but the home is probably the most common). Concerts are a very interesting phenomenon. Like museum visits, they are voluntary and people go to them with positive expectations. They are different in that they are bounded in time as well as in space. Concerts exist when they exist, not at just any old time. They usually involve a cost, sometimes substantial, and require a fair amount of advance planning. So while there are similarities to the museum visit, there are clear differences as well. One of those differences has to do with the nature of the aesthetic interaction. With music, we are clearly back in the realm of aesthetic appreciation, but of a different type. One cannot basically choose how long one will listen to a piece of music. It is as long as it is. If one goes to a concert, it might last for two hours and consist of a number of different musical pieces, or it might be an opera or a symphony. It does not come in a series of short views of works of art. Or does it? Music consists of passages, themes, melodies that are repeated and varied. Thus, even though a lengthy piece is to be taken as a coherent whole, that whole is an assemblage of parts, and those parts can be appreciated individually. Indeed, most composers aspire to take their listener through a series of emotions, thoughts, imaginings, and so forth. Although aural rather than visual, I think a concert bears a strong similarity to an art museum visit. There is the institution of the concert hall, being in the presence of others who share a common interest in this music, and the thrill of hearing and listening to the music live.

But music can be appreciated, in incredibly high quality, outside of the concert hall. It can be listened to in the comfort of one's home, or, with the advent of earphones and headphones, on a 747 or the London Underground. One might reasonably ask if even the best recording can match a live performance, and that would be an interesting question. I once attended a Yo-Yo Ma concert, many years ago, where the heating system in the theater went wonky and caused about three minutes of very loud clanging noises occurring randomly and frequently. To his credit, Ma played right through them and never acknowledged that there was anything wrong. About twenty years later, I was working with the staff at that theater and brought up the event in conversation. The response was an astonished, "You were there? It actually happened? We had heard of this but weren't sure if it were real or an urban legend." I just now listened to Ma's rendition of the prelude from Bach's Cello Suite no. 1, and the notion of different passages and themes, with beautiful transitions, and all tied together is clearly there, created by Johann Sebastian Bach, and re-created by Yo-Yo Ma.

Is there a difference between listening just now and going to a concert, even if to hear lesser players than Ma or works I like less than Bach's? Is there something inherent in the event, in the place, in the social and musical milieu? In all honesty, I think the answer here is yes. It *is* different to see it live. But I think that difference is not the same as looking at a real work of art and looking at a reproduction. If I put on my good headphones and listen to an outstanding performance of a piece of classical music, I don't see that as being a *reproduction* of a real thing. Admittedly it is not live, but in terms of it being what the performing artists want it to be, is it not better than an off night of a real concert? But the best reproduction of a Botticelli does not match standing in front of one. The differences here are interesting to contemplate. A live performance is a voluntary event, like going to an art museum. And one is not limited to a formal concert. The musical event may be a music festival, or a gathering in a home. The musical event may be the motivation for investigation into a particular work of music. It may involve conversation with the musicians in some instances. One of the fascinating aspects of considering options other

than visual art is that they all contain their own unique characteristics and opportunities; they are all worthy of serious exploration.

While we consider options, does the event have to be classical music—serious music? Will musical comedy work as well as opera? Is a boy band as
good as the Vienna Boys' Choir? If there are important differences here, what
are the characteristics that define such distinctions?

Other Possibilities: Looking at Astronomy

Over the past ten years or so, a small group of us have formed what we call
the Aesthetics and Astronomy Group and have been looking at how people
look at the images that are created from telescopes looking into deep space.
These images reproduce much better in color than in black and white, but
Figure 5.7 will provide an idea of what I am talking about.

It is an image of a spiral galaxy, not the Milky Way, but similar to the
Milky Way. Speaking of images reproducing better in color, I should mention that the wondrous colors that are seen in these images are referred to in
astronomical circles as "false color," which basically means that if you flew

Figure 5.7.   Spiral Galaxy.
NASA

out to look at the object being depicted, it would not exist in the beautiful palettes that we see in these pictures. They are showing different types of energies and wavelengths that have been detected by the satellites (sometimes images are made from the data of several satellites merged together), and colors have been assigned to the various wavelengths. There are not really hard-and-fast rules on this, but one notion that most astronomers adhere to is that things that are cold should be red and things that are hot should be blue. Astronomers seem to be naturally contrary, but they actually have good reasons for that color choice, as higher-energy wavelengths are in the blue end of the spectrum.

But what about these images and the Museum Effect? What kinds of reactions do they engender? Are they art? If we saw them in a museum setting, would it cause us to reflect in the way I am arguing art does? These questions, which our group is exploring, bring me to the final section of this chapter. The Museum Effect exists, we are fairly confident, when people encounter a number of works of art in a museum setting. In this chapter, we have stretched the notion of objects to include those that are historical, natural, scientific, written, and aural in nature. We have taken the museum and turned it into a library, a park, a music hall, and even, to a degree, a subway. We have played with the voluntary nature of moving from one object to another to listening to music as it occurs in time. And this brings me back to a very fundamental question: What is a painting like?

WHAT IS A PAINTING LIKE?

The question of what is like an art museum is one I've spent a bit of time contemplating. In thinking about possible answers to that question, a second question arises: What is a painting like? If it causes us to reflect upon ourselves, what else causes such a reaction? Where else might we look to see the Museum Effect? Is a painting like a novel, or an opera? Is it like a historical artifact or an orchid or a supernova? When an artist creates a painting (or other work of art), what is he or she trying to do? What is the intent of a work of art? What does it communicate to a viewer? If we look at the painting of Juan de Pareja by Velazquez, presented earlier, what do we think Velazquez was trying to accomplish? Would Velazquez be able to tell us if we asked him? Perhaps if we could think about what paintings are similar to in terms of other artistic endeavor, we might gain some insight into this question.

In thinking about this, one of the things that fascinates me is time. We know that when people look at paintings they do so for about a half minute. Whatever an artist has to say, the vast majority of people who look at a work feel that they have gotten the message in well under a minute. What does that say about the nature of that communication, and how does it compare to other communication? In our work on astronomical images, thirty seconds is about how long people look as well. I don't have data on historical objects, but I would imagine that they receive roughly the same amount of time. Science museums have displays and demonstrations that are multifaceted and take longer for people to view them.

Leaving history and science aside, how would we compare a painting to another creative endeavor? How would a painting compare to a book or an opera? Well, I took a sample of thirty famous novels and found that their length on average was 136,000 words. If a person reads about three hundred words a minute, it would take roughly eight hours to read a book. That will vary by person and by book, but the order of magnitude is all we really need just now. If a work of art gets thirty seconds and a book eight hours, the book takes about a thousand times longer to contemplate than a painting. Thus it is hard to say that a painting is like a book in terms of time spent. If we tried to compare thirty seconds of reading to the equivalent thirty seconds of viewing a painting, the equation seems strained at best. Reading is something that naturally takes longer to take in. Perhaps that is due to the linear nature of reading and the time needed to communicate. A poem would seem more an equivalent to a painting from the perspective of the amount of time spent contemplating it. Turning to music, in terms of time spent, a painting might be like a passage in a symphony, or a popular song. It wouldn't be a whole symphony or an opera, as they are much longer events.

We can turn this question around 180 degrees and ask how long does it take to create a painting or other creative work? Another way of putting this would be to ask how many works are created in a career? As it turns out, although one can find information on this for novelists, architects, scientists, and composers, the equivalent numbers do not exist for the visual arts. It turns out to be very difficult to say just what is and isn't a work of art. Is a charcoal study for a painting a work of art? Is the Sistine Chapel ceiling one work of art or many? I've started to collect information on the productivity of artists, and somewhere around four hundred works might represent a reasonable order of magnitude for an artist (excluding Picasso!) and around forty for novelists. So very roughly, the difference is about ten to one.

At this point in considering various arts and artists, I am most comfortable in comparing a painting to a poem. It can be something like Picasso's *Dove* or a haiku, fleeting and yet impactful, or it can be like the *Iliad* or Michelangelo's *Pieta*, with incredible depth and intricacy. In music, I am thinking more about passages in works rather than complete works, but many options are available here. My goal in thinking about this question has more to do with how it impacts us as individuals. How is it that works of visual arts, in their infinite variety, cause us to contemplate our lives, and do other forms of art do the same thing?

SO, DOES THE MUSEUM EFFECT
EXTEND TO OTHER CULTURAL INSTITUTIONS?

We have considered a number of different cultural institutions here, and even extended the thinking to astronomical images. And where are we? Well, I believe that extending to history museums is not difficult, although it would certainly await empirical verification. And I would argue that classical music venues are not much of a reach. For science museums, it seems to me that perhaps a different sort of activity is taking place. I'm a bit more reluctant to generalize to science museums, but I may be biased by thinking about the highly interactive and boisterous ones (which again, I love, but they can be a bit too chaotic to engender contemplative rumination). Libraries, I think, work in a fundamentally different fashion from art museums. In looking at them in a kind of traditional form, they allow access to great literature, and in doing so, clearly are a benefit to us as individuals and as societies, but they accomplish this noble goal differently from an art museum. There are many parallels to art museums that I can see, but also many uniquenesses. Imagine only looking at *Great Expectations* for thirty seconds, and not being able to touch it! Or consider checking four works out from an art museum to look at leisurely in one's home. The institutions, while so similar in many respects, are strikingly different in others. Each contributes to our well-being, but would require a much broader notion of how great works of all kinds enhance our lives than we can consider at this point. It is always good to have another question to pursue!

REFERENCES

Csikszentmihalyi, M. (1990). *Flow: The psychology of optimal experience.* New York: HarperCollins.
Csikszentmihalyi, M., & Robinson, R. E. (1990). *The art of seeing: An interpretation of the aesthetic encounter.* Malibu, CA: J. Paul Getty Museum.

6

How to Enhance the Museum Effect

*There are little inside stories to every art piece, little inside stories to every
artist that should be shown or heard. And most people, unless they're, you
know, really, really, really into art . . . they're just going to pass it by, and
an incredible story could be lost.*

It's just giving, it makes your mind move more.

—Two quotes on an experimental audio program at the Whitney
Museum of American Art

This chapter looks at how those of us who work in and with cultural institutions can promote and enhance the Museum Effect taking place in our institutions. Although structure of the institution, the layout of exhibitions, and
nature and wonder of our objects can be second nature to us, they are often
new to the visitor and can take some assistance to successfully navigate. I
have had the opportunity to walk through many museums and exhibitions
in those museums with the people who were responsible for organizing, displaying, interpreting, and occasionally acquiring those objects. The "inside"
stories are often more intriguing than the ones presented publicly via labels,
wall text, or audio tour information. We were once looking at a Velazquez
painting that seemed to have an exceptionally glossy finish with almost no
traces of brushwork. We asked the art historian that was giving us a tour how
Velazquez had accomplished that effect. She said, "Well, in truth, he didn't.
That painting was initially done on wood, but over the years, the wood began
to disintegrate. It was preserved by carefully removing all the wood from
the painting, leaving only the gesso and the painting, then putting in a layer
of wax, then putting canvas on that, and then ironing the canvas so the wax,

which was adhered to the painting, became affixed to the wood. In doing this, it had a tendency to flatten the original painting, which is what you are seeing." Now that is an interesting piece of information (I may well have some of the details of the process incorrect). The story doesn't really speak to the nature of the original painting, the idea of the communication of ideas from the painter to the viewer, nor any notion of how the work itself can provide a vehicle for self-reflection to the viewer. Having said that, it does make the painting more interesting—in an unintended fashion to be sure, but more fascinating nonetheless. And that fascination leads to a more careful inspection of the work, which in turn can trigger the kind of reflection that engenders the Museum Effect.

On another occasion we were looking at an exhibition of works by Jusepe de Ribera and noticed that the same individuals kept appearing in his works. One of these models had a unique face, full of expression and character whenever it appeared. We asked about that, and the curator we were looking at the works with said, "Well, you have to keep in mind that these particular works are gathered here from points far and near. They come from different churches and palaces from different cities. When you see them all here together, you see that face again and again. He was one of Ribera's favorite models, and it does seem funny to see him as a saint here and as a peasant there." Of course, one does not see the same faces multiple times when the works are in their original environments. It is only in an exhibition that draws those works together that this oddity appears. In Ribera's work one sees a running theme of the passion, the intensity of emotion that accompanies martyrdom. Ribera appears to be trying to communicate the essence of the idea of faith, of commitment to a belief that was a common thread among his saints. An exhibition allows one to see that theme portrayed again and again. At the same time, an exhibition allows a second, and unintended theme to be seen: the repeated use of certain models, which is not apparent when looking at one work. And so, a visitor might be swept away by the intensity of the works seen in a collection, and at the same time, intrigued by who these people were whose faces appear in anguish or despair in repeated paintings. Were they friends, relatives, or hired models? What was their relationship to Ribera? What is typically the relationship between painter and model? Are any of the people in this painting Ribera himself? The exhibition allows for musings that might be unique to the current configuration of works.

Let me shift gears dramatically, leaving Naples and Ribera in the seventeenth century, and go to Kotzebue, Alaska, north of the Arctic Circle, twenty-first century. We were once there on a vacation (we often take unusual vacations), and were met, as we and ten other intrepid travelers got off a small plane, and greeted by our tour guide, the reigning "Miss Arctic Circle," who told us that after a short bus ride we would visit their "wonderful museum" and see a show put on by the local children. The bus ride was literally less than a hundred yards and ended at a building that looked like it had been cobbled together from bits of other buildings no longer in existence. We made our way down some narrow passages and came out into what was essentially a small gymnasium. There were several vitrines along the sides of the walls, intermingled with wrestling mats and basketball hoops. They contained some foxes, some craft work, and skeletons of animals we didn't recognize. We saw a lovely presentation by the local children, and as "museum people" we eagerly awaited the visit to the museum. Gradually it dawned on us that we were *at the museum*. This was the gym, performance stage, and museum (the vitrines) all rolled into one. And perhaps it served other functions as well. Our guide took us up to a vitrine with a handsome stuffed fox in it and said, "This is the best piece in the museum." We noted what a fine specimen it was and I asked why it was the best piece, the same question I had once posed to the curator of the Egyptian galleries at the Metropolitan Museum of Art. Our guide proudly responded, "Because my uncle trapped and stuffed this fox." That was a first. It brought home to us what a small community museum can mean to the community. The fact that that fox was important to our guide spoke volumes. Our guide was off to college in Arizona the next year. Would she return to Kotzebue after her college work? To Alaska? Would that fox continue to be a source of pride to her? Her situation reminded me of an indigenous village I visited in Mexico many years ago where I saw young children who seemed so talented and eager to learn. If they were able to go to university, did they have a responsibility to return to their little village in the hills, or did they have the right to pursue whatever their abilities allowed them to? It is an interesting question. It speaks to the very core of what it means to be human, to be a member of a community, and at the same time, an individual with a right to one's own destiny. It was a question raised by a stuffed fox in a vitrine along the wall of a gymnasium/auditorium/museum.

Over the years, we acquired quite a few "inside stories" that never made it to the labels or in the audio tours of the works. That was fine by us, as it let us provide these morsels on our tours with friends and family. "This painting was done on a cigar box lid." "The man in the background is the husband of this lady. There had been a dog there originally." "The city behind Christ on the cross here is actually Amsterdam." "Audubon shot most of the birds that he painted." "Remington was only in the West once, briefly." "The model for this Degas painting was the Impressionist painter, Mary Cassatt." We made suggestions about including this type of information in the labels, which was sometimes welcomed and other times politely noted. The problem here is that while interesting to the average viewer, these little gems are often of no real art historical value. We would refer to them as "fun facts," and we understood why some might feel that they don't really belong in a hundred-word label, as they would crowd out other information. Fair enough. But we have found in giving tours of museums that people really love to hear those "fun facts" and they cause people to become more engaged in the work.

HOW BEST TO INTERACT WITH VISITORS?

This raises the question of how to interact with the visitors. In an art museum, or a history museum, it is important to have faith in the objects. If the works themselves do not captivate, do not hold an audience initially and encourage a return visit, then there are problems more fundamental than presentation. And some museums take a philosophical stance with regard to visitors that this faith in the objects should be honored by not cluttering them with labels that provide information about the works other than the title, artist, date, and how the museum acquired the work. "The works speak for themselves" is a not uncommon refrain.

I fundamentally disagree with that argument. If you google "cave art" and then hit the "Images" button on the google response, you will get hundreds of images of cave art. You will also get a fair number of works that look like cave art, but are in fact works made recently by people who are inspired by cave art or simply copying cave art. If I am looking at a work, I'd like to know if it is real, or a copy. If a work is the last work that van Gogh painted before his death from a gunshot wound (probably self-inflicted), I'd like to know that when I am looking at the work. If the patron of the painter appears in the work, I am interested in that and it would, in fact, enhance my viewing. Not all information in labels is particularly useful or interesting (we've become informal critics of the quality of labels over the years), but some can turn an otherwise difficult-to-appreciate work of art into something absolutely fascinating.

We were once in attendance at a meeting at the Met where a new acquisition was being discussed. It was a painting of an older woman by Delacroix (Figure 6.1). The curator in charge of working on the acquisition was rapturous about it. At first, we were a bit baffled that this was such an outstanding work. It simply seemed like a nice painting of an older woman to us.

But then we learned more about the lady in the picture from the curator. She was not Delacroix's mother, but was a person very dear to Delacroix and who became something of a mother figure to him after his own mother died. And she was not only beloved of Delacroix, but also supposedly of Talleyrand, and quite possibly Napoleon in her younger years. Really? Now we had to look closer.

Figure 6.1.   Delacroix Madame Henri François Riesener (Félicité Longrois, 1786–1847).
Image copyright © The Metropolitan Museum of Art. Image source: Art Resource, NY

We had to find the love of the artist for the subject, and also perhaps to roll back some of those years and see the young lady who caught the fancy of some of the most famous and powerful men of her time. Armed with this information, the painting becomes a completely different work. It hasn't changed a bit in terms of its physics, chemistry, or composition, but it is no longer the same. My purpose here is not to argue whether we can augment and enhance the visitor experience;

I am going to take that as a given. Instead I will look at how museums are doing that and what might be productive avenues for future work.

THE "RIGHT" WAY TO LOOK AT A PAINTING

In looking at the work of Housen and Parsons, discussed in chapter 4, we can see that there are many different ways that people look at works of art, and these ways develop as people get more experience in looking at art and/or more education in art and art history. The differences are not in amount, but in kind. Different people look for and look at different things. But it would be incorrect to say that some approaches are right and others are wrong. My mother was a fan of seascapes and forever wanted to see "water that you could touch." This led me to never getting too far from her side whenever I took her to visit an art museum. I have to say that I, too, am impressed by seascapes where the water is very realistic, but it isn't something that I go out of my way to see. I look at such works differently from how my mother used to, but that doesn't make my way better than hers.

At the same time, in talking with visitors to art museums, a common theme among them is that they want to become better at looking at art. They want to see what experts see in the works. They want to know why one work is considered a masterpiece and another is not. What should they look at first; how should they form their opinions; why do "experts" like art that seems so inaccessible to them? When looking at some modern art, these questions can border on accusation. But they are real questions for visitors—meaningful to them. What is the responsibility of the museum to help them navigate a particular work or exhibition, and to develop the skills and background necessary to do so independently?

I think the answer is twofold (at least). First, we need to encourage visitors to trust their own viewing, enjoying and reflecting on works as they see fit. There would be no point in making my mother feel bad or unsophisticated because she liked the realism found in many seascapes. And second, we need to show people that for many works, insight into the work can lead to a more satisfying interaction with it. And that the knowledge of specific works, artists, schools, and periods of art can lead to more generalizable skill in looking at particular works. And at the same time, for me, it is critical to encourage people to use works to think about the issues that are important to them in their lives.

THE BASICS: "WE ARE IN YOUR HANDS!"

In thinking broadly about how museums can enhance the visitor experience, the phrase given to us by a visitor to the Byzantine art exhibition described in chapter 2 serves as a touchstone here: "We are in your hands." Visitors, especially those who are not well versed in the subject matter you are present-ing, essentially give themselves over to the institution for guidance on how to view and appreciate the works. I will discuss several vehicles that are cur-rently in use and consider the absolute explosion of other opportunities that exist. But to begin, let me review a few ideas, some of which have already been presented in other contexts, that form the basis for thinking about how to augment viewer appreciation.

The Power of Knowledge

To say that knowledge is power is trite to be certain, but no less is it trite than it is true. If you are trying to simplify quadratic equations, knowing your squares is really helpful. It gives you more power to solve the equation. If you are trying to understand a work of Renaissance annunciation painting, knowledge of symbolism of religious iconography is really helpful. Under-standing what they are there for, what they mean, provides insight into what the painting is about. The lilies representing the chastity of Mary, the dove representing the Holy Spirit, and the peacock representing immortality all appear in religious paintings. If you have viewed a number of annunciation paintings, you can begin to compare how various artists solved the problem of working the icons into the pieces. It isn't necessarily essential to appreciating the painting, but it gives you an advantage at looking at the work. Knowing about the life of the artist, or why a work was commissioned, or that this piece was one of a series where the artist wanted to look at the different effects of light, are all helpful in one's viewing of a work.

As a case in point, you might see *The Battle of the U.S.S. "Kearsarge" and the C. S. S. "Alabama"* at the Philadelphia Museum of Art (Figure 6.2) and think, "That's an interesting sea battle painting." But learning that it is a *Civil War* sea battle makes it more intriguing, especially if you are a Civil War buff, because the battle at sea isn't typically highlighted in discussions of the Civil War. But you might then learn that the battle (and hence the paint-ing) took place in the waters off Cherbourg, France, and that it was painted by Edouard Manet. All sorts of bells go off. An American Civil War sea battle off the coast of France? Painted by Manet? The Civil War took place as Impressionism was being developed? All true. Without this information, this is a painting of a battle at sea; with the information, it becomes an object of substantial interest for anyone with an affinity for the American Civil War, or perhaps the history of the time in general.

The Whitney Museum of American Art has been a pioneer in looking at how to present information to visitors. We conducted a study with Kathryn Potts from the Whitney on an innovative audio tour program called American Voices (Smith, Waszkielewicz, Potts, & Smith, 2004). The idea behind the program was to provide visitors with a different kind of information about a work—sometimes coming from the artist himself, sometimes from a person

Figure 6.2.   Manet. The Battle of the "Kearsarge" and the "Alabama."
The Philadelphia Museum of Art / Art Resource, NY

who was an expert on the subject matter of the painting or who had particular insight into the artist. We chose four works that were included in the program, and ran a small experiment to look at the effects of the works. This involved asking sixty visitors who were in the vicinity of a work if they would like to participate in a brief experiment. If they agreed, they were randomly assigned to one of three conditions. They viewed the work:

1. as it was typically presented, with only basic information about the work;
2. with a more extensive label, presenting information about the work, and providing some context—what might be considered a "typical" museum label; or

3. with an audio segment that was devised especially for this program—the content here varied from work to work and was intended to engage the viewer in the work.

The viewers looked at the work as long as they cared to, and then completed a short questionnaire about the work. This procedure was repeated with a total of four different works, using different samples of participants each time. This allowed us to conduct a true experiment and only have to ask ten minutes of time from each participant. One of the objects was entitled *America's Darker Moments*, by Chris Burden, made in 1994. The object was a sculpture in five parts which depicted the My Lai Massacre, the Emmett Till trial, the Kent State shootings, and so forth. The audio tour stop was developed and given by the artist, explaining why he had chosen those events and constructed the piece. Figure 6.3 presents the results of several questions asked of visitors in the various conditions. It is easy to see that the audio presentation caused people to want to see more works by the artist, made it more interesting to them, made them like it more, and made them give higher responses to the phrase "It moves me."

Similar results were found for two of the other three objects. The fourth object, George Bellow's famous depiction of the Dempsey and Firpo boxing match, *Dempsey and Firpo*, was somewhat less successful. In this instance, the label text was fundamentally as successful as the audio information, although both were much stronger than the basic label. In all four works of art, people in the audio tour spent much longer in front of the works than in the basic label or extended label condition. Participants were told they could spend as long at the works as they cared to, and at first we were surprised that people spent so much longer in the audio condition, usually a minute longer and sometimes two minutes longer—very long visits given our previous work in this area. Then we realized that they were staying in front of the works until the audio was completed. Now at one level, this clearly isn't a fair comparison. But upon further reflection, it *is* the case that they spent more time in front of the work in the audio condition, and for all four works, their reactions were much more positive than in the standard condition. This small study is a good example of how to conduct work in a museum setting that is not onerous to visitors and can provide a wealth of good information to the institution.

What we can see from the Whitney study is that the information we present to visitors can dramatically alter their viewing experience. A corollary to that is what we don't present to viewers can dramatically alter their viewing experience as well. And this brings us to a bit of a conundrum. Do we provide information to the visitor, and if so, of what kind? If "the art speaks for itself," then why do we see such different reactions to the same work of art when viewed with various pieces of additional information? There is much to learn about the art, and for the most part, such knowledge enhances viewing.

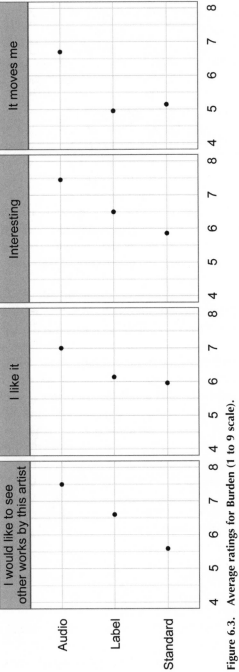

Figure 6.3. Average ratings for Burden (1 to 9 scale).

Freedom and Structure

One of the things that I have found to be true about museu/
life in general) is that there is a certain tension between freeou..
ture. When we perceive too much structure in our lives, we strive for mo..
freedom, and conversely, when we perceive too much freedom, we strive for
more structure. Take guided museum tours as an example. Have you ever
noticed how some people will hang on the fringes of such a tour, or listen in
as the guide explains something in a room? These people long for the information that they might find to be useful to them, but at the same time, don't
want the social obligation of following the strictures of the tour group in case
they might find the tour not very interesting. And so they want structure and
freedom at the same time. In a study of museum tours at the Tinio, Smith,
and Potts (2010) found that

> visitors who participated in the present study preferred low-interactivity over
> high-interactivity tours. But, consider what the interviewees are doing and say-
> ing. They want the tour (structure) and like being able to leave it (freedom); they
> want to be able to ask questions and talk to others (freedom), but almost never
> avail themselves of those options (structure). (p. 50)

In providing information and insight to visitors, we need to make it available, and to provide a framework for accessing the information (both literally
and figuratively) while at the same time maintaining in the visitor a sense of
freedom and openness in choosing and exploring objects.

The Unit of Analysis

One of the aspects that we discussed with regard to the Museum Effect was
the notion of the unit of analysis—what or who is it that we are talking about?
This issue comes around again when thinking about how to enhance the Museum Effect. The first thing to consider here is whether we should be thinking
about the person as the unit of analysis, or the museum—or individual works
of art. To a degree, to be certain, it is necessary to think of both the individual
as well as what is to be experienced, but let's focus on objects for a moment
first. An art museum is a collection of individual objects. These objects might
have a very close relationship to one another, as would be the case with Egyptian funerary pieces from the same location. They might have a relationship
but also "stand-alone" aspects, such as the series paintings by Monet, or even
the "early works" in a biographical exhibition of a particular artist. If you
consider the Impressionist wing of an art museum, or the entire collection
at many smaller museums, you are looking at a collection of objects that are

.noderately related to one another, but really more independent than not. That is, each object has its own story to tell. The relationship among the objects may be interesting in some situations, but they also have their own histories and impact on visitors.

Thus, there is often good cause for a general introduction to a gallery, an exhibition, or even a museum as a whole that provides a context for looking at the works, but then each work should probably be considered to be an individual event for the viewer. At the Byzantium exhibition that was discussed earlier, the audio tour began by saying that if you wanted to truly understand the art and artifacts being presented, you needed to understand that these works came from a time when people's lives, their religion, and their art were all closely intertwined. We found that information extremely helpful as a kind of reference point for looking at the works. It provided a context for taking the exhibition in as a whole. At the level of an individual work, we learned from a label for a particular object that it would have been rarely (if ever) seen by women before appearing in the exhibition because it came from an area of a religious site where women were forbidden to go. This engendered thinking about the work itself, but also the religious and social context whence it came. In terms of objects and groups of them, there is no single unit of analysis; one has to think of the works individually as well as what brings them together as a cohesive whole.

But what about the person as a unit of analysis? For whom are object labels, wall text, audio guides, tour texts, and so forth, written? This has been an issue we have encountered time and again in working with museums. As we know from looking at the work of Falk and Dierking, Pekarik, Housen, Parsons, as well as our own research, people who come to museums differ in their backgrounds, their goals and perspectives, their expectations and their behaviors. If we write material for one group, are we ignoring another? What level of sophistication is optimal? Should labels be short or long? There are many possibilities and approaches here, but I will cut to the chase and simply make a recommendation that we have found to be very effective and very useful: assume that your visitor is intelligent, at least moderately well educated, interested in learning more about the objects that you have, and currently only has a modest background with regard to them. In other words, smart and eager to learn. There is no need to talk down to the visitor, but at the same time it is wise to avoid esoteric vocabulary. We once saw a label that explained that a patron had "armorial aspirations," which, when we investigated, turned out that the patron wanted to have a coat of arms. In another case, we saw educational material that referred to "bibelots." Bibelots are trinkets. Who knew? The "bibelots" author is a dear friend and we had a running joke on that one for quite a while.

There is another side to this recommendation. In addition to not making the labels too esoteric, it's also useful not to simply state the obvious. We once saw a label that said that the painting was of a seated man dressed like a warrior in a red cape with a sword across his knees. Well, there was nothing incorrect about any of that except that it was quite obvious from just looking at it that this is what the painting was about. Little additional information or insight had been added here. There isn't a whole lot of space available on an object label, or a wall panel for that matter, so what goes there needs to be considered carefully.

The question arises as to what visitors should know about a particular object, or what might enhance their viewing of it. There will always be debates about the answer to that question, but as a rule of thumb, one might ask the question: Is there information we can provide about this work that will cause people to look at it longer? This might be information about the subject of the work, the artist, the time, and so on. We have found that people like to know that a painting was done on a cigar box lid, or that the artist was in love with the model, or that the painting was done so that the artist could show off his wares and get commissions for other works, or that the sun shining on George Washington's face in *Washington Crossing the Delaware* was unlikely since the crossing actually occurred at night (and the flag that is depicted in the painting was not designed until more than a year later than the crossing). These aren't necessarily important pieces of information from an artistic or art historical point of view, but they are engaging pieces of information that add interest and sometimes intrigue to a work of art.

The Paradox of Help

The idea of enhancing the Museum Effect fundamentally has to do with what a museum can do to help the visitor more meaningfully engage with the objects in the collection. This might involve taking a didactic perspective; it might involve encouraging visitors to look at works from a particular point of view or in a particular context; or it might simply involve providing information that causes visitors to become more engaged in a work. Whatever is done needs to be thought through, and if possible, perhaps tested with some interviews with visitors. One of the things that museums need to be careful not to do is to provide so much information or be so directive in how to look at something that they take away from the visitors the pleasure of discovering things on their own. This is always a concern in teaching, or in helping people in general. Whenever we do something for someone else, we assume that they will not be able to do it on their own, and we do not encourage the development of the skills to do so independently.

Consider the work of the Helmut Leder team in Vienna (discussed in chapter 4), which is mostly focused on the challenges provided by works of modern art. What kinds of information are best suited to visitors who are trying to work out what a particular object/installation means? How much information should be provided? How does that information work with the intent of the artist?

Time

As mentioned in chapter 3, time is an important factor in understanding how the Museum Effect works. Beverly Serrell (1997) has taken the idea of time spent looking at objects and exhibitions and developed an index for looking at the effectiveness of the efforts of museums. This is an interesting approach to time, and one that is perhaps a bit controversial in terms of the degree to which faith is put into staying power, but it's hard to argue that a person who spends a minute in front of a work of art hasn't had a more meaningful interaction with it than a person who spends four seconds. In thinking about how to enhance the likelihood that a visitor will have a meaningful interaction with a work, thinking about how to get that person to look longer is not a bad place to start. Thus, I basically agree with Serrell's perspective here. All other things equal, a longer look is a better look.

Insight

So what makes people look longer? What kind of information engenders lingering? It is close to a tautology to respond with "information that is interesting," but it really is a good point of departure. And what is interesting about most objects is that they have something interesting about them to tell. We simply need to figure out which information, among all that is available, our visitors would find interesting. To be sure, most labels have information that is basically "required." We will almost always tell the title, and the artist, the date, and who donated it to the museum. We might also say what the media are that the artist used. But if we go beyond that, where, exactly, do we go? There are categories of information that might be considered, including provenance, style, subject, school, and so forth, and this information is often useful and interesting to visitors.

One of the questions we have often posed to visitors is: If the curator for this exhibition (gallery, department, etc.) were here, what question would you have for him or her? We get some interesting responses to that question. The most common are "What is it worth?" and "Why is it great?" but in all honesty, even those responses aren't all that frequent. More often than not, people don't know what question they would have. What visitors want to know is something really interesting, but they don't know what that is.

And so, we have to ask the question, "What is really interesting or really important about this work of art?" In some recent work that we have been doing in looking at deep space imagery, we are spending time talking with astrophysicists about what is really interesting about the space images we are looking at. A problem here is that there is a bit of a gulf between what the astrophysicists know and what they think the general public knows. They often do not have a strong grasp of the magnitude of the naïveté of the general public. Fortunately, we are there to help them with naïveté. And the result is that we have generated some very interesting labels to accompany space imagery.

If I had to characterize the kind of information that I think is most useful to present, whether it is on labels, audio tours, or published materials that accompany exhibitions, it would be *insight*. If we can provide insight into what a picture or sculpture or artifact is about, we will capture the attention of the visitor and engender a longer look. Additionally, the visitor will appreciate the effort that has gone into presenting that information and become more receptive to additional information. Insight is hard to describe; it is a bit like the old statement about pornography: we know it when we see it! But it could be an interesting fact about the life of the artist (and many artists have lived fascinating lives), about why the work was commissioned, whom the models were, who influenced the artist, and so forth. It might even be how it was restored, what happened to it during a war, or how historical events impacted on the work. It is probably the case that not every work has a drop-dead fascinating tidbit that can be communicated, but it is true that every work has the most interesting thing *about it* that can be presented.

THE OPTIONS, CURRENT AND FUTURE

There is what we present and there is how we present it. What are the media that are available to us to present information to visitors? Those of us who have worked in the museum and cultural information field over the past thirty years would agree (I hope) that we are in the middle of what can only be considered transformative times in terms of presenting information. Thirty years ago, state of the art was an audio tape that individuals could turn on and off at appropriate times, and that ran linearly from beginning to end. There were also some interactive kiosks available at some institutions, and other than that, there were labels, wall text, brochures, and books about exhibitions. Reading rooms in exhibitions were something of an innovation. Now, I may have missed a thing or two there, but be that as it may, we have a host of new options available today, and there will be more even before this book is in print! But let us look at what the options are, current and future.

Labels and Wall Text

Labels and wall text are the old standbys of information presented to visitors to cultural institutions, and with good reason. They are present as the visitor is looking at the work of art, or entering an exhibition or exhibit room. They are a natural part of the display of works and visitors are comfortable using them. They are relatively inexpensive. On the downside, they require people to move from looking at the work of art, and processing information from an artistic, visual perspective, to moving up close to the label and reading information in a verbal fashion. This requires a real shift in mode from viewing to reading, and I think it is not a particularly comfortable shift for many people. I believe that is in part why we so often see people take an initial look at an object, read the entire label, take a second very quick glance, and then walk away. So although it is a mainstay in terms of communicating to audiences, it has always had some real drawbacks.

Wall text is somewhat different from labels in that the purpose here is to set a context for the room (or the exhibition). People read wall text typically before they look at the individual works; hence, the mode shift problem (viewing to reading and back) is greatly diminished. Wall text provides an overall context and setting within which visitors can understand and appreciate what they are viewing.

The issue to consider with both labels and wall text is the content of them more than the form (which is fixed). Having said that the format is fixed, the Denver Museum of Art, under the guidance of innovative educator Patterson Williams, developed a system for labels that let visitors choose from a number of information options by pulling out one of a number of options of slide paddles that provide different kinds of information. In retrospect, it was a kind of physical version of electronic random access to information.

Audio Tours

Audio tours have developed tremendously from a technological perspective over the past quarter of a century, and they continue to do so today. The notion of the linear tour of days past has basically been abandoned for the most part in favor of a random access approach that allows visitors to get an audio presentation on whichever work they are walking up to. These "stops" often include the option to listen to additional material that looks at the object (or related issues) in more depth, or perhaps from a different perspective. In an exhibition of the Dead Sea Scrolls at the Boston Museum of Science, there was an audio tour system that allowed for listening to an alternative perspective on the more traditional interpretations of that era of Jewish history. It was absolutely fascinating and provided a different take on the objects in the exhibition (in addition to the scrolls themselves). Some institutions have developed programs that can be accessed by calling a number on your cell phone and then accessing information at stops by entering code numbers.

As the old saying goes, however, "something is gained and something is lost" with the transition from a linear tour to random access. Although the flexibility and freedom for the visitor to see and hear about the objects that they choose are clearly desirable, one loses the structure and potential for a coherent story line that a linear tour offers. Of course, with digital media, there really is no reason to necessarily choose one over another (at least not exclusively). Think back for a second to the Byzantine exhibition that has been discussed in previous chapters. It would be possible there, in addition to information at various stops being provided via random access, to also have a structured tour of the exhibition from a religious perspective, and another from an art historical perspective. Audio tours of permanent exhibitions could be geared to various definable audiences—novices, visitors interested in portraiture, and so forth.

With regard to the Museum Effect, audio tours provide several distinct advantages to visitors. To begin, there is no need to take one's eyes off the object. One can listen to the information being provided and see what is being discussed simultaneously. Thus, one does not have to go back and forth, shift modes, or find where in the picture something is being discussed. Second, as was discovered in the Smith et al. study described earlier in the chapter, listening to the audio stop in and of itself encourages a longer look at the work. And third, with random access, the works one hears about and even what one hears about those works can be tailored to one's own desires.

There is one other potential that is still being developed and realized, and that is "third-party" tours. One can download a podcast of an exhibition or a museum and listen to the opinions of someone not directly related to the museum. Thus a broader set of perspectives can be brought to any given work of art, exhibition, or museum. Time will tell if this becomes popular, but I think there is great potential here.

Video Tours

It may seem incongruous, but there is the potential for video tours to be given in addition to audio tours. I say incongruous because it seems odd (at first, at any rate) to think of a visually based tour of a visually based phenomenon. However, imagine seeing an artist talking about the work that you are viewing, or perhaps even getting to watch it being made. One could show other versions of the same subject matter, or other works by the same artist. The options are vast. It would seem clear that an audiovisual tour would add to the experience of looking at art. But do we really want to draw the visual attention of the visitor away from the work of art? Do we want competition for the thing that is the natural object of attention? And do we want a video screen in competition with oil on wood, or gouache on paper? There is, I would suppose, an inevitability to contend with here, but the idea of a bunch of moving screens, even if just smart phones, in front of a work of art does give one pause.

In-Person Tours

Imagine that we could develop a device that had a stored knowledge set concerning art history, and in particular, the works in a given exhibition or wing of a museum. This device would also have the ability to comprehend human speech and respond to questions appropriately. The device could sense the mood of a group of people, and determine when to linger longer at a work of art, and when to move on. This device would be the tour guide, and fortunately has already been invented. Docent tours are a staple of most museums, and have been effective ways of communicating to visitors probably since not long after the beginning of museums. An experienced and knowledgeable tour guide is a remarkable resource for a museum, able to do many things that simply cannot be matched by any level of technology. But, as was found in the Tinio et al. study mentioned above, and other work, tour guides vary in their abilities, and visitors to museums vary in their receptiveness to participating in live, guided tours. Another limitation is that live tours are fixed in time and place. They are not available on demand and they do have limits in terms of the number of people who can participate.

So there are limits, but the advantages of live tours are many and can be quite profound. A tour guide can adapt to the nature and wishes of the group, and can bring an enthusiasm to viewing works that is difficult to match with technology. But how do tour guides work with regard to their impact on the Museum Effect? Tours, by their very nature, take a group of people on a prescribed visit, and the movement from one object to another, one room to another, has to take into consideration the nature of the group. A tour member who finds a work not to his or her liking is obligated to remain there until the tour proceeds. Hence, the structure becomes greater, but the freedom is reduced. Furthermore, one's attention is often split between the object and the tour guide, or other members of the tour group. It would be interesting to investigate the Museum Effect with respect to guided tours.

Reading Rooms, Catalogs, and Other Materials

Reading rooms are sites within an exhibition or gallery where visitors can stop, sit, and read material about what they are viewing. They are often quite popular within exhibitions. We have always wondered how important the opportunity to sit is with regard to their popularity. That possibility noted, the ability to read more about what one is seeing is a mutually reinforcing activity. The ability to gain knowledge within the structure of the exhibition while maintaining the freedom to move on at will is an optimal situation in many respects. Oftentimes, the exhibition catalog and other related materials are available in such rooms.

A rather ubiquitous feature of most "blockbuster" exhibitions is a small version of the museum shop that one passes through after leaving the exhibition but before returning to the museum proper. These shops are frequently the subject of derisive comments both from museum staff and visitors, but I have always looked upon them in a more kindly light. They exist to generate income for sure, but most museums are in need of such income, and if people do not want to browse in them for a few minutes, it is easy enough to pass through. But they serve another function as well, an important one, I think. One of the assignments that we took on at the Metropolitan was to determine why people didn't buy exhibition catalogs more often. Since more people *don't* buy a catalog than *do* buy a catalog, we turned the question on its ear and asked why people *do* buy catalogs rather than why they don't. That was what we really wanted to know about.

We set about interviewing individuals in museum shops at the end of exhibitions, asking them about the exhibition, and whether they were interested in making a purchase or not. One of the things that we discovered was that most people (a strong majority) will only see a special exhibition once. They frequently are at the museum that day in order to see the exhibition, and sometimes they have traveled some distance to do so. When they arrive at the museum shop, their visit to the exhibition is over. They have completed their viewing of the works. But for those individuals who were particularly taken with the exhibition, they don't want their experience, in which they have some level of investment, to end. They want to "emotionally amortize" their experience. That is, to the degree possible, they want to take it with them. At one level, this isn't possible, as the works will stay in the exhibition, and the people will leave. But they *can* take a set of facsimiles with them, and in addition, the writing of scholars discussing the works that have been so fascinating to them. The museum catalog (or similar works for sale) allows them to take a piece of the exhibition with them. They can peruse the catalog at their leisure at home, and remind themselves of the pleasurable day they spent at the museum and the thoughts that they engaged in there. We think that the ability of a quality catalog to encourage reminiscence of a day at the museum is highly desirable, benefiting both the individual and the museum (and perhaps to a degree, all of us).

Websites

The last vehicle for enhancing the Museum Effect I want to talk about is the museum website. As mentioned in an earlier chapter, the Metropolitan Museum of Art receives roughly five million visitors a year to the museum, and fifty million visitors a year to its website. In working on this book, my daughter asked me if I had seen the Artwork of the Day aspect of the Met's website and so I took a visit. It was truly remarkable! Understand that I spent eighteen years at the Met and became quite familiar with the institution and developed many favorite works of art. The Artwork of the Day section of the site scrolls through works that have been selected for being highlighted daily. One can browse through the selection of works over time. For me, doing so brought back a flood of memories, some having to do with my own reactions to the works, others that had to do with stories and events that bore some relation to the works (the *Little Dancer* by Degas that brought back memories of a study we conducted on a Degas exhibition, or George Caleb Bingham's *Fur Traders on the Mississippi* that took many, many viewings for me to develop a real appreciation for it).

We worked at the Met during its initial development of a website, and have seen the notion of museum websites grow from novelty to necessity. Websites are used to plan visits, to review works after a visit, and for many individuals, to provide the only access to certain works of art that they will ever see. Websites have become the loci for incredible creativity in terms of presentation and explanation of materials. Websites can cater to children, scholars, novices, and experts all at the same time. They allow individuals to take a respite from their daily lives and dwell for a moment or two on a great work of art, putting themselves in the presence of genius. A facsimile of genius to be sure, but our work (Locher, L. F. Smith, & J. K. Smith, 1999; Locher, J. K. Smith, & L. F. Smith, 2001) has suggested that such facsimiles are well accommodated by most individuals, and while no substitute for the real thing, offer an approximation of the real thing that is far better than not being able to view the facsimile.

LOOKING AHEAD

It is difficult to tell where technological advances will lead, but there is no question that the ability to communicate with our audiences on their own terms has grown exponentially over the past quarter century and we have every indication that it will continue to do so. What does that mean for museums? I think it is important that as possibilities expand, we keep in mind what we are about: connecting individuals with objects of importance, of genius, or historical or scientific importance. We make great works available and accessible to our communities and help individuals make sense out of them in their personal lives, their interactions with others, and how they look at the world we live in.

REFERENCES

Locher, P., Smith, J. K., and Smith, L. F. (2001). The influence of presentation format and viewer training in the visual arts on the perception of pictorial and aesthetic qualities of paintings. *Perception, 30*(4), 449–465.

Locher, P., Smith, L. F., and Smith, J. K. (1999). Original paintings versus slide and computer reproductions: A comparison of viewer responses. *Empirical Studies in Arts, 17*, 121–129.

Serrell, B. (1997). Paying attention: The duration and allocation of visitors' time in museum exhibitions. *Curator, 40*(2), 108–125.

Smith, J. K., Waszkielewicz, I., Potts, K., and Smith, B. K. (2004). *Visitors and the audio program: An investigation into the impact of the audio guide program at the Whitney Museum of American Art*. New York: The Whitney Museum of American Art.

Tinio, P. P. L., Smith, J. K., & Potts, K. (2010). The object and the mirror: The nature and dynamics of museum tours. *The International Journal of Creativity and Problem Solving, 20*(1), 37–52.

7

Investigating the Museum Effect and Other Research in Cultural Institutions

A conversation between an art museum researcher and an astrophysicist:

Museum person: "Hey, just how far is it to the moon, anyway?"

Astrophysicist: "When?"

Museum person: "Now!"

Astrophysicist: "Hard to say."

Museum person: "Would it be easier if I asked you tomorrow?"

Astrophysicist: "You think the moon is always the same distance from the Earth, don't you?"

Museum person: "You realize I would have happily taken any answer you gave me?"

Astrophysicist: "Good. In that case my answer is 'When?'"

Questions are funny things. They are like being poked by your little brother when you were a kid. They demand a response. I love questions. Well, other than, "Are we there yet?" I love questions. For much of the past twenty-five years I have tried to find answers to questions that arise in art museums. Much of that work has been at the request of someone in the art museum, typically the Metropolitan Museum of Art, but also a number of other fine institutions along the way. Sometimes the question we studied was a very practical, applied, and straightforwardly specific question in the service of the museum. Sometimes the question was vague and needed to be fleshed out and refined, and sometimes the question needed potential answers before it could be meaningfully investigated. We occasionally got to ask questions that were our very own. They were probably the most fun, but in all honesty, we enjoyed almost all the questions, and liked a lot of the answers as well.

In discussing this book with my good friend David Carr (whose own books on cultural institutions I highly recommend), he offered the opinion that the book might well be useful for students in museum studies programs and individuals in cultural institutions who would want to conduct their own research. To that end, he suggested that I include a chapter on how we conducted the research on the Museum Effect and how that might be extended to conducting other research in cultural settings. I thought about lectures I had given in the past to Deborah Schwarz's classes in museum studies at Columbia, and how such a chapter might help those students. My goal here is not to provide the "be all and end all" guide to conducting research in cultural institutions, but to give an overview of how to think about such work along with practical advice gleaned from having pulled off some pretty good work and having stubbed our toes more than once. I will use conducting research on the Museum Effect as a kind of central theme in the chapter and try to branch out from there to give a broader perspective. There are a wide variety of ways that one might conduct research in cultural institutions, and it is well beyond the scope of this book to discuss them all, or even a good percentage of them. But there are a few approaches that predominate when doing research in museums, and we will look at those here. They include survey research, interview studies, and several different approaches to evaluating exhibitions, projects, and the like in museums. I'll use examples from our research in addition to the Museum Effect research along the way.

The chapter begins by looking at what it means to ask questions in the social sciences in general, but in cultural institutions in particular. It then moves to a brief introduction into the nature of conducting research and evaluations studies, looking at models of such work, and how to choose or create research designs and measures to go along with those designs. Then four studies from our research are presented with regard to their design, analysis, and interpretation, including the main Museum Effect study. In each case, a particular aspect of the research process is explored. Following this, there is a section on how research into the Museum Effect might be extended, including other types of studies, and studies in other types of institutions. Finally, there is a summary section, looking at how research benefits cultural institutions, ethical considerations, and an overall conclusion.

THE NATURE OF ASKING QUESTIONS, IN PARTICULAR, RESEARCH QUESTIONS

In the wonderful movie *Monty Python and the Holy Grail*, the following question is posed of King Arthur: "What is the airspeed velocity of an unladen swallow?" The king replies by asking, "African or European?," which the keeper of the bridge doesn't know, causing him to fall into the gorge. (If none of this makes sense, rent the movie.) This brings up two points. First, it is good to be as precise as one can about the nature of the research question, lest one ends up in a methodological or conceptual (or physical in this case) gorge. Second, the question about unladen swallows cannot be answered by social science research.

Some kinds of questions are amenable to social science approaches; others are not. If I want to know how many gallons of jet fuel are used in a trip from New York to Los Angeles, I'm not going to conduct a survey. As my former statistics professor, Benjamin Wright, once said, "If you want to know the distance to the moon, you do not get one estimate from NASA, a second one from Harry Jackson at the sixth-grade science fair, add them together, and divide by two." So what kinds of questions are "studiable" via social science, and what kinds are not? Working at the Met provided us with a wide variety of questions and issues to deal with—we loved it. We often had to invent unique approaches to studying the questions, and we were often under a fair amount of time pressure. I recommend not trying to execute research under severe time pressure, but it is fun occasionally.

"Studiable" Questions

In order for a question to be amenable to a social science approach, it has to be answerable via some mechanism of looking at people, either just watching them (as in our time spent looking at art study), surveying them (which is what makes up most of museum research), putting them into experimental conditions and seeing how those conditions cause them to behave differently, or approximating those conditions in a quasi-experimental fashion (such as in Smith & Waszkielewicz, 2007). Sometimes, a question can only be partially answered, or can only have some light shed on it via social science methods, but in many instances, that is the most information that can be gathered. Or one might have a question that can only effectively be researched if some possible answers to the question can be proposed and studied. For example, if one wants to know what the most appealing exhibition would be, one could ask people to come up with possible exhibitions, but they are not likely to be very good at it, as it is not what they are expert at. It would be easier to present them with possibilities to evaluate. (And by the way, we wouldn't recommend doing that, either. As Philippe de Montebello, former director of the Metropolitan Museum of Art, put it in an executive meeting, "We do not go to the public to find out what would be a great exhibition. The public comes to us for that. It is our job.")

We were once asked if we could determine whether the banners that hung outside the museum would pay for themselves through increased attendance at special exhibitions. We had to think about that for a bit. Could we, with our social science toolbox, come up with a defendable answer to that question? That was a good challenge, and we took it up. How could that be studied? We started by working backward from an end result. This is often a productive strategy. We started with the notion of how the museum makes money. Well, it makes money through admissions fees and through what people spend while at the museum (food, souvenirs, etc.). It makes money in other ways as well (donations, funding from the City of New York, grants, etc.), but they would only be tangentially related to banners hanging outside the museum at best. Next we asked how a banner could increase the money the museum makes. Well, the obvious answer there is through increased attendance at the exhibition it was promoting. If we could estimate how many *more* people attended an exhibition because of the banner, and how much money they brought to the museum, then we could come up with a total estimate of the benefit of the banner. If we compared that to the costs of the banner (making it, hanging it, etc.), then we would have an answer—a rough one to be sure, but an answer that would help inform the discussion about banners. So this question is what we might call a "studiable" question. That is, one where we could shed some light on the question.

Other questions are not studiable either because the answer does not lie within the general framework of observing human beings, or the desired population is not obtainable. Many museums we have worked with, for example, want to know how to increase attendance, in particular, how could they get people who had never come to the museum to make a first visit? Here the answer lies with the group of people who don't come to the museum. In theory, those people are studiable, but in reality, for any given museum, it would probably be an expensive proposition to find those people. The reason here is that the people who could provide information that might be of assistance are not at the museum. You would have to go elsewhere to find them. We have done work in this area, but it is difficult to do, and the answers are always tentative. We have taken two somewhat different attempts at solving this problem.

In a study we did for the Brooklyn Museum, we went to places where people who might go to museums could be found: other museums, the Brooklyn Botanic Garden, and a high-end bookstore. We asked people there if they had ever been to the Brooklyn Museum, and if they had not, we asked them a series of questions about why they had not, and what might be done to entice them to go. This allowed us to gather information on the reasons people were not going. It was somewhat costly, but the answers were very helpful. In studies we have done for other museums, we asked people entering the museum if they had ever been to that museum before. If they said, "No," then we segmented out "first-time visitors" and asked them what had prompted this visit. We operated off the assumption that until that day, they were people who had never been to that museum, so they were a pretty good proxy for "never have visited, but might visit" type individuals. This is obviously a lot simpler in terms of collecting the data, but might not be quite as good at finding out why people aren't going to the museum, as these people actually were going (although they had not before).

The notion of "studiable" isn't always black and white. Some questions clearly lend themselves to social science approaches and others do not, but there are also a lot of questions where there might be some light shed on the subject (and some light is often better than no light at all), but one has to be very tentative about drawing conclusions. Let's turn now from *whether* we can study a question to *how* we could study it.

MODELS OF THE PROCESSES INVOLVED IN RESEARCH AND EVALUATION

I am a research methodologist by training. I got my PhD in a program at the University of Chicago called "Measurement, Evaluation, and Statistical Analysis." As might be inferred from the title of the program, there was a strong emphasis on quantitative work, but I also received some excellent qualitative training as well. In recent years in social science research, there has developed a bit of a war between the quantitative camp and the qualitative camp with regard to how research should be conducted. And even more recently, there is a tendency toward the use of "mixed methods" that includes both quantitative and qualitative approaches within the same study. I've been doing research for forty years now, and have seen outstanding work that is qualitative as well as quantitative, as well as exceptionally poor work coming from both camps. I'm a steadfast agnostic when it comes to such battles, although I've done more quantitative work than qualitative. I like mixed methods a lot. I cannot tell you how many times a mixed methods approach has led to a much richer understanding of a phenomenon than would have been gained from relying on one approach or the other.

But before wandering off into the intricacies of various approaches, let me provide a general way of looking at what is happening when one engages in research and when one engages in evaluation. I'll start by looking at the difference between those two terms.

The Difference between Research and Evaluation

People often use the terms "research" and "evaluation" interchangeably, but there is an important difference between the two. Research has to do with finding answers to questions that are generalizable across situations and settings, searching for what is true (or useful) in general. We have found, for example, that people who are lifelong visitors to museums often say that their museum visiting is related to family visits when they were young or to visiting during their college years. They tend not to say that it is school group visits that helped develop this pattern. We did that work at the Metropolitan, and have often wondered if it would "generalize" to other museums. Recently, in an international study of museum-visiting practices, there seems to be support for that finding being applicable in other settings. Evaluation, on the other hand, has to do with determining whether a specific program or activity at a specific site is working well (or what can be done to make it work well). Thus, there is no notion here of the finding being necessarily translatable (generalizable) to other situations. Both kinds of activity are worthwhile; it is just that evaluation work tends to only be useful to the institution in which it was conducted, whereas research might be applicable in a number of settings. Having said that, it is important to point out that evaluation work sometimes results in findings that might be used elsewhere. The distinction between research work and evaluation work is often more of a continuum than a bright line. We will look at both research and evaluation work in this chapter.

A General Model of Research

Research begins with the notion that there is something about life that we want to understand better. For those of us who work in museums, this is likely to be a question or a hypothesis about something related to cultural institutions and the individuals who visit them. Such questions might be:

- How does the way we look at art develop?
- What kinds of expectations do people bring with them to museums?
- Do museums make us better people?
- Do labels enhance the visits that people make?
- Do long labels cause traffic jams in special exhibitions?

These are all questions that we've talked about to some extent in the book. For some of these questions, there are pretty good tentative answers that can be found in the research literature on museums. For other questions, and to get better and stronger answers to these questions, more research will be needed. But to begin, we start out with a question that we want to be able to answer. That question isn't quantitative or qualitative in nature, and it does not have to be cast in the form of a hypothesis (sometimes we have a strong enough notion of an issue to form formal hypotheses, sometimes not). It is a question about life, which for us means "life in cultural institutions."

Once we have a question formed, the second step in the research process concerns how we can set up a study that will provide information that will help us answer that question. At some level of analysis, this is the toughest part of the research process. This is also where creativity might come in. There are lots of ways to skin a research question. This part of the research process involves both designing a study and either choosing or developing a way to observe (or measure) the phenomenon of interest. There is a classic text on how to find answers to questions in unusual places (Webb, Campbell, Schwartz, Sechrest, & Grove, 1981). This is the "updated" version of the text, which was originally published in 1966. It is still well worth a read to find creative approaches to getting at the information that you want. So part two of the process is how to observe what we are interested in, in some sort of systematic fashion.

The third part of the process is analyzing the data. How this is done will depend on the nature of the data and the question that has been asked. This is the part that scares a lot of people, and in truth, it can get fairly complicated. But it doesn't have to in most situations. If part two (design and observation) is thoughtfully carried out, the analysis can often be straightforward. Even though complex analyses are great fun (if that is what your training is in), we have always tried to use simple analyses wherever possible, because they are easier for people to understand.

The final part of the process is interpretation. It is amazing how often this is the part where studies fall down (or as our Kiwi friends would say, "Goes pear shaped"). There are often many possible interpretations of a research study. And while I am recommending books by others, *Rival Hypotheses* by Huck and Sandler (1979) is an excellent exploration into the issue of alternative ways of looking at research findings. Interpretation has to do with taking the results of a study and relating them to the original research question. Thus, interpretations are not fundamentally about statistics or qualitative data; they are about the question that one started out with in the first place. Interpreting the results of a study can often be tricky; it is usually a combination of thinking what the underlying causes of the results are, and then combining that with Occam's razor. That is, you want to try to get at root causes while at the same time hewing to the notion that the simplest explanation is often the best one.

One of the first studies we did at the Met had to do with an incredible show of Renaissance art from Siena (where the lady's husband proposed to her). The show was outdrawing all expectations, and the director asked us if we could shed some light on why it was so popular. We interviewed a number of visitors informally to look for initial possible answers, and followed that up with a survey of visitors as they exited the exhibition (thus employing a mix of qualitative and quantitative approaches long before the notion of mixed methods became popular). We started out with little idea of why the exhibition was so popular, so we engaged visitors in one-on-one discussions about what attracted them to the exhibition. This allowed us to hear directly and openly from the visitors, and generated some possibilities. We also talked to a number of the "old hands" at the museum to get other ideas. After this, we developed a questionnaire that we administered to a much larger sample than we could have obtained if we were interviewing everyone. Among the findings, one stood out in particular: 44 percent of the visitors had actually been to the city of Siena. This finding was basically the highlight of the study. It encapsulated the essence of why the show was so popular. Now the question was, how does one interpret that finding? What does it mean?

In talking to individuals about this finding over the years (we've presented it at conferences and symposia), a number of possible interpretations have been put forward, including:

- Shows that feature cities will be successful.
- Shows that tie in to travel are successful.
- People really love the city of Siena.
- New York contains a large number of sophisticated individuals who can be counted on to come out for an excellent exhibition.

OK, I've given the answer away! The point here is that New York City is home to a large number of individuals who can be counted on to come see an excellent exhibition. The fact that almost half of the visitors had been to Siena tells us about New York City as a potential art market in general. NYC is full of people who travel extensively, love the arts, and will come out for a great exhibition.

So we see that there are basically four steps to the research process, which we might present graphically as in Figure 7.1. We begin with a research question, determine a way to collect data on or observe what we are interested in, analyze what we've seen, and interpret the findings in relationship to our original question.

A General Model of Evaluation

Generating a general model of evaluation might be a bit trickier than doing one for research, as there are so many possibilities and so many ideas that might fit under the general rubric of evaluation, but I'll give it a try. As mentioned above, evaluation concerns a specific phenomenon. This might be an exhibition, an educational program, a particular display, an approach to presenting labels, and so forth. Evaluations are conducted on these phenomena when there is a need to know something about them. Thus, in comparison to research starting with a question or hypothesis, evaluation starts with a program, exhibition, or

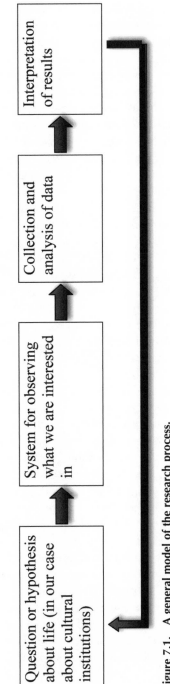

Figure 7.1. A general model of the research process.
Jeffrey Smith

an approach to doing something, and a need to know or understand something about that phenomenon. Usually, that need is to know how well it is working, but for an upcoming exhibition, it could have to do with what people already know or want to learn in the exhibition; it could also be how to improve an existing program. So we begin with an entity/phenomenon that we want to learn something about.

The second step in the process is to determine how we might answer that need. This is basically the same idea generally as the research process. We need a system for observing what we are interested in. But in generating that system, we need to be mindful of who the audience is for the study, and what actions we want to take from interpretation of the results. If we are interested in how an exhibition is working, we might follow some folks through the exhibition (perhaps before a formal opening, or perhaps even with a "mock-up" of the exhibition), watching how they visit and asking them questions about the visit. If we want to see if an audio tour is effective, we might have some visitors use it and others not, and then compare their reactions to what they were viewing (and then ask what they liked or didn't like about the audio tour). With evaluation work, there is often a cyclical approach that is taken. When conducting research, we usually rely fairly heavily on past work in the area to guide what we are doing and how we will go about it. When conducting evaluation, we often design it so that we will go through several processes and iterations of those processes, refining what we are doing from what we have learned from the previous step.

The third part of the process is analyzing the information that we have. This is often a somewhat more informal process than it is for research. The reason here is that the audience is usually the institution itself, not the general scholarly community or other museums. Thus, the checks and balances that one often sees in more formal research (reliability checks, etc.) are sometimes forgone in evaluation work. Now, so as not to anger my professional evaluation friends, this is not to say that doing this work carefully is not important. But if you are doing "in-house" evaluation work, there is only so much time and so many resources available, and you have to allocate them in the most efficacious fashion possible. So if the choice is between doing a reliability check on your analysis of a comment book, or going back into the galleries to collect data on a new question that has come out of the current data set, you are likely to forgo the reliability check. When analyzing data in an evaluation study, there is almost always the potential for going back to the phenomenon and collecting some more information as a result of the analysis. There may even be the possibility of making a change in the phenomenon (altering the exhibition or changing the audio) and then seeing once again how things are working.

The final step in the process is interpreting the results. Again, this is with regard to the original need that prompted the evaluation in the first place. But here again, there is potential for difference. The interpretation may involve a change, reconsideration, or reevaluation of what is going on. So there may be a bit of cycling back to collect more data here. In all honesty, this sort of thing happens to a degree with research, but usually in research studies, there is more of a notion of "the study is done, now we analyze, now we interpret, now we write up findings," whereas in evaluation, there is more potential for tentative answers, gathering a bit more data, tweaking the phenomenon, reconsidering the interpretation, and so on. It is more of an open-ended and potentially ongoing process. Steps two through four can involve multiple loops before bringing the evaluation to a close. I've tried to represent that cyclical nature in Figure 7.2.

Evaluation work can range from studies designed to see what a program (activity, product, etc.) should look like, through the process of testing possible designs, through formative evaluation of programs that are currently in place, to summative (summary) evaluations of overall effectiveness. We will look at a couple of possibilities below, but it should be made clear that the possibilities of what can be evaluated, and how to go about doing so, are manifold.

Choosing and Creating Designs for Research and Evaluation

Once a researcher has a question in mind or an issue to be evaluated, the next thing to do is to choose a design to use, or with thornier problems, invent a way to study the question at hand. A range of approaches already exists and can be found in a number of textbooks on the topic. One such textbook that I might recommend is by Babbie (2013). It is a general research methods text that is clearly written and at an appropriate level for someone without any background, but with a strong interest in learning.

For many research questions, one merely has to adopt a fairly standard approach and get going. However, it is always a good idea to spend a bit of time making sure that the approach you are choosing, or inventing, is going to do what you want it to do. Even with forty years of experience in designing studies, I still occasionally come up with a design that causes me to smack myself in the forehead upon reflection. In the absence of any particular need for complexity, simplicity is a virtue. With simple designs, you know what you're about. Furthermore, simple designs are easier to communicate to broad audiences. Most work in cultural institutions can be accomplished via audience surveys, interview studies, unobtrusive observation, the use of existing data, and an occasional creative approach. We will look at examples of each of these shortly.

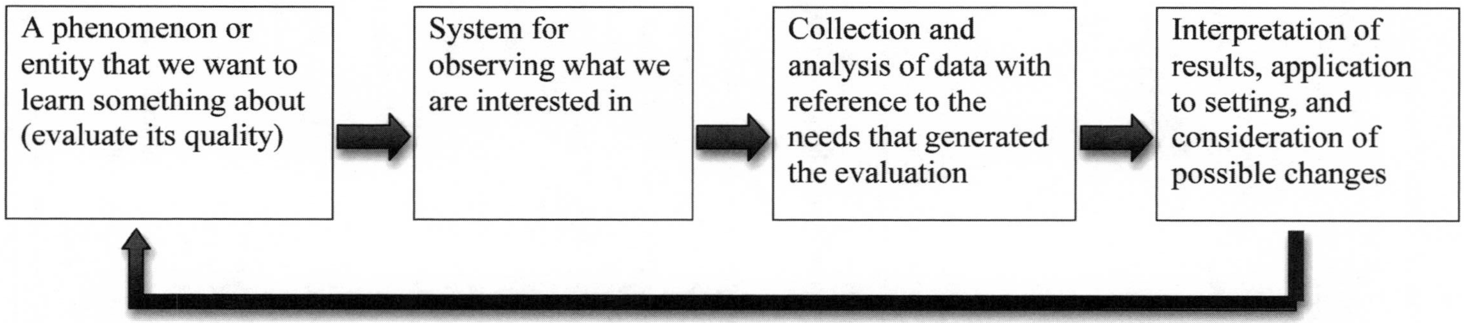

Figure 7.2. A general model of the evaluation process.
Jeffrey Smith

Choosing and Creating Observations and Measures

The design of a study concerns the logic of the study, how the data will be collected, and the rationale for making the argument that one wants to make once the study is over. A related issue has to do with how to observe or measure what it is you are interested in. Let me provide two examples. In evaluating special exhibitions, museums often want to know whether people visiting an exhibition understand who the sponsor of the exhibition is. It is important to be able to let the sponsor know that people recognize and appreciate their sponsorship. Now that seems fairly straightforward, but how would you go about actually finding that out? Well, you could survey people exiting the exhibition and ask,

Who is the sponsor for this exhibition?

and leave a blank space for the respondent to fill in an answer. Now, there might be a number of people who noticed who the sponsor was, but couldn't come up with the name while filling out the survey. In other words, they'd get it right on a multiple-choice item, but could not come up with the answer themselves. You could instead pose the question as follows:

Which of the following is the sponsor for this exhibition?

  a. Hartford and Company
  b. Minnow and Sons
  c. Mayberry Corporation
  d. Portman Limited

Or you might pose it this way:

Did you notice that the sponsor for this exhibition is the Mayberry Corporation?
_____ *Yes* _____ *No*

Or this way:

The sponsor for this exhibition is Mayberry Corporation. Did their sponsorship enhance your opinion of Mayberry Corporation?
_____ *Yes* _____ *No*

Which of these options is the correct way to approach this? Well, harkening back to the beginning of the chapter, my response would be: "When?" That is, you might use any one of them given the circumstances. We have used all but the multiple-choice option in our work (simply because it looks too much like a test question).

Sometimes you will want a response that is a scale; that is, it has more than just two (yes/no, right/wrong) possibilities. You might want to know, for example, how much art expertise a person has. First, you would have to differentiate between art productivity (e.g., studio) expertise versus knowledge about art (e.g., art history). Then you have to figure out how to construct a scale. There are a variety of ways to do this, ranging from fairly simple to mind-numbingly complex. A simple approach would be to simply ask:

On a scale of 1 to 10, where 1 = no knowledge at all and 10 = a true expert, how would you rate your knowledge of art? _____

We have actually used this question for years and found it to work quite well. It correlates nicely with more elaborate measures, and is predictive of frequency of art museum visitation and amount of art-related training. There is a lot of work that has been done in this area, and we have always found that most museum people are most willing to share their work, so ask around if venturing forth on your own seems a bit scary.

EXAMPLES AND EXTENSIONS

Armed with a general understanding of the fundamentals of the research process, in this section we will look at five examples of conducting research in cultural institutions. Each of these examples has been chosen with a purpose of illustrating a particular issue or approach that can be used in other settings. Thus, I'll present the exemplar, and then an extension of that to a more general case. We begin with the focus of this book, the Museum Effect. What I would like to emphasize in this first example is how a question goes from being an idea to being a study. The example will be about the Museum Effect, but the message here is how to think critically about what you are doing before you start doing it!

Example 1: Getting Started on the Museum Effect and Other Research Studies

The primary impetus for conducting a direct test of the Museum Effect grew out of conversations that Izabella Waszkielewicz and I had concerning her dissertation topic. She wanted to do research in art museums and wanted to explore that good feeling one often has when leaving a museum—a feeling that you are a better person, can do better things, are invigorated to do something important with your life. I think it is a notion that most of us can reso-nate with, and it was something that my wife, Lisa, and I had talked about as well, but had relegated to the status of "things we really ought to get around to doing." With Izabella wanting to work on this as her dissertation project, it got moved to the front of the line, and it was great that it did.

Before embarking on such a research endeavor, one really needs to think seriously about whether this is a question worth taking the effort to answer. Do we really want to study this question (at all) and how important is getting an answer to it (as opposed to answering a different question)? In life, there are only so many things we can do, so if we do A, we won't be doing B (or at best, we'll have to put B off for a bit). We need to think seriously about a kind of cost/benefit analysis on any research activity. How good a question is this? How likely is it to produce results that will be useful and interesting? How hard will the research be to execute well? These were aspects that we had to take into consideration in regard to whether we should look into the Museum Effect. The underlying question for the Museum Effect study was, "Does visiting a museum make you think better thoughts/encourage you to be a better person?" Now, if the results of the study indicate that the answer were "Yes," then this would truly be a worthwhile endeavor. If the answer were "No," then nobody will be particularly interested in this. Thus, the Museum Effect question in essence was a kind of "Does this work?" question. It is similar to "Is this a better way to teach algebra?" "Will this medication cure this disease?" "Can I make people be invisible?" In each case, if the answer is no, then you don't really have much that people will be interested in. So you have to ask what the likelihood of success is, and how important it would be if you were successful. And those can be tough calculations.

But Izabella brought renewed enthusiasm to the issue, so we set out to see if we could document that such a phenomenon existed. We had a rough ver-sion of what we wanted to study: *Does a visit to an art museum make people think better thoughts?* Now, where to start and how to proceed? When we look at working on a research question, we like to start by refining the ques-tion and thinking hard about a path to a successful study. We usually like to look at four related questions:

1. What do we already know about this?
2. Can we refine the question given what we now know?
3. Where is the answer likely to be found?
4. What would it look like if everything went perfectly in this study?

Each one of those questions can spur subsidiary questions and issues, and it is usually worth exploring those secondary questions as well, at least for a while. If you ponder them for too long, you will never do the study, but it is almost always useful to think carefully about them before getting too far down the road on a study. You don't want to complete a study, look at the data, and say, "I can't believe we didn't think of that before we did the study!" So let's look at those questions a bit with regard to looking at the Museum Effect.

What Do We Already Know about This Question?

It is generally true that there is nothing new under the sun. But it is also true that anything we know, we can know better. And some things *are* new. So we begin thinking about a question by asking what we already know. Sometimes this just requires sitting down and thinking about the question—listing out what you know. For the Museum Effect, we considered the question, Do people feel better about themselves as people as they leave a museum? Well, it seemed to us that we had experienced that on a personal level, so that was a start. Could we gather up some folks (friends and relatives are OK right at the beginning) and simply ask them? Has there been any research done on this already? Could we google it? Google Scholar is not a bad place to start, and now our university library system has a "Google Scholar–like" system that not only lets you see what is out there, you can access almost all of it for free (well, free to us). When we were working on the main Museum Effect research, we started by looking at what we already knew about people and their museum visits. That research has all been pretty much presented already, but let's review it. We knew the following:

- A wide variety of people come to museums and they varied pretty widely in their characteristics.
- If we talked to them or looked at what they wrote in comment books we found that they really loved their visit, with people using phrases such as: "wonderful," "incredible beauty and depth," "a life-altering experience," "an outstanding and moving visit," etc.
- Although they typically came to the museum in groups, they tended to look at art alone.
- They had difficulty singling out a particular work of art, but often said that it was the exhibition or the visit as a whole that was really what stood out.
- Although they thought they looked at particular works for a long period of time, they rarely looked for more than a minute.
- They looked at many works during a visit.
- We felt that the Museum Effect happened to us in museums, and it resonated with the friends and colleagues we asked about this—not all, to be sure, but most.

- There had been work in areas unrelated to visiting museums that described emotional responses to situations that we thought would generalize to this situation.

This was not a bad start to our efforts to see if this were a question that held potential for being worth an investigation. That is, it seemed that the Museum Effect did happen to folks, and we knew a fair amount about ancillary findings that might help us build a model of how the Museum Effect worked.

Can We Refine the Question Given What We Now Know?

People told us informally that they thought the Museum Effect was real, and we had evidence from comment books at the end of exhibitions that reinforced that notion. But what did we really mean by "people thinking better thoughts/feeling better about themselves"? How could we turn that into something more concrete—how could we "operationalize" that? There are several parts to that contention. Clearly we would need some sort of indication of the kind of thinking people were doing. We needed to capture that somehow. We would also need to have a method of quantifying improvement in those thoughts as a result of the museum visit. These were issues that would have to be resolved before moving forward.

Refining the question is a highly valuable activity in research. It forces you to think hard about just what it is you are trying to find out. And it is an excellent exercise to discuss your thoughts with someone else. It helps to clarify your thinking on the project, and can often generate new and useful insights into what should be studied. For the Museum Effect, in discussing just what we meant, we came to the understanding that we thought that people would think about their lives and where they were going, what their hopes and dreams were, how they related to others, and whether they made a difference in the world. This was still pretty much a "pie in the sky" set of expectations, but now it was beginning to get a bit more refined. Armed with what we already knew, and a somewhat better notion of what we wanted to find out, we move to where that answer is likely to be.

Where Is the Answer Likely to Be Found?

This is a very interesting question, and one that benefits from some serious thinking and often from some creativity. I recently heard on the radio of a fascinating study where researchers were trying to discover patterns of the frequency of different species of fish in various coastal areas over past decades. I tuned in too late to learn why the researchers were interested in this question, but I like to think of myself as a scholar at heart and as such, I give other researchers wide latitude in what they want to study. Besides, it's almost always the method of study I find most interesting. So, the question for these people was how could they find out what species of fish were most prevalent in various areas in the past. Now think about this for a second. You want to know which types of fish populated the waters around, say, San Diego, in the 1940s. How do you find out? Well, you could try to find some really old fishermen; that is perhaps the first thing that comes to mind (or really old fish, but often they don't like to take surveys). You might hope to find someone who has done research of this nature. You could look for newspaper articles from the era to see if fishing records were kept or if stories referred to what kinds of fish fishermen caught. Or you could do what these researchers did.

You want to know, how did they go about their study? It's *the magic of questions* that I discussed at the beginning of the chapter. Think about it. You actually want to know how some researchers found out what kinds of fish there were in the waters of various areas in the past. OK, now for the answer: *old restaurant menus*. They got old menus from restaurants in the area. The fish that appeared on the menus were what was being caught in the waters around the area at that time and that is what ended up on the menu. Look at the menus; find out what fish were in the area. I love it. But how do we know we can rely on that? Well, by seeing if it still works today when we have independent means of keeping track of how many different kinds of fish are in the sea. (And it does work.)

So where were we likely to find an answer about the Museum Effect? Well, the first place that comes to mind is in museums. That seems pretty obvious, and we'll return to that in a second. But first, let's wonder if there are any other places where we could find the answer to this question. We could conduct a survey of people in general, and ask them questions about how often they visit art museums and how much they think about the notion of purpose and doing good in their lives, and then see if the two correlate. That would be evidence of a sort, but one could argue that it simply shows that good people also tend to visit art museums. We could see if people who work in art museums seem to lead better lives than people who do other kinds of work, but again, the issue of causality arises.

It seems to be the case that looking at people in art museums is probably the strongest approach here, and indeed, that is what we did. And if a visit enhances how people think about themselves and their lives, then surveying at several different points in a museum visit seems logical as well. Whether to try to get one group of people and have them take a survey several times during their visit, or get different groups of people at different times in their visits is another methodological issue that needs to be resolved. In this case, we were concerned that if we kept asking people the same kinds of questions, they would get clued into what we were after, and would probably eventually get annoyed as well, so we opted for different groups of people.

What Would It Look Like if Everything Went Perfectly in This Study?

The final question we ask is, "What would it look like if it all went perfectly?" This is kind of the preliminary question to the rather harsh question of "So what?" If you get the answers you are looking for, do they really mean anything important? The idea here is that if you cannot answer the "So what?" question if everything goes perfectly, maybe this isn't such a good question to be asking in the first place. In this case, the answer to both of these questions was, "We would have solid evidence that art museums, and perhaps cultural institutions more generally, have very positive effects on the lives of those who come to visit." That, in my mind, is a very strong response to the "So what?" question. It affirms one of the primary purposes of having such institutions: they make us better people.

These questions are always good to ask of research. They help us determine if this is something we really want to study, and get us down the track of how to do so. We move now from looking at how the Museum Effect research got started to looking at survey research in museums.

Example 2: A General Audience Survey and How to Conduct Surveys

Quantitative research essentially involves turning observations into quantities, and conducting statistical analyses on the resulting numbers. This may seem a bit daunting to the novice, but as long as it is kept fairly simple, they are not difficult to conduct or understand. Let me provide an example for the skeptical reader. Below are selected highlights from a study we did on an exhibition of work by El Greco held at the Metropolitan Museum of Art in 2003 (Smith, 2004). They are taken from a press release after the exhibition had closed.

> During October and November 2003, a sample of 1076 visitors to the Museum completed a questionnaire concerning demographic information, visiting behaviors, and economic impact issues in relationship to the El Greco exhibition. Surveying was spaced over the days of the week and times of day to be representative of the visiting population to the Museum. . . .
>
> - A total of 574,000 visits to the exhibition were made to the El Greco exhibition during its run from October 7, 2003, to January 11, 2004.
> - Almost three-quarters (74%) of the visitors came to the exhibition from outside the City of New York. Roughly 17% were international visitors, including 24 countries represented in the sample of visitors completing the questionnaire. . . .

- Visitors to the exhibition participated in other New York City tourist and cultural activities during their visit to the City. Fifty-three percent (53%) said they were going shopping; 48% were going to dine out; 36% were going to Broadway; 34% were going sightseeing; 23% were going to Rockefeller Center; 21% were going to the Guggenheim; 18% were going to the American Museum of Natural History; 18% were going to the Museum of Modern Art; 18% were going to Lincoln Center; 16% were going to the Empire State Building; and 15% were going to the Metropolitan Opera. . . .
- The majority of the visitors (76%) self-identified as Caucasian, with 4% indicating their ethnicity as Hispanic, 2% African American, 1% Asian American, and the remainder either international visitors or checking "Other" for ethnicity. As is always the case with special exhibitions at the Met, the audience for El Greco was highly educated, with 51% of the visitors indicating that they held a masters degree or higher, and another 28% saying that they held a bachelors degree. Roughly one in five (21%) visitors was a Member of the Museum. . . .
- Visitors were asked what influenced their decision to make a visit to the Museum. The responses to this question were as follows:

I visit the Met on a regular basis.	32%
I am visiting from out of town and the Met is a "must see."	31%
I saw or heard an advertisement for the Met.	18%
I hadn't been to the Met in a while and decided to visit.	18%
I am bringing or meeting friends or relatives.	17%
I read a review about the Met.	14%
I saw the banners on the façade and they attracted me.	4%
I saw the street banners on light poles and they attracted me.	1%
I saw the kiosks outside the Museum and they attracted me.	1%

As I think you can see, even this short set of selected results presents a picture of what the exhibition was like in terms of who came to it, why, and what else they did while they were in New York City for their visit. It was part of a broader study looking at the economic impact of the exhibition on the city. *Note that there is nothing more complicated than a percentage that is used as a statistical tool here.* To be certain, this was a serious undertaking, and a lot of work hours went into it, but the statistical analysis presented here was simply not that complicated. We did some other work here on the economic impact of the exhibition that was more complex, but the information provided here was rich, informative, and could be compiled with relative ease.

Let's extend this example to the case of surveys in general. What are they and how are they constructed and used? Probably the most common type of quantitative study conducted in cultural institutions is a simple survey of visitors. Surveys are conducted on samples of individuals who come to the museum. A survey study basically consists of determining whom one wants to collect information on, generating the survey instrument, collecting the data, analyzing the data, interpreting the results, and presenting the findings. There are several critical points in survey studies. The first issue has to do with defining whom you want to survey. For example, as mentioned earlier, it's hard to find out why people don't come to the museum by surveying people who do come. Usually you want to survey your audience in general, but you may also want to survey special groups: family visitors, weekend visitors, first-time visitors, visitors to a particular exhibition, out-of-town visitors, and the list goes on. It is not hard to figure out how to segment out these groups, and frequently you will want to just collect a large sample of general visitors to the museum, and then segment out particular populations of interest. When we did work on first-time visitors to the museum, we first got an idea of what percentage of all visitors that might be, and then calculated how many visitors overall we would need to ensure a good sample of first-time visitors.

Related to this is the second issue—actually collecting the data. If you have ever been a survey taker in any kind of setting, you know that some people are more receptive to being surveyed than others. Some people seem nicer than others. Some people look like they'd like to sit at a table for a few minutes and take a survey, and others do not. Some look like maybe they do not speak English (or whatever language the survey is written in). But you cannot approach just people who look like they would be amenable to taking the survey. You have to give everyone an equal chance of being in the study, and this requires going up to folks who seem like they are going to be less receptive to your approach. Frequently, surveys will be left out somewhere (on a reception table or the like) for people to fill out if they find them and care to. This is *not* the way to seriously collect data. You have to make a sincere attempt to get a sample that is representative of the population you want to talk about (a "population" is the group of people you want to be able to talk about or generalize to; a "sample" is the group of people who actually participate in your study). You take (draw) a sample from your population.

When we do work with a museum, we usually find an area of good traffic flow where people can find a place to sit for a minute or two and fill out the questionnaire. Then we have a table and some chairs set up there. We instruct the survey takers to count off three people and go up to the next one, whoever it is. (If traffic is slow, we tell them to just go up to the next person. The key is not the number, but to have a system that requires going up to people even if they don't look like they will want to participate.) Once there is a spot available again at the table, the survey taker repeats the process. The acceptance rate should be recorded and included in the research report. People in museums are usually pretty nice about completing a questionnaire. If you really want to maximize participation, put some sort of inexpensive giveaway on the survey table in plain sight so that people will see they are getting a small thank-you for participating. It's amazing how small this can be: a postcard, a pencil, an overrun on some poster you were selling at the last special exhibition. And you also need individuals gathering the participants who are effective at doing so. Usually a very positive person with a lot of energy works best.

The third critical issue is writing the survey. There are books and books on this topic. I cannot go into great detail here, but I can give you a general idea about how to go about this, and some helpful hints that we have picked up along the way. For a more thorough discussion of surveys, sampling, statistical analysis, and the like, Babbie (2013) is probably as good a text as you are likely to find. There are books specifically on survey work, so if you are very serious about investigating this, it would be useful to get a more detailed explication. We find that the best way to write a survey is to work backward from the end point. What do you want to be able to say when you are done? Sometimes, all you want is to know a bit more about your audience. How old are they? More women than men? How big are the group sizes? Do families visit a lot? How do they make decisions about what to do with their leisure time? How do they find out about leisure time activities? What do they read/look at where you can put announcements or advertisements? But you might also be interested in what kinds of art they like most (or what kinds of books they

---

HANDY HINTS ON SURVEYS

- People can tell you better what they have done rather than what they will do.
- People do not like to write. They like to tick boxes.
- People would rather complete something themselves than have you ask them about it. (Unless you want depth, then you have to get them to talk.)
- People will only give you about 30 percent of their attention when completing a survey.
- People don't go to museums to fill out surveys, but most will give you a few minutes. Respect their time.
- Stay away from "internal use only" and little numerals under the choices. Your audience here is the people who are filling out the form, not the people who are going to enter the data. They work for you (or they are you). Make the form user friendly for the person taking it.
- Some people are much better at getting people to fill out questionnaires than others. Pick your survey administrators wisely.
- People don't like to read a whole lot. Brevity is key. Get at what you want and be done. I am reminded of a great line from the movie Zorro and Son, where the elder Zorro tells the younger Zorro, "Get in, make your Z, and get out."

read, what they know about science or natural history, etc.). Again, it can be very helpful to look around and ask around for surveys from other institutions. And when you use the same questions that someone else has, you can always compare your results to theirs. Make sure you have permission before using someone else's survey items! If you are going to build your own survey, the textbox contains a few handy hints that we have compiled through our work.

The Museum Effect research was fundamentally survey research, but with a bit of an elaboration. We took three samples of participants because we felt that if the Museum Effect were occurring, people would give us different responses at different points in their visit. Thus we drew three samples: one from those entering the museum, one from those in midvisit, and one from those who had finished their visit. This required carefully selecting where we would set up our survey stations. We didn't want to survey the same people three times. One of our touchstones in conducting research is that people do not come to museums to be participants in studies or to take tests. You don't want to overburden your respondents. We decided we would collect the entrance, midvisit, and exit surveys on different days. That way we could be certain not to be asking the same person to fill out a survey twice. The days we surveyed had to be similar days (say all Tuesdays), as we know that the weekend population for museums differs from the weekday visitors (weekenders tend to be more family groups; weekday visitors tend to be older—retired in many cases—or on vacation). If we had collected the entrance people on a Saturday and the midvisit people on a Thursday, the differences we saw might have been attributable to different kinds of audiences to the museums. Usually, the people you want to survey are a simple sample of your attendees. But, for particular reasons, you may want to only survey people from out of town, or first-time visitors, members of the museum, or people attending a given exhibition. It depends on whom you want to be able to talk about once the study has been completed.

What might a survey look like? Well, Figure 7.3 presents the survey that was used in Izabella Waszkielewicz's dissertation research. It also serves as a good model in general for conducting survey research. The first page (actually the front of a two-sided page) asks a set of questions that we used often for museum research. The second page contains the questions for her dissertation research. The "commentary" boxes were not part of the questionnaire, but have been added as commentary on the development of questionnaires. We frequently employed a "front and back" model for our surveys as it let us collect a lot of information while presenting visitors with only a single page of work. We also tended to use the same questions, and wording of the questions, so that we could compare results from one time to another, and from one institution to another. I would recommend looking for a common set of

James A. Michener Art Museum

General Visitor Survey

1. What is your home zip code or nation of residence? _____

2. Are you a Member of The James A. Michener Art Museum? ❑ Yes ❑ No

3. How many times have you visited the James A. Michener Art Museum in the past 12 months?
    ❑ First visit ever ❑ First visit in years ❑ 1 time ❑ 2-3 times ❑ 4-10 times ❑ 11 times or more

4. Who are you here with today? (Check all that apply.)
    ❑ Alone ❑ Spouse/Partner ❑ Family ❑ Organized group
    ❑ Friends ❑ Visitors from out of town ❑ Children under 12 (How many? _____)
    ❑ Accessibility Companion or Interpreter?

5. Have you ever visited michener.org? ❑ Yes ❑ No

6. What most influenced your decision to make this visit today? (Please check just one choice.)
    ❑ I saw an article about the Michener in a paper or magazine.
    ❑ I wanted to see an exhibition.
    ❑ I am bringing friends or relatives.
    ❑ Friends or relatives were talking about visiting the Michener.
    ❑ I saw or heard an advertisement for the Michener (Where?_____)
    ❑ A friend or relative asked me to visit with them.
    ❑ I saw an article about art in general and it made me think of the Michener.
    ❑ I am visiting from out of town and the Michener Art Museum is a "must see."

7. Please check all of the statements that apply to you:
    ❑ I took or plan to take the audio guide.
    ❑ I usually read the labels that accompany any painting I look at seriously.
    ❑ I usually talk with others about the art while in the Museum.
    ❑ I often become completely engaged in looking at a work of art.
    ❑ Sometimes I reflect on a work of art days or weeks after my visit.

8. Please answer the following demographic questions.

Age	Education	Occupation	Ethnicity	Income	Sex
__Under 18	__High School	__Exec./Mgr.	__Int'l Visitor	__Under 20,000	__Male
__18-24	__Some College	__Office	__African American	__$20,000-34,999	__Female
__25-34	__BA/BS	__Professional	__Latino, Hispanic	__$35,000-49,999	
__35-44	__MA/MFA/MB	__Teacher	__Asian American	__$50,000-64,999	
__45-54	__JD	__Trades	__American Indian	__$65,000-79,999	
__55-64	__MD	__Arts Professional	__Caucasian	__$80,000-99,999	
__65 and over	__PH.D.	__Sales	__Other	__$100,000-299,999	
		__Homemaker		__$300,000 or more	
		__Student			
		__Retired			
		__Other			

Commentary: *This first page takes about three minutes to complete. It gets at simple visiting behaviors and reasons for visiting. Note that it is almost all "tick box" in approach. That makes it easy for people to complete. Note also it doesn't have any of that "this space is for internal use only" nor does it have little number values under the choices. Look at question 8 for a second. The income ranges were developed so that there isn't "bunching" in some of the categories. That is, you want to choose categories so that the results are spaced out well.*

Figure 7.3a.   Survey Used in Waszkielewicz Dissertation.
Jeffrey Smith

Disclaimer: Thank you for completing the survey. Now I would like to ask you to complete one more brief set of questions. This is not part of the Michener survey, but is being done as part of my (my colleague's) dissertation research. It will take about 2-3 minutes to complete.

Directions: Below is a list of statements. Please read each of the following and rate yourself with respect to **how well you do each of these as compared to most people**. Use a scale of 1-10 where:

Not as good   About the same   Much better
1---------- 2----------3----------4----------5----------6----------7----------8----------9----------10

_____ 1. Think about the future
_____ 2. Think critically
_____ 3. Contemplate important issues in my life
_____ 4. Contemplate the purpose and direction of my life
_____ 5. Moral and ethical judgment
_____ 6. Feel inspired to better my life
_____ 7. Have a sense of mission or calling
_____ 8. Strive toward personal growth
_____ 9. I am a good listener
_____ 10. Able to take action
_____ 11. Think about others before myself
_____ 12. Consider positions and views other than my own
_____ 13. Consider myself a good friend
_____ 14. Relate well to others
_____ 15. Tolerant of people who are different from me
_____ 16. Respect the views of others
_____ 17. Able to work with others
_____ 18. Able to compromise
_____ 19. Consider important societal issues and concerns
_____ 20. Contemplate ways to make a difference in society
_____ 21. Believe that people are inherently good
_____ 22. Contribute to the well being of others
_____ 23. Motivated to make this world a better place
_____ 24. Participate in community affairs
_____ 25. Attentive to social issues
_____ 26. Motivated to donate my time to a good cause

2.   Where are you in terms of your visit   ❐ Beginning   ❐ Middle   ❐ End

3.   How would you rate your knowledge of art on a scale of 1-10 with 1 being a complete novice, and 10 being a true expert? _____

4.   How much training do you have in art history? ___None ___Some study on my own
___A course or two in college ___BA in art or art history ___MA/MFA/PhD art or art history

Commentary: This part of the questionnaire gets at the specific issues in the Museum Effect research. Here a kind of "Likert-type" scale is being used to get at issues of how people look at their lives (items 1-8), their relationships with others (items 9-18), and their views of working to improve society and the world (items 20-26). Again, this page takes about 3 minutes to complete (maybe a bit more for people who think hard about the questions).

Figure 7.3b.   Survey Used in Waszkielewicz Dissertation.
Jeffrey Smith

demographic questions to ask, for example. Perhaps borrow from the U.S. Census survey (or from the questions listed in Figure 7.3a and 7.3b).

One of the critical issues that comes up in research, particularly survey work, is how many people you need to survey in order for the results to be reliable. There is no one answer to this, but I'll try to lay out the issues involved. To begin, sample size is only one aspect of a good sample for a study. *How* the sample was selected is equally important. It was mentioned earlier that it is not wise to leave a bunch of questionnaires on a table for people to fill out as they will. You will get a sample of people with maybe not a whole lot else to do, or who wanted to sit for a bit, or who are exceptionally nice and wanted to help you out, or who had an ax to grind. That is not desirable. You need an approach that will draw a sample that is representative of the people you want to know about.

Assuming you have a good system for approaching people, and that people are generally receptive to your request to participate, the question remains: How many is enough? I'd like to be able to say, "One hundred," or "Forty," or any particular number, and let it go at that. The simple answer is "Enough to obtain a level of reliability that you are comfortable with in regard to the decisions you have to make." If you are comfortable with making statements on the order of, "The percentage of out-of-town visitors is 38 percent give or take 5 percent," you would need about five hundred people in your sample. If you were willing to make that "give or take 10 percent" in either direction, you could drop the necessary sample size to about a hundred. These are very rough estimates, and they change as the percentage approaches 0 percent or 100 percent, so best to get a bit of help on this. And by the way, the sample size is not very closely related to how big the population is. That is, a sample of a hundred works equally well for a population of a hundred thousand or one million. For most survey work that we do with museums, we try to get at the very least two to three hundred, and are much more comfortable with samples of about five hundred or more. Having said that, and before leaving this topic, if what you are measuring on people has a quantitative scale to it (say, number of times they go to museums in a year, how long they look at a work of art, or their response to a scale that you have devised), then you can get strong answers with smaller sample sizes. The logic here is that you are gaining more information per person (you know where they are on a scale as opposed to a simple "yes" or "no,") and, therefore, you can draw conclusions with smaller samples. There is a formula for estimating sample size if you know how precise you want your estimate to be and you have a rough idea of what percentages you might find. It is a bit too technical to present here, but it can be found in most research texts.

We leave questionnaire work for now and turn to a different but also very commonly used approach to conducting research in museums: the interview study.

Example 3: Constructing Meaning "In Byzantium"

In 1997, David Carr and I teamed up to do a study of how people understood the exhibition of Byzantine art, *The Glory of Byzantium* (Smith & Carr, 2001). We were asked by the deputy director of education at the time, Kent Lydecker, to conduct a study that got at what people were thinking about and how they came to understand an exhibition, in particular one in which many (if not most) visitors would not have a strong background in the subject area. We were delighted to be asked, and were greatly helped in our endeavors through the wonderful contributions of curator Helen Evans. We decided early on that we would have this be an interview study, as we wanted to hear what people had to say about their visit, and did not want to "put words in their mouths."

Interview studies are in some ways very similar to survey studies, but in other ways, very different. In a survey study, you basically start out with a good idea of what you want to know; the question is more oriented to the magnitude of a phenomenon rather than the nature of its existence. You know that you have older people and younger coming to the museum, but in roughly what proportions? You know that people come to see the art, converse with friends, be inspired, and learn more about art, but how big are each of those audiences? How many people travel some distance to get to your institution? Would they like a wider variety of choices in the café? One can, of course, put open-ended questions into a survey, but you would be amazed at how many blank answers or one- or two-word answers such open-ended items produce.

On the other hand, sometimes you want to know what your audience is thinking about things. What are their opinions? What are their preferences if the choices are wide open? Interviews allow for in-depth exploration of the thoughts, opinions, emotions, and behaviors of visitors. They are not as good for getting accurate measures of the magnitude of various issues because it is harder to get sufficient sample sizes to have really accurate estimates. Additionally, whereas in a survey or questionnaire (the two terms are used fairly interchangeably), there is the issue of people basically being limited to the choices you have determined a priori. In an interview, you can explore options and possibilities that the participants come up with. And on the other hand, the ability to get people to talk about those issues and the ability to make sense out of what they have said are very much dependent on the quality of the interviewer and the person who is analyzing the data.

We felt that *The Glory of Byzantium* represented an excellent opportunity to see what happened when visitors were taken out of their comfort zone. We were fairly confident that not many visitors would know much about Byzantine art. In fact, to make sure, several months before the exhibition was to open, we added to our general monthly survey the following question: "On a scale of 1 to 10 where 1 represents no knowledge at all and 10 represents being a true expert, how much do you know about the art of the Byzantine Empire?" Over 90 percent of the respondents gave an answer of 1 or 2, so we were confident that our suspicions were confirmed. We were wrong, of course, but we were confident nonetheless. We'll revisit that mistake a bit later on. In meetings with museum staff, we developed the following underlying question for our work: "How do people go about making meaning when the works they are viewing are not familiar to them?"

In interview research, it is often the case that the primary researcher is also the primary interviewer, and frequently the only interviewer. This has strengths and weaknesses, but that is a topic that is beyond what we can do justice to here. In this instance, we had available to us six individuals with experience in conducting and interpreting interview data, ranging from David, a veteran qualitative researcher in museum settings, to the excellent head of our research volunteer group, Nancy Posternak, who had substantial experience as a market researcher. We came up with the idea of developing a rough common core of initial questions for the interviews and then having each of us tailor and expand that list as we individually thought best. Thus, we were conducting six small studies in parallel. Each of us interviewed a set of individuals exiting the exhibition, and each of us independently wrote up a set of observations and tentative conclusions, and then we came together to combine, compare, and contrast our efforts. We found an amazing amount of similarity in our findings, much of which were fundamentally not what we were expecting when we went into the study.

The full results and more detail on the study can be found in Smith and Carr (2001), but let me present just a few highlights here. First, as mentioned, we were dead wrong in our earlier conclusion that people would not know about the works. Some did not, for sure, but many more did. The logic here is simple. If you survey general visitors to the museum, most in fact will honestly report that they do not know much about Byzantine art. Fair enough. But if you hold a spectacular exhibition of Byzantine art, those who know and love it will come out in droves. Thus, your audience for the exhibition will not be populated primarily by naïfs, but mostly by people with a strong interest in the subject.

We found that there were basically three to five groups of visitors, broadly defined. We might start with the people we expected to find: people who did not know about Byzantine art. Those visitors could further be split into two subgroups. One subgroup consisted of people who knew basically nothing about Byzantine art as they walked into the exhibition. The second consisted of people who did not know about Byzantine art, but who had taken the time to read an article or book about Byzantine art before coming to the exhibition, or who had purchased the audio tour that accompanied the exhibition. Thus, one group had no basis for understanding the works, while the other had a rudimentary basis, or support mechanism.

The second major group had a religious or cultural affiliation or link with the Byzantine Empire, and/or the Orthodox Christian Church. These visitors were coming to an exhibition of religious works that held special meaning to them. Some works on display had never been seen by women prior to their display, as they came from areas where women were not allowed entry. The Episcopalian priest mentioned in chapter 2 was one such visitor.

The third major group had an artistic or art historical link to the exhibition. And here we broke the group down into two subgroups: people with a studio art background and people with an art historical background. Their approach to the works was different, although there were some commonalities here. It was interesting to listen to the studio people talk about the mosaics and the colors used, wondering about techniques and displaying their enthusiasm to return to their studios to try ideas out. The art historians were seeing once-in-a-lifetime works, and had a much more scholarly approach to the exhibition.

As the six of us discussed our findings in the poststudy meeting, it was amusing to observe our initial reluctance to put forth some ideas that seemed a bit counterintuitive. We had set out to discover how visitors went about making meaning in this new and different kind of exhibition. We asked how they usually did this and how it might differ from how they usually go about understanding and taking in an exhibition. Fundamentally, most visitors were bemused by the question itself. "I have no idea how to do this." "I'm in your hands." "I never really know what to expect." "This is what I rely on the museum for." "I don't know how I'm going to react. That's what makes it fun." And so on.

The second thing we learned is what you saw depended on who you were. The people with a religious affiliation saw religious works. The studio art people saw ideas, colors, techniques, and so forth. The art historical people saw the history of Byzantine art laid out before them for contemplation. Then there were the people with no background, and that was the next thing we learned. The people with no background, and who had not read an article, or taken the audio tour, for the most part did not like the exhibition. They found it boring and repetitive. The people with no background, *but who had read an article or taken the tour*, enjoyed the exhibition. Many told us that they wanted to come back. But they also told us another fascinating thing: it is hard to learn about an area of art and be in awe of it at the same time. We were told by more than one visitor that they felt they would have to come back to really be fascinated by the works. This leads me to wonder which of the three (or five) groups defined here would show the biggest differences in terms of the Museum Effect. Would it be the people with a religious tie to the exhibition, or perhaps those who had no prior background, but had read about the area or taken the audio tour?

I'd like to extend this example in two ways. First, there is the always tricky problem of what do the results mean, and in a way, how much do they mean? We first try to get at the basic ideas or themes that have emanated from the findings, and then we push our understanding of those ideas and themes. We look for underlying causes, different ways of understanding. We stretch what we know like a taffy pull, trying to take it as far as we can go without breaking it. In doing interview work, it is critical to try to stay with what you've been told, and not to substitute too much by way of your own values and ideas. This can occur in the interpretation of the interviews, but it can also occur in the interviews themselves. The good interviewer keeps the participant on focus, but does not suggest correct or desirable answers, and does not talk too much. It is an interview, not really a conversation. I have to say that I am not great at this. I like to engage in a conversation, especially if the participant is an interesting person!

The second way in which we might extend the ideas from this study has to do with the fundamental differences between qualitative and quantitative research. The difference between qualitative and quantitative studies depends a lot on whom you ask. If you ask a more quantitatively oriented person, you will get a response along the lines of, "Quantitative studies are more focused on turning observations into amounts or quantities and then analyzing those quantities statistically. The purpose of such studies is typically to address a specific research question or hypothesis, and an emphasis is placed on the replicability and generalizability of the findings. Qualitative studies are more focused on processes, or explorations into issues that are less well defined. They involve gathering observations that are typically richer and more multifaceted than quantitative studies, and the analysis of such data is a complex procedure requiring insight and a constant working back and forth between the conclusions being drawn and the observations." If you ask a more qualitatively oriented person, you are likely to get a response more along the lines of, "The difference between quantitative and qualitative research is not just a difference between methods or questions; it begins with a difference in worldview, and what can be, and should be, the proper focus of research involving human beings." I lean toward the former definition, but having said that, I encourage people to consider the latter definition and recommend that those interested in the second definition explore that possibility, as it is a respected perspective in the scholarly community.

Example 4: "Origins of Impressionism" and Experimentation

I include this example because I want to show that to a degree, experimental work can be part of what we do in cultural institutions (Smith & Smith,

2003). At the same time, it is an example of evaluation work as opposed to research per se. The exhibition *Origins of Impressionism* was designed, in part, to be didactic in purpose. We were asked if we could conduct a study to see if people, in fact, did learn about the beginnings of Impressionism as a result of seeing the exhibition. Thus, we were evaluating the efficacy of the exhibition in terms of teaching people about Impressionism. It was what is called a "summative" evaluation (Scriven, 1967) in that we were not conducting the study in order to improve the exhibition. That would have been a "formative" evaluation and would have called for an entirely different design. With a summative evaluation, the goal is to find out whether the exhibition is "working" as desired.

When evaluating a program, an exhibition, an audio tour, and so forth, there is an assumption one can often reasonably make: that without the experience of the exhibition (audio tour, etc.), people would pretty much be where they were before they walked into the exhibition. If we could show that people knew more about Impressionism, in particular the beginnings of Impressionism, when they left the program than when they entered, we felt we would be able to establish the efficacy of the exhibition. Basically, the argument is that without going through the exhibition, there would be no reason for someone's understanding of the origins of Impressionism to increase significantly in any particular one- or two-hour block of time. Thus, the basic design would be to assess visitors' knowledge of the origins of Impressionism as they entered the exhibition, and again as they exited. Unlike the Museum Effect study, we decided that if possible, we would prefer to use the same individuals both pre- and postvisit. We took this decision for two reasons: first, the overall study would be tighter if we had the same people at two times. Second, we were able to give participants a nice gift for their participation: a catalog of the exhibition. Thus, we didn't mind asking them to come back to fill out a second survey. We approached people entering the exhibition and had them complete a survey prior to their visit and then return to our desk to complete a second survey before exiting. They were given an ID to return to us so that we could make sure we had both of their surveys together for purposes of analysis. They received their catalog upon completion of the second survey. Almost everyone came back for the second survey!

So the design of the study involved a pre/post comparison. But we added a twist to that design that we have used effectively in a number of evaluation settings. This is just a bit complicated to explain, but a highly effective technique. Everyone took a previsit survey before entering and a postvisit survey upon finishing their visit to the exhibition. The previsit survey asked about why they visited and had demographic questions. The postvisit survey asked how they enjoyed the exhibition and what they did while in the exhibition (did they read all the labels, did they talk with other individuals, did they take the audio tour, etc.). So far so good. The twist involved two additional sets of questions, one set about how much people knew about various Impressionist artists ("Artists") and a second asking how much they knew about the issues relating to the beginnings of the Impressionist movement ("Issues"). A random half of the visitors took the "Artists" set before their visit and the "Issues" set after they completed their visit. The other half did the reverse. This is depicted in Figure 7.4.

To simplify this, let us just focus on the questions that asked people how much they knew about the various artists featured in the exhibition. A random half of the people told us how much they knew before the visit, and the other half told us how much they knew following their visit. We could then look to see how much of a gain we saw in these ratings from pre to post. We assume that without viewing the exhibition, people would be the same. The only thing that occurred in the intervening hour or two was seeing the exhibition. Thus, we could fairly safely attribute the gains to the visit. Since we had randomly assigned people to groups, we knew that the gains we saw were not just the result of different groups of people taking the measure.

Now, we put in one final aspect. One might argue that people leaving the exhibit simply felt better, felt they knew more, and so forth, and/or they wanted to please us by giving high ratings after their visit to a great exhibition. Well, we put in a bit of a check for that. If it were true that people were just reflecting an overall positive attitude, we would expect them to rate their knowledge of all artists on the list higher than the group who took this part of the survey prior to seeing the exhibition. To test for this possibility, we put two artists on the list who were not in the exhibition. In fact, they weren't Impressionists. And for those two artists, there was no gain found from the pre measure to the post measure.

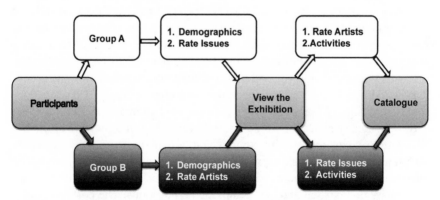

Figure 7.4.   Depiction of the design for the Origins of Impressionism study.
Lisa F. Smith

We were also able to link behaviors that people engaged in during the exhibition to the amount of gain that we saw. People who read labels, took the audio tour, and tried to make connections among the artists all were associated with higher gains from pre to post. There are many more details that can be found here. I encourage you to take a look at the article.

There are several ways that the ideas behind this study can be extended. The first way is by looking at how experimentation can occur within a single group of individuals, all of whom are participating in what the museum has to offer. Basically, we had one group of participants here, but we were able to make this into an experiment by randomly assigning them to take survey A or survey B prior to viewing the exhibition. When we then looked at gains from pre to post, we knew we were looking at differences that we could attribute to the visit and not to preexisting differences in the groups.

Second, even though this was primarily an evaluation study, we were able to build in some elements of research. The evaluation component of the study was that the exhibition appeared to be effective in teaching people about the origins of Impressionism. That was useful to us, and rewarding to the curator of the exhibition. But that finding is not really a research finding in that it doesn't really apply to anything other than this exhibition. But we were able to look at how people's behavior within an exhibition relates to the kinds of learning that go on. The results from this part of the study might well be applicable in other settings. From it we learn what kinds of behaviors seem to be associated with increased learning, and those that are less so.

Third, there is a small but useful measurement extension here. By listing two artists who were not Impressionists, we were able to guard against an alternative hypothesis that people were just giving more positive results after having been to the exhibition. In looking at the effects of a phenomenon, where possible, one should consider what would *not* be affected in addition to what would be affected. Here we were able to show that there were no gains on artists who weren't in the exhibition. In terms of presenting this information to the museum staff, and at conferences of museum educators, this was a very important (and popular) factor. We used this idea in a slightly different context in an evaluation of an audio tour program at the Whitney Museum of American Art in New York City (Smith, Waszkielewicz, Potts, and Smith, 2004) (this study was mentioned in chapter 6 in talking about the effectiveness of providing particularly intriguing information to visitors). In this study, we had samples of people using the audio and not using the audio. We argued that people with the audio would be more focused on the objects at hand, and would notice the periphery less than people without the audio. So we had visitors fill out a survey after they had completed their tour and asked them about details of the work, and also what works were next to the work.

We found that people with the audio (as opposed to those who didn't have the audio) gave more detailed explanations of the objects (as expected), but *also* these people were *less* able to tell us what was next to the works than people without the audio. That is, the audio appears to have focused the visitors in so much on the object that they didn't notice what was next to it.

Example 5: Evaluation of Easter Program: Studies That Are Communicable

The final example relates back to the story that began the book, that of the girl who was viewing the Raphael altarpiece and saw the baby Jesus. This was a program that the Met ran over the Easter holidays for kids from a local shelter. They varied in age from about six to thirteen, and came every day for a week. It was a specially funded program and we needed to conduct an evaluation of it for the funder. We couldn't count on all the kids being able to read, and we didn't want to spend a whole lot of time taking them away from the program itself. We needed something that was fairly efficient, was enjoyable for the kids, and we could communicate easily to a funder who was not sophisticated in social science. It was a fun task to take on.

We decided for a simple pre/post design for the evaluation, taking measures on the kids before the program started, and then again toward the end of the program. We had three different measures that we looked at, but I want to focus on just one here. One of the things that we wanted to do was to establish that as a result of the program, the young people had a more positive attitude toward art, and understood it better. In order to look at a more positive attitude, we decided on a measure that was directly related to the art that the students were looking at and didn't rely on reading ability. We acquired twelve postcards from the Met shop that depicted art that the students would see as part of the program. Then we went and got another twelve postcards that were photo-graphic reproductions of things we thought that the children would like such as puppy dogs and fire trucks. We put all twenty-four postcards up on a board (with art reproductions and photographs mixed) and asked each child to pick five that they would like to take with them at the end of the week. Thus, we had a measure of how much they valued the art reproductions before the program began. At the end of the week, we told them that they could choose again and make different selections if they would like. This gave us a measure of how much they valued the art at the end of the program. The difference between the number of art reproductions chosen at the beginning and end of the program is a measure of program efficacy in terms of kids valuing art. The differences were statistically significant and strong in terms of absolute growth. (By the way, we gave all the children all of the postcards at the end of the program.)

The extension here has to do with the nature of the measure that we used. We look to develop measures that are easy for participants to understand, that provide us with good variation in scores, and that are clearly related to the concepts we want to measure. But there is another characteristic of measures to keep in mind: communicability. Here we wanted a measure that could be easily communicated to a funder without resorting to a complicated explanation or a reliance on authority ("Trust us. We know what we're doing."). With the postcard assessment, we could say to the funder, "See this picture of our Raphael altarpiece? Before the program began, four students out of twenty wanted to take that home. After the program, sixteen asked if they could take it home." That communicated clearly and simply the effect of one of the major goals of the program.

EXTENDING WHAT WE KNOW ABOUT THE MUSEUM EFFECT

Having looked at a number of studies and presented some of the ideas that underlie research in cultural institutions, we can now turn to some of the work that we would like to do with regard to the Museum Effect, and how that work might be done. We begin with the notion of replication. We have seen the Museum Effect in three different institutions, all art museums. But there needs to be more work that simply replicates the finding. Most work of such nature would also involve extending the research in some fashion or another. For example, one could look at specific groups of people to see where the effect is most pronounced. We have done just a bit of that with the data we have, and it seems to be the case that people who know less about art show a larger effect. But that is very tentative at this point. It would be great to conduct a study where participants took the aesthetic fluency measure mentioned above and then broke the sample down into low/medium/high levels of fluency, and then replicated the analysis.

Another issue is to explore how the Museum Effect works through the museum visit. We know that it is at a base level before the visit starts, then elevates at midvisit, and then seems to decline toward the end of the visit. But how does that actually work? Does the curve go up rapidly at the start of the visit and then gradually decline? Does the curve move upward incrementally throughout the visit and then drop somewhat dramatically at the end of the visit? Or is it more of an inverted U-shaped curve? In order to find this out, it would be necessary to have more time periods measured in a study. Or, it might be useful to have people estimate how long they have been in the museum and how much longer they plan to stay. Then we could plot time on the X-axis of a graph, and the measures on the Y-axis. Or we could plot what portion of the visit had been completed.

A natural extension would be to other kinds of cultural institutions, as has been discussed in chapter 5 (so we won't go over that again here). But we could also look at whether looking at art (listening to music, reading, etc.) engenders a version of the Museum Effect in settings other than cultural institutions (at home, looking at art on a computer, for example, or simply reading a book). My suspicion here, and this could be studied, is that one has to enter into the activity with a personal disposition toward it. That is, I don't think we would see the effect if we somehow could assign people to reading or looking at art. I think they have to be of a mind to do so. We pretty much know that when people enter a museum or go to a concert they are in a state of mind to receive what the institution has to offer (unless they are going because of someone else's desires). But does the institution itself, the building, the atmosphere, the hushed tones, also contribute to the Museum Effect? We simply don't know, but it would be so interesting to find out!

Throughout the book, I have talked about research that we have done. This has always involved working with people—visitors to museums. It is important to keep in mind that these visitors come to the museum to do what museums are about. They come to see works of art, or objects from natural history, or scientific demonstrations. They will often gladly agree to participate in your research, but it is critical to treat them respectfully and to be sure that they are participating voluntarily and understand that should they decide, they can discontinue that participation. Ethical considerations need to always be part of the equation when one conducts research with human beings.

Finally (and really only finally for this chapter—there are many things that could be studied here), we can turn to a qualitative perspective, and look more deeply into how this process works. Our theory is dependent upon cobbling together a number of pieces of research and theoretical perspectives into the rationale behind the Museum Effect. But it would be wonderful to hear the voices of individuals as they are looking at works to see if they are indeed personalizing what they are viewing, and reflecting on their own lives as they stand in the presence of genius. One of the great things about a life of conducting research is that there are always more questions, more studies, more that we can know.

The Museum Effect is an invention. That is, it is an idea that was created to explain a set of phenomena we see in museums. Is it real? How does it work? Does it help us to understand things that are important to us, not just as scholars, but to society as a whole? I hope so. And I invite the reader to join in the search for answers to these and other questions that intrigue us about that other wonderful invention: the museum.

REFERENCES

Babbie, E. R. (2013). *The practice of social research.* Belmont, CA: Wadsworth Cengage Learning.

Huck, S. W., & Sandler, H. M. (1979). *Rival hypotheses: Alternative interpretations of data based conclusions.* New York: Harper & Row.

Scriven, M. J. (1967). The methodogy of evaluation. In Strake, R.E. *Curriculum evaluation.* Chicago: Rand McNally. American Educational Research Association (monograph series on evaluation, no. 1).

Smith, J. K. (2004). *Reaction and response to the El Greco exhibition at the Metropolitan Museum of Art.* New York: Office of Research and Evaluation, the Metropolitan Museum of Art.

Smith, J. K., & Carr, D. W. (2001). In Byzantium. *Curator, 44*(4), 335–354.

Smith, J. K., & Smith, L. F. (2003). "Origins of Impressionism": Relating visitor behavior to perceived learning. *Bulletin of Psychology and the Arts, 4,* 80–85.

Smith, J. K., & Tinio, P. P. L. (2008). Audio augmentation of museum visits: Talking the walk. In Loic Tallon and Kevin Walker (Eds.), *Digital Dialogues.* San Francisco: AltaMira Press.

Smith, J. K., & Waszkielewicz, I. (2007). *The civilizing influence of art museum visitation.* Paper presented at annual meeting of the American Psychological Association, San Francisco, CA.

Smith, J. K., Waszkielewicz, I., Potts, K., and Smith, B. K. (2004). *Visitors and the audio program: An investigation into the impact of the audio guide program at the Whitney Museum of American Art.* New York: The Whitney Museum of American Art.

Webb, E. J., Campbell, D. T., Schwartz, R. D., Sechrest, L., & Grove, J. B. (1981). *Nonreactive measures in the social sciences.* Dallas, TX: Houghton Mifflin.

A Final Word

So that is the Museum Effect: what it is, how it works, and why it is important. It is a model of how looking at art in a museum can affect people in a positive fashion. And by extension, how looking at historical artifacts, scientific exhibitions, or listening to great music might do the same thing. Is it correct? Do I have it "right"? Well, the statistician George Box once said, "Essentially, all models are wrong, but some are useful" (Box & Draper, 1987, p. 424). I like that. To be sure, there are innumerable other things that go on when people look at art (or historical objects or read great books) than are described in the Museum Effect. But I think, at times, with most people, there is a disposition to let a work speak to us in a way that is unique to us as individuals. The police officer discovers a world of genius that he had never before considered, the priest imagines himself with the incense burner, the Siena predella piece reminds a woman of a most special moment decades ago, and the Goya painting of a countess reminds me that I'm the father of a wonderful young woman. For how many of us has *Catcher in the Rye* brought us to terms with the formation of our personal identities; how many of us have been inspired listening to "The Impossible Dream," even if we might not want to admit it in sophisticated company?

This book is premature. There are a dozen studies I want to do in order to confirm the ideas that are presented here, to expand upon them, to better understand the mechanisms that underlie the theory. But one doesn't get too many chances to be impetuous at my age, so I have brashly put forward a set of ideas, and I invite you to consider them. I believe that the Museum Effect weaves together a number of disparate and difficult to comprehend findings that we and others have come upon over the years. Museum visitors come to museums to get away from their regular life and be inspired, learn, and enjoy.

They tell us that their visit to a museum or special exhibition was "incredible," "amazing," or "life altering." And yet, when we observe visitors in museums, they are mostly quiet, looking at works, or reading, by themselves, and do not appear to be ecstatic. They are actually more static than ecstatic. What they appear to be is in a kind of "zone," or, as argued here, something of a flow state. We know that museum visitors rarely look at a work of art for more than a minute, and they view dozens if not hundreds in a single visit. They often have trouble picking out a single work as special, but rather argue that their enjoyment of their visit was based on the whole museum or exhibition.

Where does that leave us? Well, I believe we can turn those observations into a narrative which is, in essence, the argument of the Museum Effect. That is, people choose to visit a museum voluntarily. They come to museums with expectations to see wondrous things that they cannot see in their everyday lives. They want to be inspired, to learn, and to enjoy themselves. They are in a receptive state of mind. They work their way from one object to the next, and while they view these objects, they think about themselves and their lives. They see themselves reflected in works of art, discover the signature of an ancestor in a faded book, find themselves in the presence of the baby Jesus. Their reflections are stimulated by a historical object, or a sculpture, or a sonnet. They think about who they are, how they relate to others, and what their lives mean in a grander sense.

Our cultural institutions provide us the opportunity to experience awe—in a brilliant Vermeer, the First Folio of Shakespeare, or a breathtaking Puccini. They take us away from our everyday lives, surround us with the exceptional, and let us contemplate who we are now and conceive of whom we might become. In doing so, we spend a small part of our lives thinking more noble thoughts, exploring grander possibilities, and envisioning a better life for ourselves and for others. We experience the Museum Effect.

REFERENCE

Box, G. E. P., & Draper, N. R. (1987). *Empirical model building and response surfaces.* New York: Wiley.

Index

aesthetics; appreciation, 77–79, 128; emotions, 79, 81; experience, 57–59; fluency, 33, 87; interaction, 76–79, 128; judgment, 79, 81
Age of Napoleon exhibition, 18–19
American Alliance of Museums, 15–16
American Museum of Natural History, 121–122
Arnold, D. 59–60
art; knowledge of, 56–62; labels, 138; as mirror, 87–89; presented online, 44
astronomy, 130–131
audio tours, 150–151

Barnes, A. C., 63–64
Barnes Foundation, 63–64
Beardsley, M., 57–58, 62
Boston Museum of Science, 118–121, 151
British Museum, The, 113–117
Brooklyn Museum, The, 160–161

Carr, D., 6, 29, 44, 158, 183–186
catalogs, 153–154
cave lions in Chauvet, 31, 92
citizenship scale, 102–108; interpersonal scale, 102–108; intrapersonal scale, 102–108; societal scale, 102–108

Civil War, The, 122–124, 141
cognitive models of how people look at art; Chatterjee's model, 75, 91; Leder's model, 77–79, 91, 148; Locher's model, 76–77, 91; Tinio's model, 80–82, 91, 92
comment books, 47–48
creating research and evaluation designs, 167
Csikszentmihalyi, M., 57–62

Dewey, J., 55, 57, 64
Dierking, L., 28
docent tours, 152–153
Doubleday, L., 3
Duchamp, M., 8–10

emotional amortization, 109, 153–154

facsimile accommodation, 27, 86, 154
Falk, J., 28
flow, 55–62, 99–100, 112
Foucault pendulum, 120
Frame, J., 5
freedom and structure, 145

Galois, E. 120–121
genealogy, 20

197

About the Author

Jeffrey K. Smith is professor of education and associate dean for research in the College of Education at the University of Otago in New Zealand. Prior to coming to Otago, he was professor and chair of the Educational Psychology Department at Rutgers, The State University of New Jersey, where he had been a faculty member for twenty-nine years. From 1988 through 2005, he also served as head of the office of research and evaluation at The Metropolitan Museum of Art. He has consulted with over twenty leading cultural institutions in the United States. He studies issues in learning in cultural institutions, educational assessment, and the psychology of aesthetics. He has written or edited seven books and over seventy articles and reviews on the psychology of aesthetics, educational assessment, and educational psychology. He received his AB from Princeton University and his PhD from the University of Chicago. He is the founding co-editor of the journal, *Psychology of Aesthetics, Creativity, and the Arts*. In 2011 he was awarded the Rudolph Arnheim Award for Outstanding Career Contributions to the Psychology of the Arts by Division 10 of the American Psychological Association.